Fly Fishing for
Great Lakes Steelhead

Fly Fishing for Great Lakes Steelhead

An Advanced Look at an Emerging Fishery

Rick Kustich and Jerry Kustich

Foreward by Lani Waller

Illustrations by Al Hassall

West River Publishing

Published by
West River Publishing
P.O. Box 15
Grand Island, NY 14072

Printed in the United States of America

First edition

10 9 8 7 6 5 4 3 2 1

Cataloging-in-Publication Data

Kustich, Rick
    Fly fishing for Great Lakes steelhead : an advanced look at an emerging fishery / Rick Kustich and Jerry Kustich ; foreword by Lani Waller ; illustrations by Al Hassall -- 1st ed.
        p. cm.
    Includes bibliographical references
    LCCN: 99-73818
    ISBN: 0-9633109-1-7

    1. Steelhead fishing--Great Lakes. 2. Fly fishing--Great Lakes.   I. Kustich, Jerry.
    II. Title.

    SH687.7.K87 1999   799.1'755
                        QBI99-999

All photography by Rick Kustich except as otherwise noted

Color fly plate photography and digital editing by Shaun Smith

Text editing by Anne Bishop

About the cover: A wild New York State steelhead

To Mom and Dad—for a lifetime of support
To Paul—for sharing his love of the outdoors
To Dan—for leading us to the trout

We haven't forgotten.

Contents

Acknowledgments   *ix*

Foreword   *xi*

Introduction   *xiii*

Part I: The Fishery

1. Philosophical Perspective   17

2. The Steelhead   21

3. Historical Background   27

4. The Modern Era   35

5. The Genetic Connection   45

6. Management Trends   53

Part II: **The Fly Fishing Approach**

7. Steelhead Behavior   99

8. Reading Water   111

9. Fly Fishing Strategy   123

10. Flies   159

Part III: **A Guide to the Rivers**

Introduction to the Rivers   197

11. Lake Superior   199

12. Lake Huron   211

13. Lake Michigan   225

14. Lake Erie   241

15. Lake Ontario   253

Epilogue: The Complete Angler   269

Bibliography   273

Acknowledgments

For a project of this nature, support comes in many ways. With a grateful spirit, we would like to appropriately acknowledge those who have helped pull this work together over the years.

Most importantly, without the understanding and encouragement from our wives Ann Kustich and Debra Doerflinger, five years of intensive writing and research could never have occurred.

The technical help received from the professional fishery managers throughout the Great Lakes has been most noteworthy, and we would particularly like to thank the following individuals for their advice and shared knowledge: Dave Borgeson, Jon George, Jack Imhof, Dennis Pratt, Paul Seelbach, Les Wedge, and especially Larry Halyk, whose effort was well beyond the call of duty.

We have had the opportunity to share time with some of the top fly fishing professionals in the Great Lakes region. Special thanks to Mike Augat, Dave Barber, Jerry Darkes, Pat Doldo, Jim Johnson, Bob Linsenman, Greg Liu, Shaun McDonald, Kelly Neuman, Jerry Senecal, Scott Smith, Matt Supinski, John Valk, and Fran Verdoliva. Regrettably, there are a number of others whose paths we never crossed.

The finished product would not be what it is without the dedicated professionalism of three individuals. Special thanks to Shaun Smith who contributed in many ways to the book's photography, to Anne Bishop for her editing skills and insight, and to Al Hassall for his wonderful artwork.

It is also important to recognize the people who have contributed indirectly in so many ways. To Annette McLean, Jeff Walker and Glenn Brackett, for constant moral support. To Jim Lorentz for showing us much about traditional techniques and Brian Slavinski who has been party to many road trips and drawn out photography sessions. To Bob Morrissey and Rob McCormick for always taking the time to share ideas on techniques and flies. And to all those we have shared special experiences with on the water over the years.

Foreword

It isn't often we get a book on fly fishing for steelhead written by two brothers. In fact, this may be the first, and I was delighted that Rick and Jerry chose me to write this foreword, although that is not the major reason for my enthusiasm. As someone once said, when asked about fishing writing: "Well, it seems more and more is being written about less and less." How true. Or so it seems, and I don't think my age is showing, even though I have been flogging the water for forty-three years now. It's just that there aren't that many new stones to turn over and it seems we keep redefining the wheel, even the one ascended and descended each season by sea-run rainbows who are asking for little more than the opportunity to keep on doing exactly that.

What we have here is the antithesis of rehashing—a very honest and genuine illumination of a subject that has unfortunately been publicly defined mostly by dark rumors, nasty little stories, and tales of dastardly deeds ranging from snagging spawning fish from their nuptial redds to angry duels and threats of death among anglers who reportedly felt obligated to fish from the shadow of one another's hip pocket. Now some of these stories are undoubtedly true, but the truth is also this: we have our own version of the same game on the West Coast and yet life goes on. There are more anglers out here each season who care and who are trying to steer the ship in the right direction, just as there are those doing the same thing "back east." That's part of what this book is about.

After years of hearing all the stories, I went back to take a look for myself last year with Tom Pero of *Wild Steelhead and Salmon* magazine and found something quite different—although I did see a pool or two on New York's Salmon River where the presence or absence of effective deodorant coverage seemed an important variable. The river, however, was beautiful, and everyone seemed to be enjoying themselves. That counts, doesn't it? In fact, I didn't see anything any more brutal than the things we affectionately call "tradition" on the West Coast.

For example: On the first morning of our visit, I watched a "line-up" of fly casters politely shooting casts into a long run whose choppy waves looked not at all unlike the ones "out here." Around eight o'clock, an angler suddenly hooked up and eventually brought a Great Lakes steelhead smoothly into the shallows of a pool somewhere on the Salmon—his first on a fly—and the simple truth is this: I was jealous. The hen was fat, silver and strong, with a nice pink stripe and a back the color of cold steel. Her pectoral fins stood out like wings. They were tinged with rose and you could see right through them. She was beautiful. For a moment, even the hallowed rivers of the Pacific Northwest had to take a backseat to this supremely gorgeous fish lying quietly in a foot of water as the angler tenderly removed the hook. I remember thinking, "My God, I thought we were the only ones who had fish like that."

Later that day, I met Rick and Jerry in a roadside café just a long cast from the Salmon. We talked about this book, and I listened as they told me what they were going to do. I think they have succeeded. This is not just another book on steelhead fishing. It is more than that. It is a pioneering, encyclopedic effort to tell the entire, and true, story of the Great Lakes steelhead fishery, and an effort to direct a new and emerging sport in the right direction.

But that is not what I like most about it. What really rings here is a dedication to the best traditions and principles of fly fishing everywhere by two anglers who care. The book is honest, straightforward and sensitive. No one who fishes these waters, or steelhead anywhere, should ignore it. It's too well done for that, and I'll share another secret: I've read it, and I've learned from it. Thank you, Rick and Jerry.

Lani Waller

Novato, California
July 10, 1999

Introduction

It's nearly impossible to reduce to words the affect that fly fishing for steelhead has had on our lives. Like a constant magnetic pull, its lure has guided us on a journey with no particular end. One marked by beauty, challenge, and adventure. Our connection to the world of steelheading has long transcended a casual acquaintance to become a deep spiritual appreciation resulting from a direct link to the natural world. The anticipation of what the journey holds in store is as thrilling as the stops that have already been made. Each year we visit new water to satisfy our thirst for exploration, yet a fair commitment is made to our familiar haunts to experience the comfort of an old friend. From our vantage point, it is a lifelong journey—and while at times physically tiring, its excitement and opportunity create an attitude that is seemingly tireless. The key to the journey is to enjoy every mile.

The objective of this book is quite simple—to create a greater appreciation for the tremendous opportunity that the rivers of the Great Lakes region provide and to design a fly fishing approach that will lead to enjoyment and challenge. Throughout its writing, the objective of this work has remained constant, but the direction required to satisfy this end was anything but direct. Every year you experience and learn, creating more information to put to paper. The release of this book is some two to three years after our original plans. In retrospect, that's a bit of a blessing as some of the information garnered in the last couple years has been integral to the completion of this work.

The book is subtitled *An Advanced Look at an Emerging Fishery*. From our view, the aspect of "emerging" has various connotations. Steelhead in the Great Lakes have a deep history but with very little tradition. Throughout the 1900's, the waters of the Great Lakes have been treated with disrespect and mismanagement. The extensive salmonid stocking programs that began over 30 years ago accidentally created a sport fishery. "Emerging" seems to contradict the fact that steelhead have existed in the Great Lakes for over a century and that the fishery which is familiar to most of us is now in its fourth decade. We have been involved with Great Lakes fishing for most of this current era, and it is clear that 30 to 40 years is not a long time in the development of a recreational fishery. The current Great Lakes fishery has been shadowed by a black cloud, as crowds and unethical behavior characterized the typical image of a Great Lakes river. Some of this imagery was contrived and exaggerated, but much was sadly true. A lack of foresight had created a carnival atmosphere across the region. It was not until the latter part of the 1980's and throughout this current decade that the Great Lakes fishery began a movement toward respectability through concerned efforts by dedicated individuals, conservation groups and professional managers. It was also during this time that the steelhead showed its ability to adapt to the various lake environs and earned the respect of Great Lakes tributary anglers as the most desirable of the transplanted salmonid species. At the heels of an expanded following of sport anglers pursuing one of our finest game fish is the development of a greater understanding of its habits along with new techniques and flies that had been ruled out years before. New management philosophies are furthering this advancement. Before our very eyes, a fishery *is* emerging—one that hopefully will know no bounds and will be able to shake past indiscretions. It is an exciting time for a fly fisher in proximity of the Great Lakes region.

We hope that through our broad coverage of this topic, we will help enlighten anglers to the entire picture that represents the Great Lakes steelhead fishery. We also hope that its emergence will live in the hearts, minds, and eyes of concerned individuals for years to come.

Part I
The Fishery

1

Philosophical Perspective

There is probably no greater thrill in river fishing than to hook either a steelhead or an Atlantic salmon on a fly. And common to the mystique of these two great anadromous sport fish are the variable synchronized factors that must all come together at an exact time and place before an angler can even expect to encounter one of these wondrous creatures. The real secret lies in understanding the fish and its world. Although any further comparison between these two legendary salmonids would be a fruitless waste of time, the many determining factors that bring each species back to its river of origin after years of ocean vagary are remarkably similar. Wherever they swim, steelhead and Atlantic salmon should be studied in the spirit of appreciation, admiration, and reverence.

During a worldwide angling history that spans centuries, the Atlantic salmon has been customarily stalked with a fly rod throughout its range in the Northern Hemisphere. However, those who chase steelhead with a fly have not been at it nearly as long. In fact, this group of fly fishing specialists *still* represents only a scant percentage of the total number of anglers who pursue steelhead with a variety of skillful, high-tech methods. With an angling past that dates back only to the late 1800's, the 20th century has produced a small, but dedicated contingent of West Coast fly fishers who have greatly influenced the sport of steelhead fishing while establishing an American fly fishing tradition in the process. From creative flies that are now classics to a variation of techniques and presentations, those who have sought steelhead with a religious fervor throughout the century have left us a spirited legacy. Despite the declining opportunities brought on by a dwindling resource, present-day greats like Bill McMillan, Trey Combs, and Lani Waller, to name a few, continue to pioneer innovative concepts, techniques, flies, and equipment that continue this tradition. In the spirit of Roderick Haig-Brown and Lee Wulff, their works are important and provide much in-depth insight based upon study, devotion, and extensive experiences. There is a wonderful world of knowledge, as well as a cadre of offbeat individuals, associated with steelhead, and these many facets combine to create the fascinating realm known as "steelheading." The sharing of ideas, the camaraderie, the eccentrics, and the hunt itself all add up to a charm that may one day culminate in the exhilarating take of this dynamic fish.

Sportsmen have been fishing for migratory rainbow, or steelhead, in many regions of the Great Lakes for nearly one hundred years. Until recently, however, relatively little interest existed in fly fishing for these freshwater descendants of the Pacific. Though the many great Michigan rivers have spawned a Midwestern steelhead fly fishing tradition of its own, there seems to be a general understanding that fly fishing opportunities for Great Lakes steelhead is somewhat limited. There is no question that the types of water containing steelhead in the Great Lakes vary tremendously. In many cases, there are no West Coast comparisons or equivalents. This belief has often been considered a handicap by many who try to judge the validity of the Great Lakes as a true steelhead fishery. Therein lies the mystery of this great fresh-water system, and for those willing to explore these waters with an open mind, the Great Lakes basin offers a lifetime of diverse opportunities.

It should be noted that some of the popular approaches for taking these Great Lakes fish on a fly rod has negatively affected the credibility of this fishery for several decades. Specifically, many traditional fly fishers have questioned the popular use of running line with weight added to the leader as a "proper" fly fishing method. Since the fly fishing potential in the Great Lakes is still unfolding, so are the techniques and riggings which match a combination of challenging fishing situations with the realistic opportunity to catch fish. It is important to understand that many of the classic fly fishing methods employed over the ages for migratory fish on both the Atlantic and the Pacific coasts are equally at home on the Great Lakes as well.

The integrity of this vast fresh-water fishery has also been darkened by images of pollution, shoulder-to-shoulder fishermen, and the legalized snagging of salmon. Many also believe that most of the Great Lakes' steelhead fly fishing is done over the redds in the spring. Though there may be some reason for concern regarding these perceptions, there have been substantive changes over the years, and the trend to improve the overall quality of the Great Lakes experience can only be viewed with much optimism.

As the 20th century winds down, critical water quality issues have been addressed from lake to lake, region to region, and there have been genuine gains in the battle of the pollutants and great steps made toward habitat rehabilitation and reclamation. With so many tributaries, crowding is no more of a problem, and in some cases less, than many other popular destinations in the country now that fly fishing has developed a solid following. The presence of steelhead in many tributaries for months at a time also offers anglers opportunities to spread the pressure out over a longer duration throughout the year.

New York State was the last stronghold of legalized snagging in the Great Lakes. This practice was encouraged to rid drainages of Chinook salmon before they died and fouled the shorelines. Although these fish readily take well-presented offerings even in the tributaries, it was commonly believed that salmon would no longer take conventional baits, lures, or flies upon leaving the lakes. And though the Chinook are a high-demand sport fish in the lake waters, ironically, these same fish were considered a nuisance to be eliminated in any way possible once they entered the creeks and rivers. For several years, many true sporting advocates were driven from the rivers by the brutally unethical practices of those who believed snagging was the only method that could extract these fish from their spawning waters. To make matters worse, many brown trout and steelhead illegally fell victim to the undiscriminating snagger in the process. Streambeds were subsequently littered with four-ounce snagging hooks, and the balls of 60 lb. monofilament left behind symbolized the sad debacle that many fishery managers admit should have never been allowed from its onset in the 70's. In 1995, the Appellate Division of the New York Supreme Court upheld the decision to ban all snagging in New York waters despite spirited opposition. And though there could be further appeals, New York is committed to ending this unsporting practice.

There has always been controversy connected with fishing steelhead on the redds. In many rivers, this opportunity is readily available, and it attracts many anglers because of the ability to spot and cast to big fish. This approach is even utilized out West, but only where spawning tributaries aren't entirely closed. Not only does this raise another ethical question, but there are also the concerns that such harassment could lead to lower spawning productivity (in rivers capable of natural reproduction), resulting in fewer natural fish for the future. Because there are steelhead available throughout the system during several months of the year, many believe the creative fly fisher can find numerous other angling opportunities while leaving the spawning steelhead alone to reproduce in peace. Even in the spring, the presence of fresh fish on the move along with healthy post-spawners can provide great sport in runs, depressions, and slots safely away from active redds.

Fly fishing the hundreds of Great Lakes tributaries presents many varied challenges worthy of any serious fly fisher's talents. Virtually every stream and river within the total system possesses a combination of characteristics that make each piece of water unique, each demanding an approach specific to its challenge. From big sprawling waters to small brushy creeks and everything in between, the astute angler can choose from many of the established West Coast techniques to some of the proven methods developed specifically for the Great Lakes. In some cases, particular situations will call for a combination of procedures or pure innovation on the part of the angler. Whatever approach is chosen, there is absolutely no reason to abandon a fly rod suitable for the rigors of steelheading and a standard fly line in any of its accepted variations from floating to full sink. The Great Lakes system is as fragmented in its approach to fly fishing as it is in the management of steelhead. Now is the time to diffuse the myths and create a new fly fishing tradition that encompasses each Great Lakes drainage, woven together as a comprehensive whole based on solid conservation, sound management, and undaunted sporting ethic.

The aim of this book is not to pass judgment on techniques and other legal means of catching steelhead. Fly fishing has its challenging parameters, and these boundaries will be explored, as will the many variable factors that influence and enhance the angler's chances of success. A presentation of rivers that are suitable for fly fishing found within the watersheds of all five Great Lakes will provide pertinent tactical information as well as ideas for travel.

Fishing can no longer be just the linear pursuit of catching a fish. Living in this modern world is much more complex than that. All of us who are active anglers share the obligation to assist professional managers in caring for *our* resource. We cannot continue to take without giving back, and that starts with a willingness to understand everything that is involved in the dynamics of our favorite waters before a fish ever sees a fly. Everyone must find ways to get involved while encouraging bold new management policies for the future. There are many factors to examine, and much to learn. As the era of the 21st century descends upon our lives, the ever-demanding forces of change necessitate that we all be the keepers of the rivers that flow through our dreams.

When it comes to steelhead, their destiny is in our hands.

2

The Steelhead

We both stood in awe. Our last glimpse of the massive fish was a silver flick as it danced its way back toward the lake in the heavy flows of the lower Niagara River. The steelhead had hammered the fly at the edge of an intimidating vortex, immediately catapulted into full view, and then had taken the express route through the boils and swells of this rapidly moving powerhouse. It took only seconds for the biggest Great Lakes steelhead either of us had ever hooked to tear through the fly line and then break off in the treacherous flow as the reel sang to the end of its backing. Though we both grew up during different polluted eras on the upper section of the Niagara, at that moment we realized this particular fish symbolized a new direction in the health of the entire Great Lakes basin. The fact that one of the most degraded sections within the whole system now supports a substantial run of steelhead is a rare positive step in a world pushed to the limits of its environmental well-being. With steelhead ascending virtually every viable drainage of all five lakes, this magnificent creature has come to represent a new age of enthusiasm for the region despite continuing obstacles that may eventually impede the ability of this species to survive in the same ominous manner as its West Coast ancestors.

Before there were ever wild brown trout swimming the esteemed rivers of Montana, the naturalized progeny of West Coast steelhead were cruising the waters of the Great Lakes. Although the true value of this fishery, widely distributed throughout the largest fresh-water system in the world, has only been recognized since the early 1980's, there has been a significant steelhead following in Michigan, Wisconsin, and Ontario for many decades. Overshadowed by the indigenous West Coast fishery, the significance of the

Great Lakes steelhead has never been highly regarded by the nationwide angling community. Furthermore, the lack of a comprehensive picture of wild steelhead potential in the Great Lakes basin has been plagued by images of industrialization, dense population, and deadly pollution. This legacy hinders many efforts to establish this as a credible sport fishery by undermining management programs needed to attain a noble end. But through increasing awareness, the value of this unique fishery, steeped in an obscure tradition of its own, has recently begun to gain respectability throughout much of the country.

It is important for all sport-minded individuals to realize that the steelhead of the Great Lakes cannot be taken for granted. Already many regional problems have surfaced that could potentially impact the fishery throughout the lakes. At this point though, the difficulties facing the survival of the Great Lakes fish are not as grave as those on the West Coast. Once the kinship between these two geographic regions has been established, beneficial exchange of information and energy between those dedicated to each fishery can result. It would seem imperative to enlist the concern of all steelhead enthusiasts throughout the country to fight for the same common cause. Steelhead, wherever they exist, belong to everyone. When these symbols of all that is wild are endangered, the very essence of human existence is similarly placed at risk, while the human spirit is diminished in the process.

A beautiful, wild Great Lakes steelhead.

Recently, a friend related to us the story of a beautiful, wild eight-pound hen he had just caught in Idaho's "River of No Return"—the beautiful Salmon River. He recounted skating his fly through the tailout of a favorite run when the fish flashed out of nowhere to grab the offering. This fish came as a particular surprise since the runs returning to the Salmon had been so paltry the past few years. Upon considering the significance of this encounter, we then dwelled on the chain of events that had to occur for their paths, angler and fish, to cross at that exact moment on that particular day. Two years before, the small smolt began a journey of over 800 miles, descending past eight dams before arriving at its oceanic destination. After avoiding commercial nets, seals, and other predators for two seasons, this mature fish re-entered the Columbia River in early fall with enough stored energy to travel 1,000 miles past the many dams, dodging Native American nets, as it ascended the river back to its home waters. Spending the harsh winter somewhere in the system, this fish began its final leg of the sojourn when the water warmed sufficiently in March, only to be waylaid and very briefly admired by an angler who had arrived after an adventuresome trip of his own into the wilderness at that very same place on the river. Destiny or chance? It was one of those discussions with no answers, but concluding with a sense of reverence for a fish possessing such remarkable tenacity.

Before man's intervention, separate species of salmonids were distributed in concise regions throughout North America. Atlantic salmon were the anadromous fish of the northeast, while its landlocked forms occupied some inland lakes and streams. Brook trout filled the eastern streams and lakes from Georgia to the Arctic Circle and westward throughout the entire northern Great Lakes region. Lake trout dwelled in the deep northern lakes throughout Canada, over to the Great Lakes, and up into Maine. The West had its many varieties of cutthroat, and their range also extended into Nevada all the way to the Pacific coast. The entire West Coast, including Alaska, laid claim to massive numbers of five salmon species as well as perhaps the most sought-after game fish in the world—the rainbow trout. Arctic char and grayling of the Arctic regions, Dolly Varden of the West Coast, bull trout and grayling of the northern Rocky Mountains, Apache trout of Arizona, golden trout of the high Sierras, and the Gila trout of New Mexico all but complete the colorful list of native North American salmonids and places them neatly into their ranges of origin. Within the Great Lake basin, it was the lake trout, brook trout, and Atlantic salmon that were the native salmonid representatives. The various whitefish species filled in respective regions throughout the continent.

Things began to change rapidly in the early 1870's when the United States Fish Commission started to redistribute our native fish throughout the continent via the steel rails. Using a special fish transporting car, the widespread introduction of the European brown trout intertwined the hodgepodge mixing of all North American salmonids by 1883. Forever afterwards, the clean lines of regional distinctions between separate species and subspecies of many salmonids became muddled. Though it wasn't uncommon for the transfers to do exceptionally well in their new habitats, gone was the genetic integrity of many strains once the distribution was complete. In many cases, hybridization of cutthroat and rainbows occurred; in others, separate subspecies of cutthroat were combined. In addition, little concern was given to the competition factor once the waters of two species were artificially overlapped. Obviously, not much thought was given to the preservation of distinctions, but at that time who knew better—or even cared? For better or worse, this is the legacy we have inherited, and except for isolated regions throughout the country, very few native stocks of salmonids have been unaffected by man's machinations. It was the fervor of this era that brought the McCloud River steelhead to the Great Lakes in the late 1880's.

The original range of the rainbow trout was widespread. Many subspecies and distinct races extended the entire length of the West Coast from the Baja of Mexico to the Aleutian Islands of Alaska. The rainbow's range is known to stretch into the Kamchatka Peninsula of Russia as well. Since the headwaters of the Columbia River begin in Idaho, the rainbow was native to its tributaries including the Salmon and Snake River drainages. This designated the furthest inland reach of the West Coast native. Kern River, Eagle Lake, Shasta, McKenzie River, Kamloops, etc. are but a few of the names that identify regional varieties of rainbow trout. Some forms were purely nonmigratory stream residents, others lived only in lakes. Some could endure extremely warm temperatures in high alkaline habitats while other hardy races could tolerate the harshest of cold climates. The beautiful rainbow trout, in whatever variation, was an impressive fish.

It is interesting to note that the rainbow was once classified as *salmo gairdneri*, while its numerous subspecies were given an additional Latin identification (i.e., Eagle Lake rainbow—*salmo gairdneri aqualarum*). The Kamchatka trout, discovered by Georg Wilhelm Stellar in the 18th century, was considered a separate species—*salmo mykiss*. "Mykiss" was the name given to this trout by the native Koryak people of the region. After years of study, however, taxonomists removed the rainbow and cutthroat from the genus *salmo* in the 1980's and reassigned them to the salmon's genus *oncorhynchus*, closely allying these trout with all six species of Pacific salmon. This was a significant step because of the notable parallels in the behavior of steelhead and salmon. Additionally, further study indicated that the Kamchatka trout was actually a rainbow trout and not a separate species as previously thought. Subsequently, all rainbows (to the dismay of some) have been reclassified as *oncorhynchus mykiss*—still honoring Stellar's original discovery as well as preserving the Koryak name.

The migratory or anadromous rainbow is the form identified as steelhead. (NOTE: technically, anadromous refers to fish migrating from salt to fresh water, potamodromous refers to similar migrations within a totally fresh-water system. To avoid confusion, however, we will use anadromous throughout the text.) A mere century and a half ago, hundreds of drainage-specific strains of wandering rainbow made their way into coastal streams and rivers from the southern tip of California to the upper outback of Alaska. Many rivers had fall, winter, spring, and summer overlapping runs—a seemingly endless pool of fish that could survive any of nature's foibles with a built-in genetic diversification that would surely guarantee the survival of this great fish. But in just 150 years, the steelhead has been extirpated from much of its original range. Progress and population has caused habitat destruction in forms of logging and development; overfishing and the need to build numerous dams to power man's lifestyle further accelerated the decline. With little or no regard for this national treasure, over 200 strains of steelhead have been obliterated off the planet, and the remaining survivors hang on by a thread waiting for some sort of comprehensive plan to save the last of these remnant Pacific strains. It is a tribute to perseverance that, despite it all, fractional wild strains of West Coast steelhead still continue to defy the ongoing trend that does so little to save this vanishing segment of our heritage. Most disturbing is the arrogant indifference that would deprive future generations of this valuable legacy.

Once thought to be the panacea for man's biological indiscretions, hatcheries have exhibited many shortcomings during the past decade. Though many will acknowledge the value of the hatchery system as a short-term management tool, these institutions cannot be relied upon as the sole solution for all our fishery woes. With regard to steelhead, hatcheries tend to ignore the genetic selectivity built into specific strains naturally engineered for individual tributaries. Mixed stock introduced into various random waters produce a weaker generic mongrel incapable, in many cases, of adapting to their new homes. In addition to diluting the integrity of existing wild strains, stocked fish display a vulnerability to disease as well. Even offspring reared from the exact same drainage and reintroduced into that same water demonstrate weaknesses in dealing with the complexities of ocean life along with other various character flaws. It would seem that, over time, much of the intangible wildness integral to the true temperament of the steelhead is all but eliminated from the hatchery form of the fish. The most tragic aspect of our reliance on hatcheries to bandage gaping environmental wounds is the critical time lost blindly venturing down dead-end paths. In the 90's, the numbers of wild Pacific stock with genetic integrity still intact numbers only in the thousands within selected drainages where there are any fish left at all. In the massive Columbia River system, for example, only three thousand wild fish returned to its headwaters in 1994. There are over one thousand miles of water in this system. The aforementioned fish caught by a friend in the Salmon River was one of less than a thousand of a unique wild strain designed by nature to travel 1000 miles—and they desperately cling to what little hope there is for survival.

When steelhead were introduced into the Great Lakes, its many unique characteristics were transported also. Despite the fact that several varieties of rainbows had been transplanted into the lakes by the early 1900's, it is believed that the initial McCloud River fish evolved into a unique Great Lakes strain with a stronghold in Lakes Superior, Michigan and Huron. Although hatcheries played a significant part in the pioneering stage of the lakes, many fish were just a generation away from the wild. Once on their own, these fish reproduced naturally, and slowly but surely wild populations increased and flourished. Identifying the true value of the naturalized, or wild, Great Lakes steelhead today is as important to the survival of this fishery as the remnant populations of wild steelhead are to the fishery on the West Coast. Whether or not these fish have any chance to thrive anywhere in the future depends on critical choices and commitments made now in the dawning of the 21st century.

3

Historical Background

The steelhead fishery did not just happen overnight in the Great Lakes. Initially much effort was expended introducing and nurturing stocks that were painstakingly transported over a series of years from the West Coast. Because of the relative lack of fishing pressure and a reasonably untainted environment in the early 1900's, these magnificent fish were allowed to populate naturally in abundant numbers throughout a major portion of the system. It wasn't until negative influences related to development in the 1940's, 50's, and 60's that it became plainly evident just how sensitive, and somewhat limited, the Great Lakes ecosystem actually is. When it comes to steelhead, we cannot forget those days: it is imperative to learn from what history has to tell us!

For a matter of perspective, the Great Lakes basin should be understood from the standpoint of natural history. In geological terms, the Great Lakes are infants. Prior to the formation of this great basin, the pre-existing geology dated back to the Pre-Cambrian Era some 600 million years ago. Then, the region was defined by mountain ranges and rivers that had formed over millions of years. The Great Lakes are a result of the Quaternary Ice Age that began over one million years ago. Resulting from a complex set of causes, ice sheets began to form during that period in the northern highlands of North America and Eurasia. Eventually huge glaciers, roughly two miles thick, spread and enveloped the entire northern area of our continent. Like a cosmic footprint, the effects of the last of the planet's five known ice ages can be traced in the scars it left behind. The North American glacier bulldozed and compressed the landscape, gouging and moving the earth's surface. In the northeastern portion of our continent, only remnants remained of the region's primeval mountain ranges. When the glacier began to melt and recede only about 12,000 years ago, the formative years of the Great Lakes began. Original rivers had reversed course, and water from melting ice began to fill the enormous, newly created depressions. Amazingly, the Great Lakes, as we know them, took final shape about 2,500 years ago—roughly during the Biblical times of ancient history. We now live in the post-Quaternary era, the period of time directly following the last ice age. Since the recurring phenomenon of massive glacier formation has been a cyclical part of the planet's natural history from its origins, essentially it can be said that the earth is now in a period between ice ages.

Life after an ice age changes dramatically. New species at all levels evolve, while others that can't cope go extinct. From a biological standpoint, the Great Lakes have not been in existence long enough to develop a substantially diverse network of life. Even the lakes' benthic drift organisms (small microscopic life) are few, and seem to be more river oriented than lake. In terms of geological time, man's intrusion into the dynamics of the Great Lakes occurred at the very beginning of the system's evolutionary process, and for better or worse, has become a major determinate in the lakes' biological development. The introduction of exotic species into the Great Lakes either accidentally or by design is man's legacy while, at the same time, symbolizing mankind's impact upon "nature's way." The steelhead, a Pacific native, is now most certainly a piece in this puzzling unnaturally "natural" process.

Did Seth Green, conservationist and New York State pioneer in fish culture, know of the great spirit of the anadromous rainbow when 7,800 Campbell's Creek ova were imported northeast to his privately owned Caledonia hatchery near Mumford, New York in 1874 and 1875? It has been surmised that originally there was no differentiation made between the eggs from steelhead or from the resident native fluvial rainbow, thus indicating a lack of knowledge about the species. Eggs from the same tributary of the McCloud River were subsequently shipped to Daniel Fitzhugh in Northville, Michigan in 1876, and they were reared at the private hatchery there on the middle fork of the Rouge River. Though fish from both hatcheries originated the Great Lakes steelhead program, Michigan's Au Sable River of the Lake Huron watershed was the first to receive fish in 1876. This was followed by the introduction of fish into New York's Genesee River, a tributary of Lake Ontario, in 1878.

It was the state of Michigan that persisted with an intense stocking program over the remainder of the 19th century. Throughout the 1880's, extensive plantings from several hatcheries located in Michigan were introduced to a number of Lake Michigan tributaries while Lake Huron's Au Sable continued to be heavily stocked as well. All fish were progeny of a McCloud River strain from either Campbell's or, subsequently, Crook's Creek. Most of the initial stocks at various points throughout the Great Lakes that decade were linked to this lineage, including the efforts of Pennsylvania, Ohio, Ontario (very limited) and, of course, New York. Even Indiana stocked its portion of the St. Joseph River in 1889.

While Michigan placed steelhead into Lake Erie's west end in 1882, the Ontario Government stocked Lake Superior for the first time in 1883 at Sault Saint Marie. Though many of Lake Erie's tributaries were deemed unsuitable for reproduction due to warm waters, low gradients, and heavy agricultural influence, stocking continued via Ohio in 1883, possibly by Pennsylvania during the 80's, and finally New York by the century's end. Under the auspices of the U.S. Fish Commission, McCloud fish were extensively introduced into the Minnesota, Wisconsin, and Michigan tributaries of Lake Superior by the 1900's.

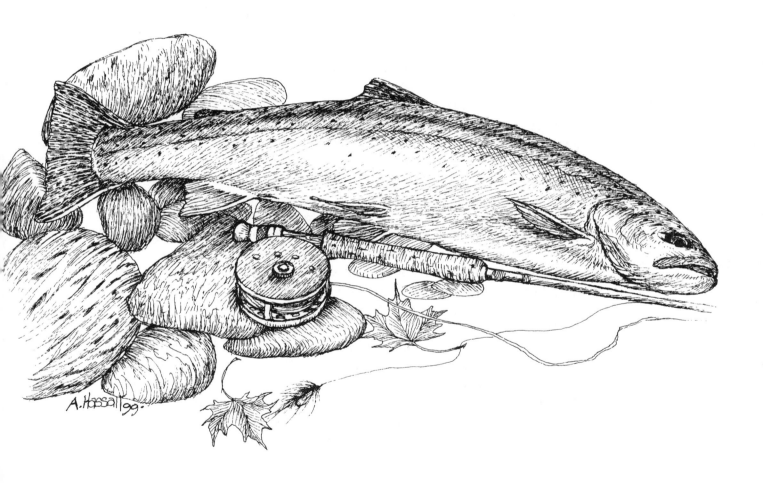

In Michigan, brood stock difficulties in 1890 led to the importation of a new West Coast strain of fish from the Klamath River. By the mid 1890's, this stock was utilized in both Michigan and New York hatcheries, and it marked the first departure from the McCloud River fish that inaugurated the Great

Lakes program. The U.S. Fish Commission, which operated Michigan's Northville hatchery since 1880 and also a facility in Duluth, Minnesota, received eggs from California's beautiful Redwood Creek in 1895 and 1896. Ensuing transfers of eggs from Oregon and Washington by the turn of the century were also recorded. Exactly how the introduction of these new strains of fish affected the integrity of the original stocks is not certain. It seemed quite clear that the systematic stocking of the lakes was intended to establish a self-sustaining population of rainbow trout throughout the entire system. By the 1900's, there were impressive indications that the migratory rainbow, most likely the McCloud strain, was doing very well in many tributaries of Lake Michigan and Lake Huron.

The success of the entire program was judged by commercial and sporting catches in the lakes and by the returns in individual drainages. Lake Michigan's Pere Marquette River recorded some of the earliest returnees by 1886. Good catches occurred in the Boardman River by 1890 and the Little Manistee by 1901. In fact, good spawning runs were known in several rivers from the Muskegon River northward on Lake Michigan's east shore by the 20th century's first decade. During this same period, runs became established in Michigan's Au Sable and Pine Rivers on the cross state Lake Huron shoreline. Though there were no recorded fish coming back to Michigan's Lake Erie streams, returns to this state's share of St. Mary's River in the Northern Peninsula were impressive. This strait connecting Lake Superior to Lake Huron indicated an increasing naturalized population of fish. It is unclear how Michigan's other Lake Superior rivers fared in the upper peninsula during this period. Great numbers of fish on the western end of the lake, spreading northward into Ontario, were noted during the early 1900's. In Lake Erie, the only early returns were recorded in several Pennsylvania streams by 1895. New York continued its stocking of all Lake Ontario's drainages, but any indication of natural reproduction was rare at this time.

When the Province of Ontario started its hatchery program in 1914, natural reproduction had already been established in some of its Lake Superior tributaries, including the St. Mary's River. By 1912, there had also been some fish introduced to the Georgian Bay drainages of Lake Huron by the Canada Department of Marine and Fisheries, and these rivers were receiving major runs by the 20's. Eggs from the St. Mary's region initiated the project at Mount Pleasant, which expanded to another hatchery in Normandale by 1917. Ontario's hatchery system was never a major production, it just barely supplemented a gradually expanding natural stock throughout the north shore of four lakes and the south shore of Lake Huron as well. The first official Lake Huron plant from this hatchery system was in 1922. Lake Ontario's Canadian shoreline received some fish by the late 20's, and even Lake Erie's water probably received some benefits from the Normandale hatchery. Wild fish continued to show up consistently in many of Ontario's tributaries throughout the century.

The rainbow fishery developed separately in each lake at its own pace throughout the 20th century. At the headwaters of the entire system, Lake Superior's anadromous fish were doing very well by the 1920's. Spawning runs in the west and north were well established, and there was by then much evidence of growing populations from the easternmost St. Mary's River southward along the Michigan and Wisconsin northern shorelines. Although the Province of Ontario stocked a few north shore rivers in 1934, 1951, 1952, and again in the late 60's and early 70's, Ontario's Superior rivers supported natural runs throughout the century. By 1920, the state of Minnesota finally started to take an active role in management and continued to enhance the lake's growing rainbow populations with a stocking program of its own. Up to this point, the U.S. Fish Commission handled Minnesota's waters. Lake Superior remained relatively unscathed by the abusive practices of colonization, and its fishery maintained itself even during the difficult years of the 50's and 60's when all the other lakes were facing difficult times.

By 1913, tremendous numbers of fish were evident in Lake Michigan from the tons of rainbow being netted commercially each year—a practice that was banned by the mid 1920's. While several of the aforementioned Michigan tributaries continued to spawn many fish, it wasn't until the late 20's that just a few of Wisconsin's Lake Michigan rivers started to show some reproduction. This lag was indicative of tributaries much less suited for spawning than the spring-fed flows of Michigan's waters. Indiana tributaries, including the St. Joseph, showed no evidence at all of natural reproduction. Illinois has no permanent tributaries along its short reach of Lake Michigan.

The 1950's was a bad era for much of the Great Lakes system, and Lake Michigan poignantly reflected the deterioration of these great waters. The anadromous rainbow population plummeted there by the mid 50's, a slide that had started with the arrival of both the sea lamprey and a bait fish called the alewife from the Atlantic coast. The effects of pollution and overfishing hastened the decline of many of the lake's species of fish. Not until the lamprey was controlled and an extensive planting program started in the 1960's was there a vast improvement in rainbow populations by the 70's. Progeny from the Manistee River were introduced into many of the Michigan rivers as well as Wisconsin's.

During the 20th century, Lake Huron maintained its low-profile status as the most unknown of the five Great Lakes. Less affected by man's abuses, a trait it shares with Lake Superior, fish populations there were also negatively impacted by the lamprey infestation well into the 50's. Similar to Lake Michigan, the runs of large fish utilizing Ontario rivers in the Georgian Bay region were impressive. Although initial stocking to its waters was very minimal in the late 1880's, the Saugeen, Bighead, and Nottawasaga displayed notable runs through the 20's. Fish had also naturally spread southward to the Maitland and Bayfield Rivers by the mid 30's. The rivers in Michigan's Huron watershed were exhibiting the same success. Lake Huron's lengthy Ontario north shore has few significant fishing rivers. Despite a general lack of historical information, there were indications of good rainbow populations on that side of the lake also. Since the Province of Ontario's stocking program has been irregular and rather insignificant from its inception in 1917, Lake Huron's Ontario population to this day is still very dependent on natural reproduction.

Lake Erie was never believed to have tremendous steelhead potential because of its shallow nature and warm seasonal streams, but there were always a few fish on the Lake's eastern streams of Pennsylvania and southwestern New York. Though there was record of some fish by the late 20's on the Canadian side of the lake, once Ontario started stocking its Lake Erie shoreline in 1936, significant runs of fish have been noted in its streams since that time. The state of Pennsylvania has actively stocked Lake Erie at times throughout the century; and during the last two decades, the numbers of fish released by the Keystone State have been massive. New York has also released a steady number of fish during this time. The Michigan streams and the attached Lake St. Claire have never been productive steelhead waters on the eastern end of the lake.

Although some of the earliest Great Lake plants occurred in the Lake Ontario watershed through the efforts of Seth Green's Caledonia Hatchery starting in 1878, New York's tributaries were never noted for supporting much natural reproduction. The smallest of the Great Lakes received good numbers of fish from the New York Fish Commission through the 20's and beyond. By the 1940's, there were only a few New York rivers with known natural reproduction, including the now renown Salmon River at Pulaski. The Province of Ontario began stocking its tributaries in 1927, and continued until 1936. Then there were no more records of stocking until 1954. During that period, there appears to have been a substantial naturalization of populations in some of Ontario's streams entering the lake east of Toronto.

The fact that Lake Ontario's massive numbers of Atlantic salmon had disappeared by mid 19th century and the subsequent inability of the lake to support naturalized runs of steelhead on the New York side pointed directly to the deleterious effect of man's presence on the shoreline of its waters. Lake Ontario was the first lake in the system to have been colonized by European settlers, and it didn't take man long to upset the balance of what must have seemed to be a limitless bountiful resource. Though specifically endemic to Lake Ontario, the Atlantic salmon was the only native salmonid to be entirely extirpated from the system. The introduction of rainbow offered some hope to fill the void created by the loss of the salmon, but the same problems that would impact both species were never addressed. Dams built on virtually every New York tributary blocked all spawning opportunities for the native salmon, and it would be these same obstacles that would impede the steelhead program. The insidious effects of pollution, starting in the 19th and continuing through the 20th century, combined with the sea lamprey's death grip essentially left Lake Ontario barren of sport fish by the 1960's. Though some fish made it through the worst of times, particularly on the less-affected Canadian shore, Lake Ontario's steelhead program was in dire shape by the end of the 1950's.

Between 1954 and 1970, the Province of Ontario stocked many of its tributaries once again, and New York also became actively involved in Lake

By the 1970's, steelhead were widely distributed throughout New York waters.

Ontario's steelhead program starting in the early 70's, stocking Chambers Creek progeny from Washington State. At the same time, the state began to address Great Lakes water quality after decades of degradation.

The history of steelhead in the Great Lakes has been one of peaks and valleys since the inception of the program. Within the system, there always seems to be one region doing well while another area battles one problem or another. The fact that the 1990's can still boast of such widespread steelhead sportfishing opportunities, despite ongoing impacts, is not only a tribute to the fish, but it also honors those managers from a bygone era who dreamed of a better tomorrow—five lakes full of rainbow trout.

4

The Modern Era

The modern era of Great Lakes salmonid management began in the late 60's after the acknowledgment of critical problems facing the system. While water quality, contaminants, habitat degradation, lamprey control, and dealing with the explosion of alewives became primary rehabilitation targets, it was during this period that the individual states were empowered to actively become involved in massive stocking programs. These programs not only restored the eroded naturalized and indigenous salmonid populations that occurred throughout the first half of the 20th century, but they also catapulted the count of Pacific salmonids to unprecedented levels as these fish became vital factors in the reformation of this dysfunctional system. With little knowledge of exactly how they fit into the natural scheme, the Pacific salmonids now occupy an important ecological, sociological, economical, and political niche. The steelhead, which had survived naturally to varying degrees throughout the century, were considered a significant element in this unfolding picture.

In the mid 1980's, the entire fishery management scheme for the Great Lakes was critically analyzed for the first time. According to Dr. Paul Seelbach, prominent research biologist for Michigan's Department of Natural Resources (DNR) Institute for Fisheries Research, there was little documented information when he began his in-depth Michigan steelhead studies in the early 1980's. The information base, however, on all species of salmonids (steelhead, salmon, char, brown trout, and Atlantic salmon inclusive) within the system has increased considerably during the 90's. The knowledge gained from the many ongoing studies and scientific research projects has become the basis for the close scrutiny given to the multidimensional management plans being developed throughout the basin for the next century.

The modern era marked the first time that the individual states started to take an autonomous role in enhancing sportfishing opportunities in the Great Lakes' waters. Up until the mid 1960's, the federal agencies were governing activities on the Great Lakes in conjunction with each state. These changes were precipitated by Dr. Howard Tanner, then Chief of Fisheries in Michigan. Subsequently, management practices were undertaken, in many cases, independently by each of the states and the Province of Ontario. It has only been within the early 90's that an interest in comprehensive cooperative management practices has come about. Up until this time, the sovereign rights of each state and province have dictated a fragmented approach to salmonid management. Although the volumes of material garnered from the many recent studies have been freely shared by the biological community, acting upon the information gained by the representative governing bodies has been a difficult process to implement.

A driving force in much of the management considerations is the high expectations of the Great Lakes' recreational angler. Sportfishing has become a billion dollar per year industry in the 90's, but the demands the sportsmen and their insatiable appetite place upon the fishery may be hard to sustain in the future. Many anglers have been spoiled by tremendous success rates since the 60's. But just as thousands of new anglers have begun to "discover" the salmonid fishery on their doorsteps during this period, a transition in the system has begun. Although the just-plant-more-fish mentality illustrates the simplistic ignorance that drives these demands, partial solutions lie in the responsibility of the Great Lakes sportsman to willingly understand the why and wherefore of future management schemes. The fight to eliminate the unsportsmanlike snagging of salmon throughout the lakes serves as a sad example of how difficult initiating change can be within the ranks of some anglers.

Unfortunately, many anglers seem content to ignore the changing dynamics within the lakes, and at the same time they use the general distrust for governmental agencies as an excuse to conveniently dismiss what biology is telling us. While it may be important to manage to the needs of the fishermen, the ability to sustain the fishery in a balanced ecosystem has come into question during the late 80's, and much biological evidence points to many changes occurring within the ecosystem. Sportsmen must understand their role as a variable factor contributing to these changes. As new management programs are developed, it would be helpful for this element to take a creative role in this process. Rather than placing unrealistic demands upon the fishery, more harmonious suggestions could be considered. In other words, it may be time for anglers to accept limitations that are not only more in line with reasonable expectations, but also more beneficial to the fishery.

Sifting through the ever-increasing pile of biological data is a task being undertaken by the states and the Province of Ontario in an unprecedented effort to determine a program that maximizes Great Lakes fishery potential while preserving the integrity of the system. For those of us specifically interested in steelhead, it is perhaps best to understand this fish in a broader context. An excellent keystone book, *Great Lakes Fishery Policy and Management: A Bi-National Perspective*, has recently been published, and it extensively covers the many intricate factors that compose this fishery. In particular, the section on Pacific salmonids by Dr. John Kocik and Dr. Michael Jones offers the best overview to date on the place the transplanted West Coast salmonids occupy within the Great Lakes aquatic community.

There are several present-day management schools of thought that range between two extremes. The enhancement theory proposes that since the system itself is so impaired, an active stocking program, particularly for Pacific salmonids, must be maintained to enhance the status quo for the good of the economy dependent upon this fishery. The restoration theory supports a return to management of endemic salmonids and other native species as a priority; but the damage done to the system is so irreversible that this may not even be a plausible concept. Efforts to restore Atlantic salmon back into its native ranges of Lake Ontario have met with very little success. While the lake trout has made a strong comeback in all five lakes after serious declines throughout the 20th century, the brook trout's widespread demise remains a troubling reminder of human impact and, at present, only a few native strains of this beautiful char struggle for survival in isolated locations. Others would like to consider the place of naturally reproducing salmonids, particularly steelhead, in the plan. While some question whether an "introduced" species should have this right of special treatment, many believe there is a role, particularly for wild steelhead, and it requires continuing research and evaluation. This same school believes enhancing the natural with a balanced number of hatchery-reared fish is the only way to maintain a quality fishery. In this way of thinking, understanding the ways of wild steelhead takes on profound importance.

Justifying the attention given to the presence of the Pacific salmonids in the Great Lakes has become a major focal point for some. However, the fact remains that much of the system has changed, and the resulting situation has to be dealt with from that perspective. Upon accepting this fact, it may be hard to quantify the true impact of Pacific salmonids, positive or negative, upon the entire system in terms of what is ethically right or wrong in the sense of historical authenticity. In the hundred-plus years of the steelhead's presence, these fish have occupied an apparent benign niche independent of the historical "what should be's." This trout's versatile nature links it to a wide array of food options, not necessarily upsetting the status quo even if the ecosystem wasn't impaired.

Hatcheries can enhance runs where sufficient reproduction is not feasible.

The success of the salmon species as a game fish, particularly in Lakes Michigan and Ontario, is linked to the overabundance of both the alewife and rainbow smelt that had grown disproportionately without a substantive predator base in the mid 20th century. The man-caused chain of events that brought the lamprey, alewife, and Pacific salmonid together dramatically illustrates the alteration of the Great Lakes' ecosystem as well as the interconnected dependency of exotic and endemic species seeking equilibrium in a closed ecological system. By 1960, it was believed that 90% of the total fish by weight in Lake Michigan alone were alewives. With such an abundance of bait fish, the situation couldn't have been better for coho and particularly Chinook salmon in the early 60's. Chinook populations correspondingly ballooned as these schools of salmon fed voraciously upon the multitudinous numbers of free-swimming alewives and smelt. It seemed that these introduced salmonids found a natural home in a setting that had long parted from the traditions of its natural history.

Many would theorize that man's influences are just another factor in the evolutionary process of the planet. Although this does not excuse excessive and abusive activities, it does acknowledge man's role in nature's way. In this context, accepting the Great Lakes for what they have become and managing them as such may be the wisest approach. Although the pendulum with regard to water quality and habitat has swung back toward environmental soundness, this does not repair the damage that has been done, nor accounts for the "acceptable level" of degradation that is simply a by-product of man's ever-increasing presence. Whether or not Pacific salmonids belong in the Great Lakes seems moot at this point. Because these salmonids require quality habitat to survive, they will always remain important indicators to the present health and condition of Great Lakes waters. Furthermore, the Pacific salmonids' usage of tributaries also provides additional information about the quality of the source water in virtually every drainage throughout the lakes.

With regard to cold water salmonid fisheries within the continent, comprehensive specifics have been sketchy. While most pertinent data dates back only to the 1960's in many areas, the concept of managing a quality trout and salmon fishery in an equally qualitative environment has surfaced to the level of significance only within the past two decades. The Clean Water Act of 1972 prompted many changes in our country's waterways. Subsequently, fish and game agencies throughout the country began to hire many more biologists to study existing fisheries in relation to management policies, and from these efforts notable fisheries were rehabilitated and many new ones evolved. In some areas, however, particularly on the West Coast, much ground has been lost during this same period despite knowledge gained. While not nearly enough time has lapsed to discuss trends in any fishery, periodic or cyclical, it would appear that on the short term every fishery goes through phases based on climatic, man-caused, disease-related, etc. influences. In the long term, these problems may seek their own resolution. But when it comes to angler expectation and an economy based upon sportfishing, long-term solutions often are not satisfactory. The angling public wants consistency, and this group exerts many demands upon managers. Since short-term solutions can somewhat be manipulated, decisions affecting the fishery are often based upon sound biological input and, at times, not so sound politics.

During the 90's, a phase of transition has begun to develop in the Great Lakes, and the Pacific salmonids are the indicators of this event. Much of the management in the Great Lakes during the modern era has centered around stocking massive numbers of Pacific salmonids since the 60's, particularly Chinook salmon. Because these fish thrived on the huge schools of free-swimming alewives and rainbow smelt, the salmon got big quickly and many businesses were established to accommodate the glut of interested anglers. In effect, this became a put-and-take fishery on a grand scale. People liked to catch a lot of big salmon, and they also liked to eat them.

The steelhead during this era had a relatively small cult following of loyal supporters and were pursued primarily in the tributaries of Lakes Superior, Huron, and Michigan. Most fishing activity took place for salmon offshore, and only incidental numbers of steelhead were taken in the process. While the massive stocking programs continued, questions arose as to the capabilities of the lakes to sustain this program. Although angler demand seemed insatiable, there was a limit to the number and size of fish these lakes could reasonably expect to produce. Supporters of endemic Great Lakes species were also voicing concerns about the effects of stocking on the rehabilitation of native populations.

Steelhead followers enjoyed much success as well during this period. The naturalized populations that had survived for one hundred years were substantially supplemented by hatchery fish. The interest in steelheading began to grow in the late 70's. Almost unnoticed, tremendous steelhead opportunities developed during the 80's in both Lake Erie and Lake Ontario, but these fish were overshadowed by the large numbers of salmon and the desire of many anglers to pursue them. To date (mid 1990's), it is believed that 294 million Chinook salmon have been planted in the Great Lakes.

During the late 80's, the alewife and rainbow smelt populations began to crash. While both size and numbers of Chinook in all lakes decreased, the ability to sustain the king salmon was scrutinized. The decline in forage fish certainly could be linked to the ravenous appetites of the salmon, though at this point it is uncertain whether this was the only factor that has contributed to this decline. In Lake Michigan during the late 80's, Bacterial Kidney Disease (BKD) was additionally responsible for wiping out large numbers of Chinook, especially naturalized populations, and still the forage continued to decrease. Some theories link the independent down cycle of the alewife community to an overwhelming stress factor on the Chinook populations that manifested itself as BKD. For reasons that are purely speculative at this time, the prey base in all five lakes seemed to have dropped off significantly, and this is a link in the chain of life that the salmon cannot do without. Some believe that the decrease in prey is purely cyclical. In the case of the alewife, periodic population declines are not uncommon. The introduced salmon and alewife populations would appear to be seeking a balance in a system that is trying to sort through years of ecological confusion. After all, 30 to 40 years of co-existence is really not that long of a period to firmly establish any patterns of consistency or predictability of populations.

As of 1996, populations of the alewife and Chinook seem to be back in balance in Lake Michigan as great runs were reported for that lake's tributaries. Whatever the cause for the past declines, Lake Ontario has been severely affected as well, and a joint decision in 1993 was made by New York and Ontario to immediately reduce the numbers of stocked salmon. Some believe that, by 1996, the forage base has rebounded even in Lake Ontario, but techniques to quantify those claims have been weak. Whether or not a management plan can be devised to maintain a proper balance within the bounds of the actual present-day carrying capacity of the lakes remains to be seen. An adjustment in angler expectation may be in order as well. Since it has been deemed that the alewife is now such an important factor in managing this modern era of the Great Lakes, many believe that it is imperative to

The modern era has created high-quality fly fishing opportunity for steelhead.

understand the factors contributing to prey limitations within the system. In early 1996, New York's DEC decided to get opinions from an independent expert panel of scientists to gain insight into the pelagic fish community of Lake Ontario. Under review is the bioenergetics of the alewife in relation to winter die off and predator base (lake trout and Chinook). There is also the consideration of reduced phosphorus/nutrient loading due to improved environmental laws coupled with the efficient filtering system provided by the recent exotic invader, the zebra mussel. Lake Ontario's cleaner water may negatively impact the population of the benthic (microscopic life) community which, in turn, is a vital component in the young alewife's diet. From a predation point of view, the alewife and even smelt contain an enzyme that breaks down thiamine in their predators which, in turn, can lead to death. Exactly how all these factors interact is not clear, but it does seem more evident than ever that the Great Lakes fishery can only be as good as its prey base allows it to be.

In reaction to the lack of large catchable numbers of salmon, anglers have begun to target steelhead in the lakes during the 90's. Steelhead have become the main object of pursuit for charter boat captains as well in Lakes Michigan and Ontario. This event has been the most significant factor affecting recent steelhead management plans. Because the quality of the fishing in the Great Lakes had reached a world-class level, the number of anglers increased dramatically during that period as well. The catch-and-keep-lots-of-fish mentality created by the salmon fishery was now turned loose upon the steelhead. Large groups of anglers desiring to catch and keep many steelhead has not boded well for populations of the migratory rainbow in all the lakes (lake trout have been similarly affected as well). Legal limits designed for taking salmon now seem inappropriate for these large trout, yet without a flinch, many steelhead are stashed into coolers. There seems to be no question that when steelhead are targeted, their numbers cannot withstand this kind of assault at a sustainable level either—even if the populations are supplemented by hatcheries. Although steelhead may have a better chance to subsist in the system because it can utilize a broader food base than the salmon, the dependency of these fish on the alewife and smelt is still unclear (i.e., managers in Lake Michigan consider the alewife an important aspect in the diet of its steelhead). Consequently, angling pressure and a food source that is not completely understood by managers could spell problems for this long-standing, successful Pacific salmonid of the Great Lakes. Statistics support downward population trends of steelhead at present, but the numbers have not crashed. A steady decline of steelhead in Lake Superior, Lake Huron, and, to a certain degree, Lake Michigan has caused much concern; and this trend has been directly linked to angling pressure and liberal limits.

In the late-developing lakes, the situation has progressed somewhat differently. Lake Erie never had a tremendous salmon fishery, but its rehabilitated walleye program has intrigued fishermen throughout the east. While this world-class walleye program developed, steelhead were ignored for most of the 80's. Lake Erie's massive stocking program, especially by Pennsylvania, has maintained a put-and-take scenario that still seems to be going strong despite the Canadian government's concern about overstocking in United States waters. A commercial fishery for rainbow smelt in Canada is blaming this artificially large population of steelhead for the reduced numbers of smelt in this lake. The Ministry of Natural Resources questions this lake's capability to sustain this number of steelhead, especially in the wake of the system-wide salmon declines.

The problems facing Lake Ontario's salmonid populations are complex. Toxic residue in the fish prompted official warnings not to eat fish caught in Lake Ontario and, as a consequence, there has been a voluntary catch and release within its waters for years. Although some still kept fish to eat them and others to get eggs for bait, many fish were released to be caught again. Populations of lake trout, steelhead, Chinook and brown trout grew to astounding numbers during the late 80's and fishermen's success rates reflected that fact. Efforts to restore Atlantic salmon have been slowed by the fish's lack of response in the lake as well as experiencing rearing difficulties in the hatcheries. Although there are few streams suitable at present for reproducing the *salmo salar*, there still remains a firm commitment on both sides of the border to re-establish a spawning population of this one-time prolific indigenous salmonid despite apparent setbacks.

In a sense, the concern for decreasing salmonid numbers in Lake Ontario occurred almost overnight. Although the crash in forage base rumored since the early 90's may only be a cyclical phenomenon, it adds another variable to the management puzzle of the modern era. Expectations may have to adjust to this lake's true carrying capabilities. As in Lake Michigan, the decrease in the number of Chinook prompted the charter boats to target steelhead in the deep waters of the lake. Liberal limits and a charter boat industry geared toward keeping many fish had reversed the voluntary release programs of years past based upon the fears, and even state recommendations, not to eat fish from this lake. Whatever the reasons, recent decreases in both the brown trout and steelhead runs, particularly within United States waters, have raised some serious questions for Lake Ontario.

The modern era of the Great Lakes has produced a complex fishery that demands a comprehensive plan. Each state and province is actively processing all the elements of Great Lakes fishery management. Steelhead have risen to the status of primary importance within the past decade. At present, the state of Michigan is formulating a steelhead management strategy for Lake Michigan which places a detailed focus upon the value of this lake's naturally reproducing fish. Since the hub of the system's historic steelhead fishery has centered in Michigan, it would only seem reasonable that this state lead the way in creative management of the species. Active fishery managers throughout specific regions of the Great Lakes have derived beneficial information from a variety of research projects applicable to a general understanding of this wonderful fish. These discoveries have fueled regional management plans, and the willful sharing of this data has inspired broader-based strategy programs as well.

5

The Genetic Connection

For years, the public has been led to believe that the elaborate system of hatcheries set up throughout the United States was the guaranteed cure-all for the multitude of woes facing our weary and degraded cold-water fisheries. Indeed, hatchery-manufactured salmonids rehabilitated many ailing fisheries during the 60's, 70's, and 80's; all of us who fish have enjoyed the fruits of these facilities at one time or another. The reliance upon artificially produced fish, however, has undergone much critical analysis within the past decade. While no one can deny the effectiveness of the hatchery system as a useful management tool, a blind faith dependency upon this modern era curative has led to many other deep-seated problems too complex to fix with planted fish. On the West Coast, for instance, the complacency created by hatchery programs has allowed a lax vigil over cold-water habitats. Dams were built, mountains denuded, and the ocean overfished—all resulting in diminished returns of anadromous salmonids. The belief that hatcheries could fill the void and mend the problem has proved generally to be false. Although the program in many cases has demonstrated an ability to address short-term fishery needs, hatcheries have evolved only as a Band-Aid solution that all but covers up the true nature of the uncertainties that beset our fisheries. Since 1991, over 300 separate stocks of West Coast salmonids have either gone extinct or have become endangered.

In the Great Lakes, the hatchery concept plays somewhat of a different role. Sustainable steelhead runs are maintained in regions of the Great Lakes where streams are incapable of naturalized reproduction. In most cases, feral brood stock is utilized; that is, eggs are gathered only from fresh-run fish each year and then reared to smolt size before being released back into or near streams of origin. While this hatchery concept still makes many purists uncomfortable, the valuable and exciting fishery provided in these areas cannot be overlooked. Some ideological conflict does occur, however, where naturalized runs are overlapped or supplemented by hatchery fish. Since Great Lakes managers have grown increasingly aware of the valuable contributions of the system's "wild" steelhead populations to the well-being of the Great Lakes' steelhead program, much recent attention has been directed to understanding the limitations of hatcheries in light of genetic integrity.

The field of genetic research in relation to our salmonid populations is a relatively new science with many technical complexities that even fishery biologists and managers have difficulty understanding. The diversity of West Coast salmonid strains has provided the basis of information that can be applied to the wild stocks of Great Lakes steelhead as well. It is important to realize that we do not all have to be geneticists to understand the significance of genetics. In simplified terms, scientists have merely confirmed through the genetic coding of DNA molecules what many sportsmen and biologists have suspected for years. Locked in the molecular makeup of the wild salmonids of the Pacific are the secrets of the species' survival. This is true also for the naturalized steelhead stocks of the Great Lakes which have had, in some cases, over twenty generations to adapt genetically to specific Great Lakes ecosystems. In other words, the particular intricacies needed for surviving unique situations have been imprinted genetically upon individual strains of fish over the ages. Genotypes, therefore, are the individual strains that carry the secrets for specific drainages. Such variability as summer, fall, winter, and spring runs are but a few examples of differences between strains that are rooted in the genes. But as genotypes disappear, so do the secrets. Hatcheries not only failed to recognize these subtleties, they cannot recreate in a generic fish the complexities it takes to replace the genotypes that no longer exist. Lost on the West Coast are the many widespread seasonal runs. Also, in many instances, strains that have been genetically engineered by nature for distinct ecosystems have all but vanished.

What does all this mean from an angler's point of view? Since those of us who fish are among the greatest beneficiaries of a healthy fishery, it would seem mandatory that we all understand the many factors that affect fish populations. This "hands on" understanding will not only satisfy our curiosity, but such angler involvement can also be an important factor in the management of these fisheries. When it comes to our steelhead on the West Coast and in the Great Lakes, the scientists have already provided much evidence that emphasizes the importance of wild stocks in both systems. We have learned that it is not only essential to cultivate an appreciation for these wild fish, it is paramount as well to realize that we cannot afford to lose the source of biological truth these last remaining stocks have to offer.

The importance of wild fish management was first noted in the 60's on Montana's Madison River. Although brown and rainbow trout were not native to these waters, they had naturalized in much the same manner steelhead had in the Great Lakes over about the same time period. Through observation, negative impacts to the wild residents were discovered when hatchery fish were planted in the same space. So irrefutable was the evidence to renowned fisheries specialist Dick Vincent that Montana's Fish, Wildlife and Parks (as this agency is known now) opted to manage all of the state's world-famous trout rivers exclusively for wild fish. This bold move has become the benchmark for wild fish management, because it was based upon empirical observation and critical thinking rather than genetic studies.

When it comes to wild fish management, there is a limited baseline of information available. It has been the tradition in North America that wild salmonids have been left to fend for themselves, and when populations begin to fail, recovery is based upon hatchery programs rather than an understanding of wild fish dynamics within its habitat. Although genetic research at least provides some factual foundation and insight into the complex makeup of wild salmonids, this field of study cannot be the only criteria. Noted fishery research biologist Dr. Robert Behnke acknowledges the benefits of genetic research, but he also warns about trying to justify the management of individual races of salmonids solely upon DNA sampling.

A wild steelhead smolt from a Great Lakes tributary.

This concept can only be understood in the broader context of biodiversity. Biodiversity is the belief in the interconnectedness of all species on the planet—all evolving to fill a specific niche in the earth's biological scheme. As natural global changes occur, certain species evolve to adapt to these changes over time while others, unable to cope, become extinct. To many simple-minded legislators concerned with a conservative pro-industry agenda, a biodiverse planet is unattainable in this age of man. According to this mind set, if a species goes extinct because of man's activities, that just emphasizes mankind's role in the "natural" scheme of things. Mankind's activities have so accelerated environmental changes that many species and their regional variations cannot adapt within only a few generations. Understanding biodiversity when it comes to fish is even more complicated because of genetic diversification within many species. Although legislators point to the fact that, for example, West Coast steelhead as a species are not extinct, this does not account for the many specific races that have disappeared.

To understand genetic diversity within the salmonid species, Behnke emphasizes the importance of recognizing the "range of adaptiveness" of these fish. Adaptiveness is the quality responsible for specialized traits and characteristics that have developed within strains of salmonids to cope with unique aspects of specific habitats. Some strains, for instance, are comprised of small fish, some large, some are great leapers while others are adapted for long distances—all these are genetic diversifications that fall within the range of adaptiveness. Some types of diversity in specific races, however, have not had the biological time to significantly imprint on any detectable hereditary material. Therefore, it may be impossible to provide "hard factual" data to sufficiently influence decision makers whose policies may determine the future of our fisheries. This is where critical thinking and logic based upon scientific observation becomes significant. Adaptiveness cannot be quantified, but it can be observed. Preserving this range of adaptiveness is the root determining factor for preserving the existing strains of wild salmonids wherever they exist. Logic itself would dictate that a one-fish-fits-all generic replacement is not sufficiently diverse to offer any viable solution or hope for the long-term future of our salmonid populations. Although genetic studies provide much insight, these studies alone cannot provide the fuel to solve the problems facing fishery management.

The key, therefore, lies not so much in a comprehensive understanding of genetics, but in how to effectively use the ongoing information obtained from this evolving field of research, particularly in conjunction with our hatchery system. Michigan's Dr. Paul Seelbach believes strongly in his state's wild fish, though he also emphasizes the importance of the hatchery in the scheme of the entire Great Lakes steelhead management program. He notes, however, that wild populations in the lakes are being given more serious consideration these days than ever before because of the data gathered since the mid 80's.

Preserving wild stocks, where they exist, is of vital importance to the Great Lakes fishery.

This same trend is reflected in West Coast management and serves as a great example of the interconnected philosophies spanning thousands of miles. Idaho's Salmon River illustrates the effective use of the hatchery system to preserve a strain of fish adapted to a journey of a thousand miles. The construction of eight dams on the Columbia system has created an insurmountable obstacle for steelhead of the upper Salmon River. Inconsistent flows during the spring fail to push smolts sufficiently down to the ocean. Long, warm reservoirs create thermal blocks impeding the return of the adults in the fall. On both ends of the journey, these steelhead face peril. Although most wild natives have been decimated, the Salmon River genotype has been preserved in a produced fish that maintains the genetic qualities it takes for the long journey. The Salmon River hatcheries literally flood the system with smolts and barge them downriver in the hope that a very small percentage survive the two-way journey.

To many serious sportsmen, there is little solace to be found in these hatchery fish. The mitigation efforts of dam construction have preserved the run, but have done little to save the wild stocks of Salmon River fish. Although token numbers of wild fish still exist, normal mortality in dwindling numbers of naturally reproducing fish presumably reduces the numbers ever reaching the smolt stage, therefore leading to a spiraling cycle of decline in wild fish. By the mid 90's, there were only an estimated one thousand wild steelhead returning to the Middle Fork of the Salmon River which enters the Salmon a few hundred miles below its headwaters. The Middle Fork is not supplemented by hatchery stock and the trends are dismal. It would seem that, without man's artificial help, the true wild native cannot survive mankind's contraptions.

Hatcheries have also preserved a strain of large fish in the Clearwater River, another tributary of the Columbia flowing out of Idaho. However, to those who fish these waters, it has become quite apparent that the hatchery fish does not at all compare to its wild counterpart in either heart or soul. Although certain traits are kept alive in a hatchery fish, there clearly is a quality lost in the process—the spirit of the wild steelhead. In addition, it seems that hatchery fish accumulate and then perpetuate weaknesses as well as characteristic flaws that eventually are exhibited in these fishes' ability to survive in the long term. Both the Salmon and the Clearwater indicate the value of a hatchery system on the one hand and the shortcomings on the other. When habitats are so severely altered, options are few.

Another strain of West Coast steelhead (important to the Great Lakes fishery) also provides additional insight into the preservation of specific genetic characteristics. The well-known Skamania steelhead is named after the Washington State county where the Wausugal River system is home to this unique strain. This fish is derived from a naturally occurring small run of summer steelhead that has developed a great leaping ability because only the heartiest progeny were able to jump a high falls to continue onward to the upper reaches of the river. This resulted in a naturally selective, but small and limited, stock of well-adapted fish. It was this trait that the hatchery sought to preserve in a summer run strain. Since this fish could tolerate warm temperatures, it is considered the ultimate summer steelhead; and consequently, hatchery stocks were widely utilized throughout the West Coast. There has been concern, however, that genetic weaknesses could occur in the future since the pool of fish tapped for eggs was so small. Initially, some Great Lakes managers expressed worry about introducing this new strain upon the well-established naturalized Great Lakes steelhead populations if, in fact, there is some substantial weakness in the future linked to this strain. Although it may be too early to investigate whether these fears have any foundation, for now there is no question that the Skamania provides some exciting summer and early fall fishing opportunities where they occur throughout the Great Lakes system.

Some may think that making the genetic connection in Great Lakes steelhead has little merit because these introduced fish have origins based upon a mixture of several strains throughout the system. Also, it may be argued that these fish really haven't had the time to develop any significant genetic imprinting to specific reaches within the lakes to make a difference. Although these points will be discussed on a lake-by-lake basis later in chapter six, managers on Wisconsin's Brule River and Michigan's Little Manistee have realized the importance of these particular "strains" of Great Lakes steelhead for years. Without the benefit of scientific genetic support, these strains have been preserved through hatchery programs because of the belief that important adaptations have begun to evolve within these fish since 1880 (and over twenty generations) to warrant special attention. Whereas Brule River fish are specifically targeted for rehabilitation in that river only, the Little Manistee strain is more widely stocked along Michigan's Lake Michigan shoreline to supplement naturalized populations. This strain is stocked in other parts of the Great Lakes as well. The importance of the Little Manistee strain has been recognized for decades, and it remains a vital cog in Michigan's wild steelhead program.

For the average sportsman, understanding the connections between wild fish, genetics, and hatcheries may not only be complex, but confusing as well. In the Great Lakes, many studies have just begun, and we all must realize that such science is a work in progress, revealing bits and pieces of a total picture that may take generations to comprehend. Encouraging these studies and heeding the insights revealed may be the most important role sportsmen can play in the process. We don't have to be scientists to appreciate what scientific studies can teach us. In general terms, there is enough factual support to indicate the importance of wild fish to any system that supports them, and it is imperative to nurture all the data these fish can reveal. For these reasons alone, there should be a priority placed on wild fish management whether it be the West Coast or the Great Lakes.

In the Great Lakes, there is an evolving belief in the philosophy that supports wild steelhead. On a lake-to-lake, state-by-state-by-province basis, plans for the 21st century are being developed now that emphasize wild fish management based upon the growing understanding of naturalized steelhead in the system. The lessons to be learned, particularly from the West Coast, are sad and harsh: there is no way to manufacture replacement wild steelhead strains once they are gone. The steelhead of the Great Lakes are direct descendants of diversified West Coast fish, and many have had over 100 years to meld into the fresh water way of life. It has become extremely evident that these naturalized citizens of the Great Lakes cannot be squandered in the same manner as their West Coast relations.

6

Management Trends

Fishery biology is a science based upon accumulated data gathered primarily in the field. Although long-term trends are best understood from years of collected scientific input, widespread fact gathering in most fisheries has a relatively short history. Still, as factual pieces are systematically compiled like the parts of a puzzle, the big picture takes shape as revealing insights unfold. At best, a fishery is a work in progress, ever changing, no beginning or end, and man's part in manipulating controllable factors is now a part of this evolutionary process. A portion of our angler dollars finances the men and women who are building a data base of pertinent facts that will contribute to a broader knowledge of the waters we fish.

Understanding the dynamics of the fresh-water steelhead fishery is as diverse as it is complex. The Great Lakes management agenda is often thought of as a put-and-take program, not only by many familiar with this expansive volume of water, but also those viewing it from afar. While it is true that the hatchery-raised fish still figures prominently into the strategy in certain sections of the system, wild fish make up a substantial portion of the runs in many other regions. The importance of historically naturalized populations has been undeniably recognized as the foundation upon which the future hopes of the fishery program must depend. Management perspective has changed dramatically over recent years as more and more importance is placed upon identifying wild stocks and the drainages that can support them. The increasing costs of producing hatchery fish and the disease potential now associated with these artificially reared rainbow are a few issues receiving considerable attention during the 90's from biologists around the country.

The wild card that overshadows the ability to effectively manage the Great Lakes fishery is the continued influence of the 140 or so exotic plants and animals introduced into the system since the arrival of the white settler. Many such interlopers are responsible for much of the habitat alteration and degradation found throughout the world. Much loss of biodiversity can be linked to introduced species as well. Freed from a system of checks and balances within their native range, exotics will often overrun their new habitats and out-compete existing native species. Under the right conditions, their numbers may explode and their populations at that point are very difficult to control, let alone eradicate. Ironically, the Pacific salmonids fall into this category despite becoming an important and somewhat manageable part of the impaired Great Lakes ecosystem. While other exotics have failed to get permanently established, some have the potential for widespread devastation.

The sea lamprey (*Petromyzon marinus*) is probably the most infamous of all exotics ever to spread through the Great Lakes. Although there are four species of lamprey native to the Great Lakes, it was this ancient introduced exotic dating back 450 million years that was the problem. This snaky fish has been responsible for destroying tremendous populations of sport fish for decades. The sea lamprey migrated from the Atlantic Ocean. Once it established in Lake Ontario during the 19th century, it spread through the entire Great Lakes via the Welland Canal system. Historically, it was thought that the lamprey entered the Great Lakes through the St. Lawrence Seaway, but there were too many rapids for the lamprey to utilize that path. The Erie Canal provided the actual route. The eel-shaped parasite has been able to adapt to fresh-water existence in much the same manner as the Pacific fishes have been able to do. In the process, however, this parasite with a toothy disk-shaped mouth has wreaked havoc on Great Lakes large predator fish populations, particularly lake trout. By latching onto a fish, it sucks out all of its host's bodily fluids until it is dead.

The state of Michigan was the first to conduct any comprehensive study of the sea lamprey in the 1940's. It was then recognized that, without a firm understanding of this creature there was absolutely no chance of dealing with it. By 1949, the United States Fish and Wildlife Service became involved, researching ways to control this devastating predator. Of the 3,000 tributaries that enter the Great Lakes, it was found that the lamprey utilized 371 of them for spawning purposes. Like other anadromous fish, the lamprey swims upriver looking for suitable gravel. When the eggs are fertilized, they hatch about 20 days later. The small larvae burrow into the gravel and live in the stream from 3 to 13 years before they begin their parasitic career in the larger body of waters. Although concrete barriers were built on some select tributaries and electrical barriers were used as well to block upward migration of the lamprey, during the mid 50's, all attention turned to a selective chemical treatment used to destroy the lamprey in the vulnerable larval stage. It was found that when the chemical TMC (3-trifluoromethyl, 4-nitrophenol) was synergized with a small amount of a certain molluscicide, it could effectively ferret out sea lamprey larvae with minimal damage to other native species within the stream. A highly regulated process pumped select amounts of the poison into the stream based upon its dynamics. By choosing particular periods of the year, based upon the life cycle of native species, the risk could even be minimized further. The only permanent damage to native species using this process are the other native lampreys. By the mid 60's, the decline of lampreys in treated areas was dramatic. As funding became available, every affected area was treated. There has been some indication that the rainbow trout are able to survive lamprey predation to some degree, but as the lamprey numbers increased in Lake Michigan, populations of rainbow correspondingly declined by 1950. Although Georgian Bay steelhead seemed to withstand the lamprey onslaught to a certain degree during the period, their numbers rebounded considerably during the late 60's after lampricide treatment of the spawning streams. Ongoing methods of lamprey control, such as electrical barriers, have been developed (used historically for control counting of lampreys as well). This method has been questioned because of the impending threats these procedures pose to the migrating wild steelhead at times of spawning as well. It is important to realize that the sea lamprey has not been eradicated, just controlled. The process is ongoing.

Another exotic that has caused much concern recently is the zebra mussel. Introduced via the ballast of overseas freighters, this mussel is fingernail-sized and is native to the Caspian Sea region of Asia. Discovered in the Lake St. Clair area in 1988, these mussels have been found in great numbers throughout Lakes Erie and Ontario, and they continue to spread elsewhere in the lakes. They have severely reduced and eliminated native mussel species. This prolific mollusk sticks to anything and virtually covers, in great numbers, everything to which it becomes attached.

Fears are that this mussel would alter the food chain significantly while eating itself out of house and home on the Great Lakes' plankton supply. Each mussel filters one quart of water per day. The result of this activity in Lakes Erie and Ontario has been crystal-clear water and the rebirth of native weeds that have not been able to grow for decades because of the lack of clarity. To this point, it seems young fish use these weeds for cover, leading to an increase in various fish populations. So far the impacts of the zebra mussel have been difficult to assess. At present, it would appear that its populations may be declining into equilibrium with the system, but the ongoing effects of these shellfish are vigilantly being monitored.

The European ruffe is probably the most feared of recently introduced exotics. At the very least, it represents the kind of ongoing threat that constantly besieges the biological integrity of the Great Lakes. Found in the Duluth area of Lake Superior, this small but pesky member of the perch family has already proven its ability to alter ecosystems where it has invaded lakes in both Europe and Russia. Since it is highly reproductive, can eat a wide array of foods, and its spiny features make it difficult for predator fish to eat, the ruffe has all the ingredients it needs to out-compete existing species of fish. Its rapid spread through the western end of Lake Superior is alarming, and recently the ruffe has been discovered as far north as Thunder Bay.

Exotic species have been and will continue to be a major force in the dynamic makeup of this fresh-water system as the Great Lakes continually seek some sort of balance in an environment severely altered by man's presence. With a return to a native state not even an option, the best we can hope for is a system of management strategies that may be able to artificially keep all the forces—good and bad—in check.

An important element in the overall fishery management trends within the entire Great Lakes basin is the role of the Great Lakes Fishery Commission. This joint Commission between the United States and Canada assumed duties on July 1, 1956, and these duties were twofold: (1) develop coordinated programs of research in the Great Lakes and recommend measures which will permit the maximum sustained productivity of fish stocks which are of common concern based upon the findings and (2) formulate and implement a program to eradicate or minimize the sea lamprey population in the Great Lakes.

The direction of the Commission through the 90's was defined by the Strategic Vision, a plan which reflected the ecological and institutional complexity of managing the basin as well as renewing the Commission's commitment to an ecosystem management approach for the five lakes. There are three components of the vision:

1. To foster healthy Great Lakes ecosystems
2. To formulate integrated management of the sea lamprey
3. To form partnerships with institutions and stakeholders, which includes all the states and one province

A high priority of the Commission is to conserve biological diversity through rehabilitation of native species, communities and habitats. Along with encouraging the protection of healthy ecosystems, the Vision encourages natural reproducing fish populations and self-regulating fish communities. Among considerations that provide sustainable benefits to society, the Vision supports the value of fisheries with increased contributions from wild fish. And though Pacific salmonids are not native to the basin, the Commission recognizes they do have an acknowledged role. Specifically, populations of wild steelhead will play an important part in the future evolution of the Great Lakes ecosystem.

What follows is a lake-by-lake account of studies and policies that will define management trends into the next century.

Lake Superior

From the beginning, the steelhead's existence in the most undefiled of the five Great Lakes has been characteristically a rugged one, but they adapted well. Although these first fish stocked near the Sault Ste. Marie region were of McCloud origins, subsequent plantings in the Duluth area mixed several other strains of West Coast fish into Lake Superior as well. How these strains intertwined with each other is anyone's guess, but the assumed blending of fish with varied West Coast heritages developed into the naturalized steelhead that have existed in Lake Superior for over 100 years. The resulting progeny are a typically slow-growing but hearty breed of small fish well-suited to the extremely cold Superior environment.

Within Lake Superior waters, the adult steelhead must endure the most severe of conditions affecting survivability and growth rates. Steelhead grow best between 51 and 68 degrees, yet the average annual surface temperature

Jerry Kustich displays a hearty Lake Superior steelhead before its release. Scott Smith photo.

of Lake Superior is only 41 degrees. Its average small-size adult can be directly linked to a growing season of only 66 days when surface temperatures are above 55 degrees—none over 60 degrees. By comparison, fish in some areas of Lake Michigan have 133 days of 50 degrees or more—and 73 of those days are over 60 degrees. Biologists indicate that during austere seasons of very low temperatures, fish numbers are negatively impacted. Under these extreme conditions, spawning in Lake Superior's tributaries is a challenging struggle.

Understanding the wild steelhead of Lake Superior is a complex matter. A lake-wide genetic study by eminent authorities Drs. Charles Krueger and Bernie May proves that genetic variations definitely exist between separate populations of Superior steelhead, and these variations can be detected in drainage-specific fish throughout the lake. The fact that there is little overlapping of fish from one drainage to the next is an important discovery, and these differences can even be seen in various tributaries with limited spawning potential and small numbers of returning fish. This discovery is especially significant with regard to the tributaries of the north shore.

From Duluth to Sault Ste. Marie, the tributaries into Lake Superior flow out of the geological region known as the Canadian Shield. These spate drainages are typically high-gradient, rocky, fast-moving streams and rivers with little groundwater influence. From a steelhead point of view, the most important characteristic of these tributaries is the most limiting one as well. A great number of streams and rivers have impassable falls that block the movement of migrating steelhead at some point, thereby restricting populations, in some cases, to very short lengths of streams. Consequently, many of these drainages are limited in the number of fish each can produce. Since returning steelhead are then concentrated and confined, they become easy targets for the technically adept steelheader. Further, because most runs are drainage specific, angler influence alone could considerably impact certain populations of fish. Unpredictability of runs, high water, inclement weather, etc. probably have saved populations from complete obliteration at the hand of the steelheader. Although there have been notable decreases in north shore runs since the early 1980's, it is still undetermined whether the problems are linked to in-stream or in-lake survival. There is no question that anglers have had a great impact upon this limited resource, and the recognition of this influence has been a major step in managing remaining wild stocks throughout Superior.

The composition of many south shore rivers differs considerably from that of the opposite shoreline. Winding through mixed forests, some heavily logged, many are lower gradient and gain some flow from groundwater and springs. One of the most important wild steelhead rivers in the entire Great Lakes basin is Wisconsin's Brule River that enters the lake from the south shore some twenty miles east of Duluth. Historical data shows this river to have been a significant steelhead fishery back into the 1920's, and that the Wisconsin state record rainbow comes from its waters. But it is the insight this river has given into the nature of Lake Superior steelhead that is perhaps its most notable asset. Brule River studies conducted by Dennis Pratt and Bill Blust are among the first to recognize the importance of keeping specific strains of Great Lakes steelhead intact, and the findings have greatly influenced the comprehensive management picture of Lake Superior.

When a series of combined events in the early 1980's led to seriously depressed steelhead runs in the Brule by the mid 1980's, there was a realization that things needed to change quickly before this valuable aspect of Wisconsin heritage was lost. Research by Rob Swanson on Wisconsin's Pike Creek in 1985 revealed the significance of repeat spawners in that system. Through the study of scale samples, the percentage of repeat springtime spawners in Pike Creek was able to be determined, and this became a useful and easily obtainable index of the status of spawning stocks. This significant discovery served as a model for other Lake Superior tributaries and formed the basis for additional studies and management practices. Applying this knowledge to the Brule River gave even more insight into the impact of increased fishing pressure and the ability to sustain angler harvest on the river during that period. The findings that runs were comprised of 50-60% repeat spawners pointed heavily to growth and recruitment restrictions in the severe habitat of the lake. In other words, fish harvested one year were directly taking fish from the next year's run while depleting overall spawning potential at the same time. It was found that a six-year-old fish from this environment is only 26 inches and may have spawned three times already. A 28-inch fish that had spawned five times was eight years old. In addition, these models hold true for most regions of the lake. First-time spawners occur between 16 to 20 inches. Methodical harvesting of prime spawning-age fish was seriously depleting the run on the Brule. Understanding this revelation led to strict regulation changes in 1989. By 1994, a one fish over 26 inches limit was enacted on the Brule to insure that all returning steelhead spawn at least one time.

During this period, Brule River's depressed runs have been enhanced by hatchery-reared fish. Managers, however, recognized the value of keeping the Brule River strain intact, so eggs taken only from ascending Brule River adults are utilized and then returned as smolts. The hatchery, in this case, was viewed as an effective tool to work with native stocks rather than an excuse to overwhelm the river with generic replacement steelhead. As the Brule River run continues to be restored, the state of Wisconsin has admirably engaged in an active angler education campaign to encourage those who pursue these special fish to voluntarily release all steelhead and to responsibly recognize their potential impact on the resource. In addition, seasonal closure of prime spawning water allows fish to reproduce without the added stress of

The fish way on Minnesota's Knife River. Jerry Kustich photo.

angling pressure. It should be noted that steelhead populations in Wisconsin's other south shore streams are maintained naturally.

Minnesota's share of north shore tributaries has also been plagued by serious declines in naturalized runs during the 1980's. With only 180 miles of tributary streams accessible to steelhead, limited spawning capabilities combined with increased angling pressure have severely impacted this fragile network of waters flowing into Superior. Although this localized system produced a historically notable wild steelhead fishery from 1940 through 1960, decreases in populations were first noted in the 70's. The streams in the Duluth area account for 136 miles of accessible river, 120 miles are included in the Nemadji, Blackhoof, and Knife River drainages alone. The balance of steelhead-attainable streams on the upper shore all the way to the Canadian border are both small and short, but all support runs to varying degrees.

In an effort to enhance offshore fisheries, several domestic strains of rainbows were introduced to Lake Superior during the 70's. These were lean times for the lake thanks to the lamprey, so the eventual successful stocking of Kamloops rainbow was welcomed by area anglers. During that era, wild steelhead stocks were supplemented by the release of Michigan's Little Manistee strain, but these efforts were only moderately successful. In 1989, eggs taken from the Knife River were reared in the French River Coldwater Hatchery to smolt size and then released into both the Little Knife and French

Rivers in the spring of 1990. Returns of these fish were alarmingly low. As the wild stocks continued to decline throughout the 80's and supplemental stocks failed to pick up the slack, concerned fishery managers and sportsmen realized the need to deal with the problem.

In 1991, the Minnesota Department of Natural Resources formulated the North Shore Steelhead plan that would be enacted between the years 1992 and 2002. The long-term goal of this plan is "to stop the decline of adult steelhead and to gather the necessary information to rehabilitate wild steelhead stocks." To understand why steelhead are declining, the DNR and anglers needed to know more about the steelhead and whether wild fish are better adapted to survive the rigors of Lake Superior than hatchery-reared fish. Krueger and May were contracted to search for genetic variations within specific Minnesota waters. Using the electrophoresis process, they found there were genetically identifiable populations of wild steelhead in all Minnesota tributaries with additional significant variations among samples within certain streams. There was a differentiation between hatchery and wild stocks, and in rivers where applicable (i.e., Knife, Baptism, Devil Track), there were genetic contributions from the Little Manistee strain mixed with existing wild stock. Surprisingly, it appears that no steelhead had ever mixed with the Kamloops lake strain. The implications of these findings was to formulate the plan in order to preserve stream-specific strains by stopping the introduction of new strains of rainbow into the area. If stocking does occur, the brood fish must come from specific streams and they must not be mixed with any others from different streams. Streams that have good potential for natural reproduction or that have limited fishing potential will not be stocked.

In addition to these genetic studies and revised stocking strategies, the plan addresses habitat issues, monitoring stations, economic impact studies, and restrictive regulations. A one unclipped, over 28 inch fish per day limit virtually implies a catch and release mandate. Dealing with the Midwest meat fisherman mentality on behalf of quality wild fisheries is no easy task in the Great Lakes, and for this commitment alone, Minnesota deserves much praise.

There has been substantial efforts to study the exact reasons contributing to the decline of Minnesota steelhead. The increase of exotic species in the lake, coupled with a rebound of indigenous lake trout, may be undermining survival of natural recruits once they reach the lake. Studies also have shown that Minnesota fish spending two years in-stream survive better than one-year recruits. Since in-stream water conditions vary greatly on north shore tributaries, there are many factors that could prevent the regular development of two-year-old smolts. In an effort to load the system with fry, a fish trap is set up on the French River. The eggs are then hatched in the hatchery on the banks of the river and immediately released into the river when the egg sac has buttoned up sufficiently. In this case, it is a matter of numbers—more fry may eventually lead to more smolts.

On the Knife River, an improved fish way may hold the key to survival of that particular strain of steelhead. The trap there is monitored daily to allow only wild fish up to the 70 miles of spawning water above the river's natural barricade. In 1997, a smolt trap was added to create both a safe passage for dropping down smolts while at the same time getting an actual count of wild smolts produced in the Knife that enter the lake. These numbers can then be correlated to future return counts of adult fish which, in turn, could determine whether the steelhead problems lie within the stream or in offshore waters. From that information, further strategies could be developed.

It will take years to determine whether the implementation of wild fish management can lead to a restoration of quality steelhead fishing on Minnesota's north shore. Managers feel that Minnesota steelhead runs have always had a high degree of irregularity due to the intense variability facing these fish every step of their existence. Since little effort was given to quantify these runs over the years, only speculation and spotty records can determine the potential of this fishery based on historical actuality. As of 1998, the runs continue to struggle. At this point, the fate of the wild steelhead that swim in Minnesota's waters hangs in the balance of the great unknown.

During the 1980's, the same patterns of population decline were also being seen on Ontario's portion of the north shore despite some longer drainages and many more rivers. The average size of fish decreased significantly as well throughout the period.

Based upon the concerns expressed by the serious local steelheaders, the Lake Superior Management Unit of Ontario's Ministry of Natural Resources (MNR) led by avid steelhead supporter and biologist, Jon George, developed a three-year co-operative program in 1991 with the North Shore Steelhead Association of Thunder Bay to study the situation. Western rivers were studied first, then eastern rivers were added to the program in 1993. Swanson's model of repeat spawners became the basis of the study. Data was gathered by workshop-trained anglers from across the region. Using sampling kits, anglers were requested to collect length, sex, and scale sample from all rainbow trout caught (kept or released), plus any other fish they witnessed caught during their time on the river. The Sault and District Anglers Association and the Sport Fishing Development program of the City of Sault Ste. Marie conducted these creel surveys in the eastern district. All data was gathered along with the scale and sent to Jon George for evaluation.

Scales from the anal area were pressed on plastic acetate slides and examined on a microfiche reader for spawning checks. These checks show up as a jagged scar, and multiple scars indicate the number of years individual fish had spawned. Maiden fish, of course, exhibited no scars at all. The number of fish released vs. the number kept was tabulated on a per tributary basis, and subsequent data from following years were evaluated to determine the influence of harvest rates on repeat spawners.

In the final analysis, it should be no surprise that rivers with high harvest rates had significantly lower repeat spawners when compared to drainages that had high release rates. As repeat spawners decrease, so does the population. This does not even address the genetics lost when repeat spawners coded with survival skills of over 100 years are reduced to table fare. In essence, this simple experiment validated the concerns of management and anglers throughout the entire Lake Superior system.

Although it was determined that male mortality is naturally higher than that of female spawners, recommendations based upon these findings were that fisheries managers should attempt to maintain a 55% repeat spawner program (both sexes) in Canada's Lake Superior waters. Regulation changes were utilized to attain these goals. A daily bag limit of one fish under and one over 20 inches was enacted. Although this replaces the liberal 5 fish over 20 inch daily limit, many feel that this new regulation is not strict enough to deal with the spiraling population decreases.

Until the mid 1990's, the only active stocking program on the Canadian north shore was handled by Sault Ste. Marie Sport Fishing Development in nine tributaries up to Pancake Bay northwest of the city. Eggs derived from angler-caught fish were taken and reared at the city hatchery. The eggs were mixed and matched (along with the genetics) and returned as 5-6 inch fin-clipped yearlings the following spring. Though this was a rather minor enhancement program, it was feared that the mixture of returning stocks could adversely impact and dilute naturalized runs based upon knowledge garnered from other regions in the Lake. A lack of funding has put this program on hold.

Michigan's Upper Peninsula shoreline along the southeastern section of Superior falls into the category of management obscurity. With the state of Michigan's main thrust of attention given to the Lake Michigan tributaries and, to a lesser degree, its Lake Huron shoreline, the Lake Superior tributaries seem too far removed to manage them with the same dedication seen throughout the rest of the basin. However, Paul Seelbach's and Barry Miller's research regarding the dynamics of hatchery and wild steelhead on the Huron River corroborate findings in other sections of the lake. Although the river was found to be fairly unproductive from a wild fish standpoint, with runs comprised of 54% three- to four-time repeat spawners, supplementation with stocked Little Manistee strain fish was certainly a futile effort with a return rate of only 4 fish per 10,000 stocked. The recommendation to stock with a local wild steelhead progeny and limit the harvest of wild fish parallels the conclusions of Wisconsin, Minnesota, and Ontario in their respective waters.

Little else is accurately known about the balance of Michigan's south shore rivers. There is thought to be about 40% natural reproduction in the popular Two-Hearted River and also in the Sucker River. Although both of these tributaries receive supplemental stocks of Little Manistee fish, many are harvested annually thanks to a three-fish daily limit. It has not yet been determined whether the Lake Superior genetics have been diluted by the stocking of Lake Michigan fish.

The waters of Lakes Superior, Michigan, and the northern portion of Huron are subject to Native American treaty fishing rights dating back to the early 1800's. A series of federal rulings have guaranteed the rights of the Chippewa, Ottawa, and Menominee nations to fish these waters. These rulings were made in the states of Michigan and Wisconsin as well as the Province of Ontario. Though some gill netting was banned in a U.S. District Court during the late 70's, the U.S. Court of Appeals subsequently ruled that no treaty fishing rights could be regulated unless it is shown that fisheries are being depleted.

In 1985, a consent agreement between Michigan, the U.S. Department of the Interior, the tribes, and other organizations was enacted by the U.S. District Court, and it provided mutually understood rules and management guidelines to be followed in the aforementioned waters until the year 2000. Again, some gill net restrictions were set up and regulations banning the netting at the mouth of tributaries were also put into place.

While the effects are only speculative, some natives have targeted steelhead with gill nets in various locations within American and Canadian waters of Lake Superior. No matter what side of this sensitive issue an individual's belief lies, ethical or otherwise, the end result is still the same—a reduction of steelhead numbers in the lake. On both sides of the border complaints exist, even from tribal members themselves, about the use of nets in the mouths of tributaries during spring spawning runs. Abuses are difficult to control, and agencies quickly drop this political hot potato when any questions are asked about the subject.

The steelhead populations in Lake Superior are unique within the entire Great Lakes system because they have had the opportunity to develop unaffected by negative influences for a longer period of time than any other lake. From a management and an angler point of view, it is encouraging to know that this historically obscure fishery has inspired official cooperative efforts and shared knowledge to address the problems facing the fishery there today. There is still much not known about the life and times of Lake Superior's wild steelhead, but it can most likely be concluded that the restrictive environment within the lake as well as the tributaries severely limits the overall number of steelhead this system can produce. Despite the fact that every suitable stream in the system supports self-sustaining populations of steelhead, these same streams may not be able to support the continued increased angling pressure by an unenlightened public. Once each tributary has been colonized, it appears that each population is then genetically oriented to that specific drainage; this fact makes particular streams and rivers extremely vulnerable. It would also appear that the complexities of the lake limit the abilities of a hatchery system to meet the demands of anglers who desire to keep much of their catch. Over the years, the natural selection process has resulted in specialized Lake Superior strains expressing life characteristics and patterns suitable for survival in the most pure, sterile, and rugged water of the Great Lakes system. Failure to recognize these facts and deal with them accordingly could result in a irreversible population collapse of wild fish in future years.

Lake Huron

Lake Huron begins where the strait that is referred to as the St. Mary's River rapids ends. St. Mary's continues into Huron's north channel—a narrow piece of water dotted with and formed by several islands. Manitoulin Island is the largest and, along with the projected Bruce Peninsula from the southern shoreline, forms the massive Georgian Bay. Many speak of this body of water in terms of these two separate components: the Lake and the Bay. Lake Huron's shoreline can be divided into four distinct segments as a result of its odd configuration.

The north shore of Lake Huron, which also includes the northern shore of what is known as Georgian Bay, is the longest stretch of shoreline without any significant steelhead water for the fly fishing enthusiast. Although it is known that some small streams that flow into the lake in that region support wild fish, these streams are considered having only local importance. Some sources have indicated, however, that this region may hold some surprises for those who like to explore, especially the few bigger drainages. The tributaries of Manitoulin Island also are known to be productive water for wild fish. The St. Mary's River is the main influence on the north shore, and though the river supports many naturalized fish, it would be impossible to identify or quantify specific strains in that region for several reasons.

The Ojibway Indians called the rapids "the meeting place" (Batwating), for it was there that hoards of whitefish could easily be dipped with nets from the bountiful crystalline waters. These rapids were well-suited for rainbow also. Native rainbow lived within the river and additional annual runs of fish from Lake Huron moved in also to successfully spawn in the spring. It is believed that fish migrating from Lakes Erie and Michigan can be found in the river as well as fish dropping down from Lake Superior. In the mid 1980's, a spawning channel was completed paralleling the main river separated by a concrete dike. The water entering the head of the river is controlled by a retaining dam; thereby, a regulated flow can be released into the spawning channel each spring to successfully assist reproduction of the steelhead. Salmon also spawn in the channel later in the year.

Although Ernest Hemingway drew attention to this area in the 50's for its famous hard-fighting rainbow, St. Mary's River supported a renowned naturalized fishery in the early 1900's based upon the fish stocked there by Michigan in the late 1890's. The St. Mary's popularity remains strong and this trend continues into the 1990's. The city of Sault Ste. Marie envisions much economic potential capitalizing on the fishing along its banks and within the area. The Sport Fishing Development program was initiated in 1986 to stimulate the area's sportfishing industry through better management, habitat rehabilitation, regulation changes, and hatchery assistance. In 1987 the Sault Ste. Marie Municipal Fish Hatchery was built to rear eggs collected from sportfishers each spring, and subsequently reintroduced into area tributaries including the St. Mary's River. A lack of funding put this program on hold in 1995. For several years, though, these fish were stocked on top of others that showed up in the river from Lakes Superior, Huron, Michigan, and even Lake Erie. Although many fish spawn successfully in the main section of the river as well as the controlled flow spawning channel, these naturalized fish are most likely a hodgepodge of strains. According to the city managers, it was not believed that these fish alone can sustain the demands placed upon the fishery given the Lake Huron daily limit of five steelhead, and it has history to support those fears.

Lake Huron falls into the realm of the forgotten as far as fish management is concerned. In Michigan, comprehensive studies dedicated to understanding the dynamics of its wild stocks have been limited despite the fact that it supported the first established run, on the Au Sable, in the 1890's. Populations along the Michigan shoreline remain steady and healthy. While the area is supplemented annually by the Little Manistee strain fish, the few streams along this shoreline support very good naturalized populations also. The Au Sable is a rich-flowing river similar to those that flow into Lake Michigan, but hydroelectric dams limit its spawning capabilities. The Rifle is another of that shore's rivers supporting wild steelhead that dates back to the initial days of the program in the 1800's.

The Bighead and the Nottawasaga Rivers that flow into Georgian Bay have always been recognized and managed for their wild fish capabilities. With 70 or so miles of gravel, the Bighead is one of the best-producing steelhead rivers in all of Canada (including the West Coast). The larger Nottawasaga has been historically regarded for its rather large strain of fish. Its tremendous base flow originating from the Niagara Escarpment, providing both consistent temperature patterns and high-quality water, encourage fish movement as well as excellent rearing habitat. The Nottawasaga fish may also have the greatest genetic diversity within the entire Great Lake's basin.

Bob Morrissey swings a fly on the Bighead River.

It is believed that fish entering the Pine and Boyne Rivers, tributaries of the main river, are unique strains. Another separate strain also spawns in the upper Nottawasaga. Recent studies indicate the possibility of other strains as well. Since a particular chromosome found in these fish links all strains directly back to their West Coast heritage, the fish of the Nottawasaga may be the most genetically pure of all wild Great Lakes steelhead—and between 20,000 to 40,000 of them return to this large drainage annually. Because of its consistency, the Nottawasaga supports Skamania during the summer and early fall as well.

Lake Huron has supported a healthy rainbow population throughout the century. Although the lamprey populations beginning in the late 1930's wiped out the lake's lake trout population, the rainbow populations actually expanded during the same period. It is speculated that climatic conditions contributed greatly to this event. When Hurricane Hazel severely hit the region in 1956, the ensuing floods cleared many tributaries of man-made and natural blockages that had accumulated throughout the years. Subsequently, the 1960's brought a series of good water years that resulted in excellent spawning conditions. By the mid 1980's, rainbow numbers reached an all-time high in Georgian Bay. The decline of the lake trout may also have resulted in less predation on young rainbows. This factor may have accounted for the prosperity of steelhead during the same period in Lake Superior as well.

During the late 80's, declines in both the numbers of immature rainbow trout harvested in the open water and the numbers of mature adults returning to spawn in southern Georgian Bay tributary streams have been observed by anglers as well as the Ontario Ministry of Natural Resources (OMNR). In response, the Lake Huron Management Unit initiated a study between 1993 and 1994 to analyze all the available data that could be gathered from various sources. The goal of this review was "to develop a plan for protecting and rehabilitating rainbow populations in southern Georgian Bay and to provide guidelines for maintaining a sustainable recreational fishery for the species throughout all of Lake Huron." In 1994, the Rainbow Trout Review Public Advisory Committee (PAC) was established to work in partnership with OMNR to develop a Rainbow Trout Management Plan for Lake Huron. It consisted of 25 members representing angling associations, the fishing tackle and charter boat industries, and environmentally active groups.

The study collected data from fish way counts, angler surveys, and biomass monitoring programs. A review of the information gathered demonstrates empirically clear evidence of declines in the numbers of rainbow trout returning to spawn in the Georgian Bay tributaries based upon the analysis of repeat spawners. Climatic factors periodically have influenced recruitment—from summer stream discharge flows and water temperatures to winter severity. These recent declines seem directly linked to overharvest by sportsfishers combined with depressed numbers linked to climatic factors. From the studies, it appears that annual harvest is in excess of a staggering 50% of the total rainbow spawning population for southern Georgian Bay. Overharvesting in both the lake and in the stream has negatively impacted runs on the Bighead, Sydenham, and Beaver Rivers, among others. Due to heavy harvest in the middle section of the Nottawasaga, the Boyne River strain has all but crashed despite just moderate declines in the main river itself.

The PAC and OMNR believe that the long-term health of the steelhead population depends on several factors. First, strategies must be devised to protect and enhance the coldwater stream ecosystems on which the fish depend for spawning and juvenile rearing habitats. Then, regulation changes should be considered to address the problem. A two fish per day 19 to 25 inch slot limit was proposed. Other recommendations included river-specific season closures, a catch and release only regulation in specific locations, and new sanctuary waters. All parties agree that ensuring the sustainability of Huron's steelhead populations will require a concerted effort on behalf of all individuals and organizations concerned about this resource. As of 1999, the daily limit has been reduced to two steelhead per day for most of the Lake Huron and Georgian Bay tributaries.

It is interesting to note that the rivers entering the main portion of Lake Huron have not suffered the same fate as those of Georgian Bay. Although there has been fluctuations in populations within these tributaries throughout the 80's and 90's, most have been linked to climatic inconsistencies. There is a tendency to view Lake Huron and the Georgian Bay as separate entities, but any regulation changes occurring in the Bay will be applied to the main body of the lake as well.

For much of the century, the region has relied upon wild steelhead, and it will continue to do so for the most part. The Community Fisheries Involvement Program, started in 1982 and run by local volunteers in conjunction with OMNR, conducts a localized supplemental hatchery program targeting a few of the waters near Owen Sound using a variety of stocks. Along with a few smaller tributaries, the Sydenham River gets a regular infusion of hatchery steelhead reared from its own egg-producing fish. Despite naturalized runs, the complex Saugeen River system, which empties into main Lake Huron southwest of Owen Sound, also gets a supplemental stocking. The lower reaches of this river get heavily fished, particularly the section below the cement lamprey barrier. For many years, OMNR plants were considered for rehabilitation purposes, though in many cases the plants supplemented naturally reproducing stocks. Today, many question the stocking policies which provide angling opportunities that are not naturally sustainable. More importantly, there are concerns about the loss of important genetic variability when these localized plants occur on top of wild and naturalized fish.

Since many tributaries of Lake Huron historically demonstrate excellent fish-rearing capabilities, it has been recognized that some strategic projects

Habitat rehabilitation by conservation groups has been the key to the building of wild runs in Ontario.

could further enhance these wild stocks. For instance, there is a vast section of water above the barrier on the Saugeen capable of sustaining wild steelhead populations. New improvements at the fish ladder section of the cement blockage are hoped to increase upstream migration of the many fish that run into this system. Fisheries managers look at the upper river as a vast frontier to expand a viable self-sustaining steelhead fishery in future years. The Maitland River, another of the fine wild producing steelhead rivers in the area found south of the Saugeen, has actually seen an increase in its wild populations thanks in large part to rehabilitation efforts on several of its small spawning tributaries.

Lake Huron's role in the Great Lakes steelhead program has been a quiet one, but it has certainly not been insignificant. All of its suitable tributaries support populations of wild steelhead. Since many of Lake Huron's hearty larger steelhead seemed to have weathered the lamprey attacks of the 50's and 60's, a continuity with regard to its strains dates back to the turn of the century. The state of Michigan noted in the early 70's that a tagged Lake Huron fish was caught a year later in the Long Point area of Lake Erie. Subsequent fish in Lake Erie were also identified as Lake Huron's. Who knows if this pattern of migration did not exist throughout much of the 20th century.

Lake Michigan

Though historical accounts are sketchy, the state of Michigan has led the way in Great Lakes steelhead culture for over 120 years—and still counting. Blessed with shorelines on three separate Great Lakes (Michigan, Superior, and Huron) early fishery pioneers must have recognized right from the beginning the potential of the quality tributaries that ran into each of these lakes.

Most fishery biologists believe the present-day "Michigan Strain" steelhead is closely linked genetically to the original McCloud strain fish. Modern-day egg gathering occurs solely in the Little Manistee River, and this Lake Michigan tributary has never been stocked. Dave Borgeson, the former Assistant Chief of Fisheries for the Michigan Department of Natural Resources, believes that Lake Michigan maintained a substantial wild steelhead population even through the bleak years of lamprey devastation. The rainbow trout that survived the lamprey gauntlet were able to feast on the growing number of alewives as the population of these fish ballooned. Because steelhead spawned in the upper reaches of tributaries and the young steelhead stayed there until they were past the size of vulnerability to the alewife, the migrating rainbow figured prominently into the rehabilitation plans of Lake Michigan after lamprey populations were controlled in the 60's.

In the mid 1960's, the state of Michigan recognized the unlimited potential for recreational fishing on the Great Lakes. Drs. James McFadden, Howard Tanner, and Wayne Tody were all names associated with drawing up and implementing the Management Program for Michigan's Sport Fisheries in 1965. Dealing with the abundant alewife population became of paramount importance. Massive periodic die-offs of these fish not only pointed to the severity of the overpopulation, but the repugnance of dead, rotting fish piled along the shorelines provided (through sight and smell) a clear indication of a system totally out of balance. Although Chinook, coho, lake trout, and some new strains of steelhead were introduced as a major part of the alewife control plan, maintaining the naturalized steelhead runs through stream management was given the highest of priorities. Borgeson states emphatically that the state of Michigan has always believed in and strongly supported its wild steelhead populations.

There is good reason for Michigan's historically successful steelhead program. Its rivers in the northwestern part of the state are among the richest nursery waters in the world. The stable flow produced by a constant groundwater discharge provides the most ideal of conditions for spawning steelhead. Fortunately, Michigan's Department of Natural Resources has recognized the value of this treasured resource. Not only has the state been the focal point for Great Lakes steelhead management from the onset, it still leads the way in the late 20th century. In an effort to understand the dynamics of steelhead in Michigan waters, the work of DNR's Dr. Paul Seelbach has provided much valuable insight for the entire Great Lakes basin. Realizing the tremendous lack of background information on this important Pacific species in the early 80's, Dr. Seelbach set the standard for all the steelhead research that has been undertaken to this point throughout the lakes. The subsequent sharing of data throughout all managing agencies in the Great Lakes has led to a more unified approach of dealing with steelhead populations based upon a common understanding.

Seelbach's comprehensive studies have resulted in a series of reports that lead to a clearer understanding of steelhead dynamics within the lakes and their tributaries at all stages of the fish's development. Perhaps the most important study was that of winter steelhead populations in Lake Michigan and the relationship between in-lake and in-stream harvest. This work established 72% of all Michigan steelhead harvested in 1985 were taken by stream anglers. By 1993, 61% of all Michigan steelhead harvested were taken offshore in the open lake. Since the lake itself used to act as a traditional refuge for growing steelhead, this reallocation of fishing pressure during the 90's has resulted in new concerns for the fishery—especially the wild fish populations. While in-stream harvest targets only sexually mature returning fish, the lake harvest targets fish at all ages. Although imposed size restriction regulations can address some of these concerns, any further increase in the

Jerry Kustich with a wild Michigan steelhead on the Pere Marquette River.

total steelhead harvest can start to affect the right age/size structure of returning fish needed to maintain natural populations. Eventually the concerns of over harvest and increased stocking to maintain anglers' "needs" has the potential to alter the genetic makeup of Lake Michigan fish. Seelbach concludes that "management scenarios which result in drastic changes to age and size structures of steelhead populations should raise caution flags and be scrutinized carefully from a genetics standpoint."

Taking all this data into consideration, the state of Michigan has developed a long-range steelhead management strategy for Lake Michigan. The plan recognizes the biological necessity to protect and enhance wild stocks to insure the future abundance of both natural and artificially produced runs. This plan is multidimensional and calls for continued stream inventory and study, age harvest regulations of wild fish, and stream habitat protection while controlling biotic system-wide threats. In addition to restoring existing habitats, the potential of new areas will be explored by eliminating dams and bypassing waterfalls. Hatchery fish augmentation will follow the strictest guidelines that have the least impact on wild stocks. The ultimate goal of the plan will be to maintain a beneficial recreational fishery while not sacrificing Michigan's wild steelhead populations in the process. If successful, this strategy not only serves as a lake-wide model, but establishes a philosophy that could insure the survival of a unique resource well into the next century.

Lake Michigan's steelhead program takes a unique twist at its southern tip where the St. Joseph River empties into the lake in Michigan. By the early 1800's, a bounty of fish from the St. Joseph basin attracted many European settlers to this river valley shared by Michigan and Indiana. At that time, the river's fishery for bass and sturgeon was considered to be the best in the Midwest. But the consequent population growth led to the need for hydroelectric dams, and along with them, the decline of a wonderful fishery. When plans developed in the 1960's to rehabilitate the Lake Michigan fishery, Michigan's DNR stocked millions of salmon and steelhead into the system with great success. After a fish ladder at Berrien Springs dam opened another 10 miles of Michigan water in 1975, possibilities for similar upriver projects were born. In 1978, an ambitious cooperative developed between Michigan and Indiana, and by 1980, the two states signed an agreement known as the St. Joseph River Anadromous Fishery Plan. The U.S. Fish and Wildlife Service became a third partner, providing both technical assistance and some cost share funding through the Anadromous Fishery Conservation Act. The idea was to construct fish ladders at the next four dam sites, which would then get salmon and steelhead into Indiana's loop of the St. Joe.

The project proceeded very slowly, meeting many setbacks. Another operational management agreement between the states was signed in 1988. When the St. Joseph Interstate Anadromous Fish Project, as it is now called, was completed in 1992, fish had access to some 63 miles of river up to the city of Mishawaka. The initial plan came complete with innovative access sites and a new fish hatchery.

This proud award-winning bi-state project opened many miles of the St. Joseph River for large numbers of urban anglers while providing Indiana a significant role in the Great Lakes steelhead program. At the same time, pressure from some of Michigan's quality northern rivers was diverted as well. The river provides a year-round fishery with Chinook running in early fall, Michigan strain steelhead entering in late fall and extending through winter, and the Indiana Skamania returning in early summer running into early fall.

At the turn of the century, the McCloud plants of steelhead were sketchy and never amounted to anything of significance within Indiana's waters. Indiana experimented with Washington strain steelhead for the waters within its borders during the early 70's, again with little success. In 1975, the experimentation extended to importing Skamania eggs from the hatchery in Washington to a hatchery in Indiana. The plans at that time were to develop an in-lake fishery for the limited Indiana shoreline. When disease prevented the import of eggs from Washington in 1980, the Skamania returning to a couple of small tributaries within Indiana during that period provided the basis for a homegrown source of eggs that has expanded into a self-sustaining hatchery program. It was this program that provided the basis for the fishery that has developed in the Indiana section of the St. Joseph River during the 90's.

The success of this hatchery program was a result of much trial and error. Once the initial problems of infections and funguses were conquered in the early stages of the egg gathering process, the Skamania proved to be very hatchery friendly. With the construction of the new hatchery in 1983 at Mishawaka, efficient production increased and Skamania fingerlings were introduced into the system as early as 1985. It wasn't until the early 90's, with the completion of the last fish ladder, that the fruits of Indiana's efforts could be enjoyed within its own waters.

Despite the fears related to the effects of a hatchery-manufactured strain of fish on the existing wild and naturalized strains in Lake Michigan as well as in the other lakes, the Skamania program has been a fascinating undertaking. Its success has provided a summer fishery throughout the Great Lakes for a few rivers that can supply the needed criteria during the warm months of the year, and Indiana's eggs were the initial source for these select tributaries. On the St. Joseph River, the Skamania begin to ascend its waters in May, at about the same time the "Michigan Strain" steelhead from the previous fall start to return to Lake Michigan. Although there is some natural reproduction acknowledged in the St. Joe system, it is not considered significant.

The west shoreline of Lake Michigan is largely characterized by urban sprawl from Chicago to Milwaukee, Sheboygan to Green Bay. Although this is the most urbanized continuous portion of the entire Great Lakes, it is not without important steelhead rivers. Unfortunately for the state of Illinois, there are no tributaries to call its own, so wild fish management is out of the question. However, the state has explored its offshore options to contribute to the in-lake and shoreline fishery of that region. Historically, Illinois was only minimally involved in the original plants of Great Lakes steelhead. In the late 1980's, experimentation began with a Skamania program as well as a domestic strain of Arlee rainbow. To a degree, the Skamania show regular returns to the local waters, although its older tagged fish have been caught as far away as Lakes Huron, Erie, and Ontario. The sedentary Arlee did not show the same proclivity for long-distance travel.

Further northward, several significant tributaries flow out of the beautifully varied countryside of Wisconsin through the populated regions of the state and into Lake Michigan. Although these streams are characterized by sand and gravel runs, the farm-related runoff often is responsible for off-color flows. Despite Wisconsin's consciousness of wild steelhead demonstrated in the management tactics on the Brule River that runs into Lake Superior, wild fish management in this region is not quite so probable. Unlike the Michigan rivers that enter Lake Michigan on the eastern shoreline that provide excellent wild fish habitat, Wisconsin's rivers do not have the same advantage of spring-charged flows and the accompanying ideal water temperatures. Even in the early development of the Great Lakes fisheries, it seemed evident that most of Lake Michigan's steelhead were supplied by the Michigan rivers. Natural reproduction has been surmised on the Oconto and Kewaunee River systems as well as in a few little creeks on the Door Peninsula, though little evidence exists to support any substantial spawning along Lake Michigan's east shore from the Wisconsin tributaries.

The Wisconsin Department of Natural Resources (WDNR) is an operative force in Lake Michigan fish management, and it has maintained an active salmonid stocking program during the modern management era, starting in earnest about 1963. A "spring strain" was the rainbow stock initially utilized by the state. This stock was eventually developed into both a fall and spring run carryover brood stock. This method of stocking provided a peak run in 1977, but sharp declines continued until 1985. Disease and other weaknesses associated with this stocking technique could have been to blame. The increasing use of fingerlings rather than yearling fish was also linked to low survival rates in the lake. Wisconsin determines the viability of its steelhead runs by angler catch rates, and by 1985, annual catch plummeted to about 25,000 steelhead, down from over 90,000 in 1977. Wisconsin abandoned its fingerling stocking program during 1985 and started stocking yearlings.

In 1988, WDNR enacted a comprehensive Lake Michigan Steelhead Fishery Management Plan that addressed many facets of the steelhead issue. The plan called for identifying probable strains to be used to revamp the program. Three strains of steelhead were chosen—Skamania, Chambers Creek from Washington State, and Ganaraska from the Province of Ontario. Since the three have different run time orientations—summer, winter, and spring respectively—it was determined that these stocks could best provide fishing opportunities for a long duration throughout the season. Each strain also requires a specific set of criteria best suited for unique characteristics, and once this data was understood, strains were stocked into tributaries according to optimal chances for survival. Times of the year and size of the steelhead stocked in each drainage were also prime considerations.

Wisconsin has created a significant fishery on Lake Michigan's western shore.

The plan also investigated the most efficient ways to produce the fish by improving upon the several hatchery facilities the state has available. Fish weirs were constructed on both the Kewaunee and Root Rivers, and these locations were to be the primary fish gathering stations to provide the needed eggs for the hatchery. Only feral stock would be used, and each strain would be identified by clip marks and bred separately. Habitat and stream rehabilitation, together with improved fish passage facilities to increase fish accessibility were important aspects of the plan as well. There was also consideration given for developing more natural reproduction in these tributaries. No local strain has withstood the test of time, however, and the future of the fishery in this area will most likely always depend heavily upon the hatcheries.

In early 1995, Wisconsin instituted its Lake Michigan Integrated Fisheries Management Plan that would carry through to the year 2001. The plan addresses all phases of lake management for all species while addressing the needs of sports and commercial fishermen within the boundaries of a sustainable fishery. Sensitivity to offshore steelhead and the concerns of other managing states are also major considerations. Comprehensive efforts as demonstrated by this plan may hold the key for the future well-being of the entire Great Lakes fishery.

After Bacterial Kidney Disease had wiped out much of the lake's naturalized Chinook salmon populations in the late 1980's, commercial charter boats and sportfishers turned from their preferred quarry to the copious numbers of steelhead swimming in the lake during that time. Much has been learned about the habits of steelhead while in the lake. When conditions are right, steelhead can consistently be found along temperature breaks well away from shore. This temperature break, or thermocline, will often host steelhead feeding readily in the top twenty feet of water. Fishing the famed "scum-line" presents little challenge to large boats trolling planer boards. These boats cover a lot of water and the steelhead are quite vulnerable to this technique.

In 1994, the four states possessing shoreline along Lake Michigan agreed to a universal five-three-two creel limit. This is a total limit of five salmonids with no more than three of any one species and only two lake trout. Salmonids include steelhead, brown trout, Chinook and coho salmon, lake trout and whitefish. Though a step in the right direction, this regulation will only provide marginal protection for wild steelhead since the previous limit was three per day as well and, under this regulation, this is still possible. However, by spreading the limit over several species, it is hoped that the steelhead harvest will be reduced. With growing realization of the importance of wild fish in the system, there is a push for a more restrictive limit of three fish total over 15 inches in length for the lake and tributaries. Still not perfect, this would allow a greater number of fish to spawn.

Lake Erie

Lake Erie is comprised of three distinct basins, and a brief understanding of the morphology of each plainly reveals the lake's limitations. The western basin is the smallest, comprising 12.8% of the total area and 5.1% of the volume with an average depth of 25 feet. Limited tributaries and annual warm periods usually force the salmonids toward the cooler eastern waters. The central basin is the largest, containing 62.9% of the lake's total area and 63% of the volume with an average depth of 62 feet. This transitional zone extends from Cedar Point, Ohio to Presque Isle Peninsula in Pennsylvania. And although it has normally supported populations of salmonids, particularly during the colder seasons of the year, studies now show that more and more steelhead may be utilizing the central basin year-round to take advantage of an increasing food supply. (This shift may be linked to the extreme clarity in the eastern basin due to the zebra mussel.) The slate-bottomed tributaries of this basin flow out of Ohio, and with little groundwater support, these drainages depend on rainfall for cool discharges. Finally, the deeper eastern basin extends from Presque Isle Peninsula to the upper Niagara River in New York, making up 24.3% of the surface area and 32% of the lake's total volume with an average depth of 80 feet and a maximum depth of 210 feet. This basin provides excellent year-round conditions for the rearing of steelhead, and the tributaries entering this "lake within a lake" have historically been known for most of the lake's prolific steelhead runs.

Overall the most shallow of the Great Lakes, Lake Erie's summertime temperatures soar, and since most tributaries around its entire circumference drain fertile and flat agricultural land, most of these waters run warm in the summer and muddy during wet periods. The streams of the Norfolk Sand Plain are the exceptions, however, consistently registering temperatures ranging from the mid 50 to mid 60 degree range. Historically, the lake has offered excellent fishing opportunities for walleye, bass, yellow perch, and a subspecies of walleye called blue pike. This particular fish was unique to its waters. Commercial fishing, lampreys, and finally the accumulation of pollutants that clogged and dirtied its waters led to the total disintegration of this warm-water fishery by the 1960's. These conditions also caused the probable extinction of the blue pike. Remnant populations of rainbow, along with random populations of native warm-water species, survived during that period. (It should be noted that with the exception of the blue pike, many of the indigenous warm-water natives are once again thriving.)

Modern-day studies of several tributaries entering the eastern basin of Lake Erie indicate significant recruitment from natural reproduction even in the 90's. It is therefore likely that many catch reports from the lake's eastern basin during the century were supplemented by a self-sustaining population of steelhead. Although Lake Erie has never been known as a stronghold for Great Lakes steelhead, it is apparent that its waters have quietly developed a significant niche during the 20th century.

When it comes to wild steelhead, Ohio's Department of Natural Resources claims that their state's tributaries are not capable of any self-sustaining natural populations. All of Ohio's prime steelhead streams empty into the central basin of Lake Erie. Its slate-bottom tributaries run low and warm in the summer and get little reprieve from any spring water source. The Ohio stream closest to the eastern basin, Conneaut Creek, is a rather long meandering drainage with some gravel and localized spring recharge. Natural reproduction is known to occur in the Conneaut, but according to Ohio's fishery managers, the numbers of wild fish from this source are too insignificant to manage.

Over the years, its hatchery system engineered a strain of fish that was both durable and could tolerate the warm temperatures of the central basin. The so-called London strain was the amalgamation of crossing three distinct strains of steelhead, and the result was the chosen stock used for many years in Ohio's rivers. Since the mid 1990's, the Little Manistee (Michigan) strain has totally replaced the London strain in Ohio's management scheme. Because this strain has naturally developed for over a century in the Great Lakes, it has proven superior in many ways to the London strain for Ohio's waters. The Michigan strain grows much faster, and its survival rate is three to one better than its predecessors. Consequently, those statistics even support a reduction in the number of fish the DNR has to stock annually. Only four rivers are identified in the state as suitable for annual plantings: Conneaut Creek, Grand River, Rocky River, and the Chagrin River. But like most streams throughout the entire Great Lakes system, other small tributaries in Ohio will get stray runs under the proper stream conditions. The Ashtabula River is another tributary of significant size within the state, but an EPA Superfund Site on its lower end prevents the state from actively stocking and managing its waters. However, DNR reports that the Ashtabula does indeed get a decent stray run of fish.

It has never been clear why commercial reports showed consistent catches of steelhead in the eastern reaches of the lake at the turn of the century and beyond. It can only be speculated whether or not these were naturally reproduced fish during that era. Pennsylvania acknowledges some supplemental reproduction in its waters these days, but not significant enough to manage for specifically. Its streams are characterized by much slate and little spawning gravel.

In 1986, the Pennsylvania Fish and Boat Commission (PFBC) outlined a Steelhead Management Plan for Lake Erie. The objectives were as follows:

1. Establish a steelhead fishery that can sustain a harvest of 20,000 fish from Pennsylvania's waters.
2. Develop a non-captive brood fish population adequate to support Pennsylvania's steelhead program.
3. Preserve and enhance the differing seasonal components of the steelhead run.
4. Minimize the genetic contribution of domestic hatchery rainbow to Lake Erie stocks.

5. Minimize the risk of introduction of new diseases to Lake Erie
while maintaining the genetic diversity.

During the modern era of the Great Lakes, PFBC started active plantings in 1961 when 15,000 fingerlings from West Coast stock were introduced into Pennsylvania's waters and the program continued intermittently until the mid 1980's. When the Steelhead Management Program was adopted, eggs were then taken from spawning adults returning to Pennsylvania's streams. Egg collection and fertilization has been done in the late fall/early winter and in the spring to maintain the seasonal spawning attributes of progeny. Disease introduction was minimized by eliminating alternate egg sources from outside the Great Lakes.

From 1989-1994, PFBC has stocked close to one million smolts annually, combined with another 60,000 from a private trout association, into its 13 major tributaries. These numbers seem particularly staggering when it is considered that Pennsylvania's Lake Erie shoreline extends for only 41 miles. PFBC believes that flooding its waters with smolts compensates for high mortality potential due to bird and fish predation along with angler harvest of these juvenile steelhead. Many of Pennsylvania's stocked fish show up in Ohio, New York, and Ontario tributaries, providing excellent sport throughout the eastern basin. But this is not without political fallout. The Province of Ontario is concerned about the genetic commingling of Pennsylvania hatchery strays with its own wild stocks. Also, the Canadian commercial fishery for rainbow smelt blames the decline of harvest on the overabundance of stocked trout and salmon in its fishing waters. Although these are only unsubstantiated allegations, it does point to the types of problems that can develop when several governing bodies try to manage streams that share a common body of water. And though it seems that the Canadian commercial interests are more disturbed with the damage stocked lake trout are doing to the smelt populations, this perceived overstocking of steelhead raises the red flag of concern as well.

The Lake Erie story takes an interesting turn in the waters of New York. The state's Department of Environmental Conservation (DEC), in cooperation with local sportsmen and Trout Unlimited, have been conducting surveys in the tributaries of Cattaraugus Creek to evaluate the extent of wild fish reproduction in that system. According to Bill Culligan, Supervising Aquatic Biologist and Lake Erie Fisheries Unit Leader, the contribution of wild steelhead into New York's waters cannot be ignored, and assessing exactly what that is in terms of percentage of the total run is the purpose behind these studies. Despite irregular stocking of this region in the early 1900's, there was good tributary fishing for steelhead available in New York during the 1950's. The wanderings of fish from elsewhere in the eastern basin or from other parts of the Great Lakes, for that matter, could have been contributing factors responsible for those fish populations. But possibly, there could have

Electrofishing a tributary to the Cattaraugus Creek. Jim Lorentz photo.

been a significant historical foothold of wild fish populations in New York's tributaries during that period also.

Led by Senior Aquatic Biologist for Lake Erie's Cold Water Program, Floyd Cornelius, studies began in 1995 on Spooner Brook, a small spring-fed tributary of the Cattaraugus. The numbers of young, naturally born fish were significant. These studies will also extend to other feeder streams on the "Cat" that have been known to get runs of fish for years. The verification of these isolated populations could have significant ramifications for this wonderful 40-mile tributary of Lake Erie. A recently completed study of the scales of returning adult fish indicated that approximately 25% of the Cattaraugus run is comprised of wild steelhead. Also, genetic workups ought to reveal some insights into the history and origin of these runs. Studies of other shorter lake tributaries, such as Chatauqua and Canadaway Creeks, thought to have reproduction are also planned in the future.

The results of these wild fish surveys will no doubt have important and far-reaching implications for the region's steelhead management plans. For over 30 years, an environmental program has been in place within New York State designed to protect habitat while giving wild fish the best opportunity possible to reproduce and survive. Known as the Classification of Waters system, this tool has the potential to greatly influence the dynamics of this resource while, at the same time, altering the way steelhead are currently perceived by anglers and fishery managers.

When Lake Erie was sucked into the black hole of environmental destitution during the dead years of the 60's, its fish populations were devastated as well. Whether some wild steelhead survived to provide a continuum to the past can only be speculated. In the aftermath of the Great Lakes Water Quality Agreement (an international agreement signed between Canada and the United States in 1972 clearing the way for the implementation of the federal Clean Water Act of 1972), the lake's ecology began to slowly improve. New York State's first official step into the planting process occurred in 1974 when Washington State's Chambers Creek strain steelhead were used to stock the region. This strain is largely responsible for the restored runs on the Salmon River, and is the basis for the Salmon River strain now utilized in the regular New York steelhead stocking programs within both Lake Erie and Lake Ontario. New York plants its Erie waters with Salmon River progeny on a yearly schedule.

A wild Cattaraugus steelhead.

There are many factors influencing the management of New York's Lake Erie steelhead heading into the 21st century. The Skamania stocking program was put on hold when whirling disease showed up in New York's Caledonia Hatchery in 1995. This sobering event once again pointed to the problems inherent in a hatchery-based fishery. The proliferation of Pennsylvania fish showing up in New York's tributaries has yet to be evaluated. At first glance, this does not seem like it should be much of a problem, at least from an angler's point of view. But if specific strains of wild fish are determined to significantly exist in the Cattaraugus, for example, then there will be some concern for dealing with the effects that stocked fish from several other sources within the lake may have upon these wild stocks. It is important to reiterate that the genetic benefits of wild steelhead can never be understated or taken for granted.

The most consistent wild steelhead production in Lake Erie most likely occurs on the Canadian shoreline. According to Larry Halyk, Senior Management Biologist for the Ontario Ministry of Natural Resources, Ontario's tributaries have limited reproductive success when compared to other regions of the Great Lakes, but it is not insignificant. Although a couple small creeks entering the central basin exhibit some reproductive success, most natural reproduction is restricted to Long Point Bay tributaries draining the Norfolk Sand Plain and the tributaries to the large Grand River, all entering the Lake's eastern basin. This sand plain provides abundant groundwater seepage and relatively cold, stable flows to the area's tributaries. These conditions compare favorably to those that occur on the famous rivers of central Michigan.

It is no accident that the Normandale hatchery seems to be a major factor in the historic development of this north shore fishery. The origin of the initial fish taken from a hatchery on the St. Mary's River was not clear. Ontario planted some McCloud fish near Sault Ste. Marie in 1883. Several primary sources for other steelhead strains, beginning with Redwood Creek in the mid 1890's, possibly showed up in hatcheries on Lake Superior and Lake Huron between 1912 and 1913. Normandale stock was expanded in the mid 30's with a British Columbian Kamloops strain and a fall spawning strain of unknown origins from Minnesota. In 1947, another shipment from Sault Ste. Marie of McCloud fish were added, and by 1956, the last known infusion of fish came from Merrit, British Columbia. This combination was known as the Normandale strain, and it could primarily be traced back to the original McCloud stocks.

By 1929, a brood stock at Normandale had been developed to be used for the steelhead stocking program throughout Ontario. Although there were no formal plants of Lake Erie until 1936, reports of Normandale escapees seem to recur in documents from that time. There was no regular stocking of that region. Since Normandale Creek is a Long Point Bay tributary, it is quite likely that other area streams were colonized at that time. Noting the quality of these tributaries, it was quite likely much natural reproduction was also occurring. By the 1950's, there were substantiated reports of wonderful fishing for a particularly dynamic strain of steelhead coming from Big Creek and its tributary, Venison Creek. Other Long Point Bay tributaries provided equally excellent fishing into the early 60's. It can only be speculated whether these fish were exploring any of the American rivers and contributing to that fishery during the 40's and 50's. Unfortunately, added to the disasters occurring in the lake during the 60's was habitat degradation due to dams and sedimentation of the tributaries from intensive tobacco and vegetable farming. By the mid 1960's, fish numbers declined drastically. Numbers continued to decline in the 70's despite heavy stocking. Although, by 1970, much had negatively changed in the area's fishery, things began to improve in the early 1980's when habitat problems were addressed and fewer fish of better genetic quality were stocked. Because of an outbreak of BKD, the Ganaraska strain steelhead (which evolved from original Normandale fish) replaced all existing brood stock at the Normandale Hatchery in 1981, and this strain is now utilized as the Ontario source for its stocking program.

Heading into the next century, Ontario's north shore tributaries show great promise. About twenty thousand Ganaraska yearlings are stocked into Big Creek annually by the Ministry to contribute to the recovery of steelhead runs in that system. These fish supplement runs of wild fish and also spawn successfully to some degree. The genetic impact of these fish on the steelhead that have been naturalized in the Big Creek system for many decades is unknown. It is also not known if there is any link genetically to original stocks that survived through the 50's. The only other Canadian stocking in the lake occurs in the central basin. A private club annually plants the waters near Port Stanley, providing some fishing in what is considered marginal water. The purpose of this stocking, though, is not to provide stream fishing but rather to enhance angling in the open waters of the lake near Port Stanley.

Although Big Creek probably offers some of the best fly fishing opportunities in the Long Point area, smaller creeks such as Fishers, Normandale, and Young Creek produce many steelhead. In fact, Young Creek also supports natural reproducing runs of cohos, Chinook, odd-year pinks, and some browns, giving an insight into the quality of its habitat. The once-famous Venison Creek is on the comeback after decades of sedimentation as well.

Ever since a barrier dam was removed on the Grand River near Brantford in the late 1980's, steelhead have been colonizing several of its quality tributaries in good numbers. Lower Whiteman's Creek possesses all the right ingredients and has become a steelhead nursery. Because the Grand River has not been stocked, its fish are likely strays from the Long Point population and the United States stocking programs. The Grand offers some exciting opportunities for exploration of its bigger water, and according to Larry Halyk, its developing populations may offer a new steelhead frontier for the future.

In response to increased interest in the steelhead of the Ontario portion of Lake Erie, in 1997, the Lake Erie Management Unit of the Ontario Ministry of Natural Resources began to develop a rainbow trout management strategy for this region of the lake. The initiative is comprehensive and includes an assessment of each tributary for wild production and habitat suitability. Catch success and biological data (size and age structure, scale samples, etc.) is obtained from an angler diary program as well as the monitoring of three fish ways. Genetic analysis of selected wild and hatchery populations is performed, and the resulting data is being utilized to govern hatchery programs in relation to specific wild populations of steelhead. Additionally, this project is linked to New York's DEC efforts on the Cattaraugus Creek. This initiative represents yet another attempt to understand the important contribution of wild steelhead populations in those streams capable of supporting natural reproduction.

Lake Erie's warm-water fishery has overshadowed the potential offshore steelhead opportunities over the years. Without substantive in-lake fishing pressure as experienced in Lake Michigan, the result has been bountiful runs of steelhead pursued by a growing number of anglers in the lake's few tributaries. Although rainbow trout are not regularly targeted in the lake, there is a growing contingent interested in developing that pursuit, and only time will tell if the streams will be affected by such activities. For the time being, significant steelhead runs occur in virtually every one of its tributaries from fall through spring. Despite this fishery's dependency on a massive stocking program around the entire lake, natural reproduction in several streams from Ontario's shoreline to Ohio could definitely influence how the fishery will be managed in the future.

Lake Ontario

At the lower end of the system, adversity has been no stranger to Lake Ontario, the smallest and the deepest of the Great Lakes. As last in the chain, it could also be considered the most complex. Beginning with colonization and the loss of the indigenous Atlantic salmon in the first half of the 19th century until the years of the lamprey and the debilitating pollution of the 1950's, a lake environment suitable for a healthy fishery has been rooted in a series of obstacles. Deforestation, farm runoff, early sea lamprey infestations, chemical and toxic dumping, among many other abuses, painted a bleak prognosis for this deep, vast body of fresh water. The fact that the Canadian side of the lake was not as affected by man's activities has more than likely been this lake's saving grace. With virtually every tributary flowing into Lake

Ontario on the American side interrupted by dams close to the lake, it was these small northern rivers that were able to maintain a habitat conducive to the natural rearing of steelhead. Although these drainages have suffered from historical agricultural degradation, reforestation of the Canadian north shore in the 40's directly led to improved water conditions by the early 70's capable of supporting high numbers of healthy young fish.

The main force influencing this deep lake is the Niagara River, which supplies 75% of all Lake Ontario's inflow. Its average 200,000 cfs is a volume of water greater than most other large rivers in the world are capable of carrying. This huge river is actually a 37-mile strait that connects Lake Erie to Lake Ontario, and in very dramatic fashion, over half of its 328-foot drop occurs at Niagara Falls. After years of environmental abuse on the river, the Niagara's negative impact on the waters of Lake Ontario has been significant.

Playing a major role in the formation of our nation, the Niagara has always been a river of vital importance. Before the arrival of European settlers, the Seneca Indians regarded the Niagara Frontier as sacred hunting grounds and, as a member of the six Indian nations of the Iroquois Confederacy, protected the region from western intruders. Once matters were settled after a series of wars, including the French and Indian War, the Revolutionary War, and the War of 1812, events began to unfold that led to the complete environmental disintegration of the region by the mid 20th century. Because of the potentially cheap water-generated power the region had to offer, industry developed at an accelerated pace. Waste of all kinds was conveniently swept away by the roaring waters of the river. Commercialization of the spectacular Niagara Falls brought in great numbers of visitors while the whole area continued to grow and prosper economically as the country entered the age of industrialization.

After over 150 years of environmental degradation, a Remedial Action Plan (RAP) was developed by the New York State Department of Environmental Conservation (DEC) in cooperation with citizens concerned about the river's revitalization, and an action committee comprising of representatives from 26 diverse but interested groups was formed in 1989. The mission of the RAP is "to restore the chemical, physical, and biological integrity of the Niagara River ecosystem...(while) protecting and enhancing the human health, fish and wildlife, aesthetics and recreation, and the economy of the Niagara River Area of Concern."

Though various stages of rehabilitation have already taken place from Lake Erie to Lake Ontario since the 1970's, the RAP is thoroughly comprehensive and its 1993 summary delineates long-range goals and the implementation procedures. The toxins threatening the fish and the survival of aquatic life listed in this plan are disconcerting. PCB's, mirex, chlordane, dioxins, and polynuclear aromatic hydrocarbons are but a few chemicals cited specifically, not to mention concentrations of heavy metals in sedimentation.

Jim Lorentz with a large Niagara River buck.

Although conditions have improved considerably, there will always be much to rehabilitate. The RAP is the essential tool needed to ensure that the future biological management of the lower Niagara River and Lake Ontario will continue to flourish.

The overpopulation of alewives and rainbow smelt, combined with the decrease of predators as a result of the lamprey in the 60's and 70's, led to heavy stocking of Pacific salmonids through the 70's and 80's. For a combination of reasons, a decrease in forage base in the lake during the early 90's has called for a corresponding decrease in Chinook salmon stocking. It is not exactly certain how the decrease in forage directly affects the survival of steelhead; indirectly, the lack of Chinook in the lake shifts increased angler pressure to both lake trout and steelhead populations. In the absence of comprehensive wild steelhead assessments within the lake, the true effects of this increased attention in terms of naturally reproducing steelhead can only be speculated.

The review and subsequent status report of Lake Ontario's pelagic fish community in 1996 by the technical panel of scientific experts discussed in Chapter 4 has been a very important move in the overall management scheme of the lake. It has become critical for the future health of the fishery to understand the dynamics between the biomass of prey and its limitations with respect to the specific stocking of Chinook and coho salmon. More importantly, an understanding of all factors influencing the life cycle of both the alewife and rainbow smelt populations has been recognized as a priority issue for the balanced health of this complex ecosystem.

Acknowledging the need for continued research, the panel made some conclusions based upon available information, scientific data, and observation. Bioenergetic models were developed and evaluated. Although the alewife population increase in 1995 was likely due to a reduction of stocked salmon in 1993 interacting with other complicated in-lake factors, it cannot be assumed that a return to increased stocking numbers is the next expected course of action. Managing the Lake Ontario salmonid fisheries through stocking is a tightrope act between return and risk. Current stocking rates will maintain a fast-growing salmon based on alewife as the primary forage fish. A return to higher stocking rates will likely increase the salmonid population, but also increases the risk of disease (such as BKD) and slower growth rates. The panel emphasized that managing a fishery for maximum yield is a prescription for disaster since it is often not possible to know the maximum sustainable yield until it has been exceeded.

Although these conclusions should greatly influence the angler's perspective of this fishery, it is not exactly clear how steelhead fit into the management scenario and future decisions of return versus risk. If there was ever a reason to consider the status of wild steelhead in Lake Ontario, it certainly would be now. A valuable work that has established some baseline information relating to the ecological genetics of an introduced species was put forth by Lucy A. Dueck and Roy G. Danzman in 1996. The study of successful steelhead colonizations was designed to provide useful insights into "the evolutionary dynamics of adaptations" within Lake Ontario. Ultimately this work would attempt to quantify variability in populations distributed throughout the lake. Specimens from several sources on the north and the south shore would be sampled. Important in these studies, however, was first to trace the origins of steelhead populations past and present. The results would compare recently stocked strains to the established naturalized populations.

Historically, Lake Ontario seemed to receive the least amount of attention from the steelhead pioneers who had targeted the upper lakes. About 1940, creeks west of Toronto received fish from Codrington Hatchery of primarily Normandale origins. Intermittent plants of Normandale fish occurred through the mid 1960's. There is much evidence supporting natural colonization of Ontario's streams throughout the middle part of this century. It is important to realize that much of Lake Ontario's original Canadian steelhead population developed naturally. Although New York's south shore produced very few fish, Ontario's north shore tributaries seemed to have developed into a productive nursery for these migrating rainbows.

Despite the presence of self-sustaining rainbow trout populations in the lake's watershed, massive stocking programs occurred in the Province of Ontario's water starting in 1968. As the effects of the Clean Water Act started to take hold, New York's stocking of Lake Ontario began in 1973. These programs were enacted in response to forage overpopulation and angler demands for increased sportfishing opportunities. New York stocked 2.5 times the number of fish during the period that peaked by the late 80's. Close to 15 million rainbow were introduced throughout the period. In New York, Chambers Creek winter strain became the main strain of choice after several others exhibited shortcomings for one reason or another.

Simply stated, Dueck's and Danzman's studies found that Ontario's naturalized populations were highly differentiated when compared to the tributaries of New York. In other words, the north shore fish had developed unique genetic characteristics different from those on the south shore. Additionally, a subdivision may be developing between Ontario's Ganaraska fish and those of a few neighboring tributaries, including Wilmot Creek. New York's fish showed the overwhelming influence of stocking several strains upon the genetic character of its original populations. Understanding the specifics is best left up to the scientists, but the conclusions of the study (translated into language the average angler can understand) may be capable of providing substantial data crucial for the future management of the resource. Whereas genetic population structures have "largely been ignored" for introduced species throughout North America, insights gained from such studies may now become a valuable management tool.

The rainbow trout is the most widely distributed salmonid in the world thanks to an aggressively comprehensive stocking effort. The ability of the rainbow to adapt readily to its local environments gives insight into the true nature of this salmonid species. Lake Ontario, in particular, offers the valuable opportunity of observing a population of fish in the process of genetically adapting to its new environmental range. According to Dueck and Danzman, "study systems of introduced fish are useful contemporary models in ecological genetic research, since introductions and stocking are analogous to initial founder and dispersal events for colonizing species." Although the situation in Lake Ontario is by no means pristine, it does afford a unique observation into the evolutionary determination of an introduced species adjusting to its role in an era impacted by unbridled human activity.

As habitat conditions improved on most of these north shore tributaries over the past 25 years, the rearing capabilities did as well. These rich tributaries contribute many steelhead annually to the Lake Ontario community. Even during the bleak 60's and 70's, some fish survived the negative conditions to continue the genetic connections to the past. The progeny of the Ganaraska River has emerged as another identifiable Great Lakes strain of steelhead, and it is the result of a process that developed naturally in a lake that seemed forever doomed. This strain replaced the traditional Normandale stock in the early 1980's, and it is used for various, but minor, supplemental plantings throughout the region. Fishery managers emphatically state that brood stocks are not retained anymore. Eggs are taken yearly from feral fish.

To this day, south shore tributaries are maintained by annual stockings of Salmon River progeny and Skamania. In the mid 1990's New York's interest in assessing its potential and eventual management of wild fish in Lake Erie will hopefully extend to Lake Ontario. The tributaries of the Salmon River will receive primary attention. Irondequoit and Sandy Creeks near Rochester both appear to support some natural reproduction as well. It is believed by those who regularly fish the Niagara River that a number of fish caught there annually are wild, but it is not known if these fish are of Niagara River origins. There is need for New York to understand the contributions of its naturalized fish to the lake community in much the same manner as the Province of Ontario.

The DEC's interest in re-establishing the Atlantic Salmon populations may also have potential benefits for New York's wild steelhead. The elimination of dams and construction of fish passages could assist in the spawning process of both species. This has been witnessed to a certain degree on the Black River near Watertown. Similar to the Grand River entering Lake Erie in Ontario, there is a developing steelhead fishery in the upper reaches of the Black now that fish can pass through a lower dam site, providing new

A.Hassall/99.

opportunities for both the fish and the fisherman. Oswego River and, possibly, Oak Orchard Creek hold the same potential for future management practices.

As mentioned above, much attention has been directed to the loss of forage base in recent years. There has also been some concern about Chinook and steelhead recruitment as well. It is feared the survivability of stocked juvenile salmonids has dropped in recent years as well in conjunction with the decreased forage base. In fact, the juvenile salmonids may have become forage. In 1997, there was a proposal from the DEC to participate in a joint salmon and trout pen rearing project with the Oak Orchard Business Association. The purpose of the project is to enhance the fishery in Lake Ontario as well as the Oak Orchard area of the lake by the use of rearing pens placed in the lower portion of Oak Orchard Creek. It is believed that the use of these pens will increase survival by allowing the fish to grow larger while, additionally, acclimating to the environment before release into the wild. Also, the process will promote proper imprinting. This cooperative effort may prove to be another effective tool in managing a region with limited spawning capabilities. Only time will tell.

These are exciting times on the Great Lakes because many of the studies discussed will provide solid foundations for the future fishery of the system. Another important work by Lucien A. Marcoliese and John M. Casselman of the Ontario Ministry of Natural Resources details a definitive scale sample methodology for discriminating between indigenous and hatchery rainbow in Lake Ontario that has a very high rate of success. According to the report, since it has been difficult to assess the overall contribution of indigenous fish to the lake population because unmarked hatchery fish have been stocked, indigeny must be measured if the structure of the population is to be known and appropriate decisions are to be made for managing this popular sport fish. This method can be adapted and utilized in the other Great Lakes as well.

What is good for the Niagara River is obviously most beneficial to all of Lake Ontario's water. With a vast improvement in water quality, steelhead populations flourish, but not without hatchery assistance. The Province of Ontario still only plants supplemental fish from its Ganaraska River brood stock while New York's fish are reared from Salmon River heritage. The Skamania program was dealt a serious setback in 1995 with the discovery of whirling disease in the Caledonia hatchery leading to the extermination of the entire stock. Natural reproduction is noted in some of New York's waters, including the Salmon River's tributaries. New York's DEC is investigating ways to open more spawning habitat on rivers historically blocked by man-made dams.

Controlling sea lamprey predation will always be a problem, and the increasing harvest of fish by charter boats in the open lake is beginning to show impact. Ironically, the high contamination level of all fish swimming

Rick Kustich hefts an above-average Lake Ontario steelhead.

Lake Ontario over the years has led to a voluntary catch and release ethic practiced by many that has resulted in a spectacular fishery. With the perceived decline in the lake's forage base and the de-emphasis of the Chinook salmon fishery, the charter boats have targeted steelhead. Despite the fact that there are health risks to be considered when eating a Lake Ontario fish, charter boat clients keep many steelhead annually. Fortunately, there is a movement at present pushing for a reduction in overall limits within Lake Ontario—particularly for steelhead.

Although the reputation of Lakes Erie and Ontario have been tainted by all the negativity associated with pollution and massive stocking programs, the credibility of both lakes continues to grow as the new wave of studies proceeds to reveal true potential. Unfortunately, it is this reputation that has also tarnished the image of the entire Great Lakes system. However, the knowledge gained by the many studies conducted within all five lakes to this point by dedicated managers cultivates the respectability needed to take this fishery seriously.

The future of the Great Lakes depends upon sound management and the support of educated anglers. It should be noted that every manager and fishery biologist we have contacted has shared a sincere personal interest and passion for the Great Lakes fishery. They deserve our respect and confidence. Decisions can no longer and should never be made based upon the emotional demands of the unenlightened. The truth is our fishery managers are the experts and we should value their scientific input. Although there is still much to be learned, it is wisdom that must lead the way, and it is only with a spirit of cooperation that a quality fishery can be maintained well into the 21st century and beyond. If we can all work together in the spirit of cooperation, much good can be accomplished for present and future generations.

The Great Lakes are analogous to a long flowing river, starting with crystalline pure water in the upper reaches and ending in the lowland reaches of Lake Ontario as its water exits to the Atlantic Ocean via the St. Lawrence Seaway. All five lakes are bonded together by more than a common ribbon of water, however, and the steelhead are but one link in the chain that includes many other positive and negative factors as well. The pristine waters that flowed prior to the arrival of the European settlers are gone forever, and the impaired ecosystem that has been passed on to us all requires our concerned and diligent stewardship. There is little room for error—past mistakes have at least taught us that. In the end, what is best to foster natural reproduction of Great Lakes fish, including steelhead, is probably the most healthy direction the management of the entire system can take.

Part II
The Fly Fishing Approach

A. Hassall 09

A Steelhead Gallery...

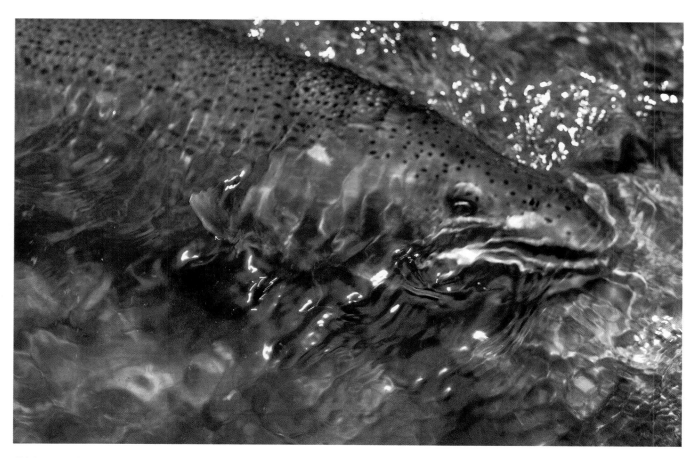

Shimmering dreams...

*First one
through the
pool...*

A late spring...

Pure silver...

Power to spare...

A touch of chrome...

A lone autumn angler...

Released to fight again.

7

Steelhead Behavior

The dynamics of fly fishing for steelhead requires us to understand its ways. One must have a systematic approach to consistently encounter fish in the varied waters of the Great Lakes region. This understanding not only helps us to be successful, but will allow us to appreciate this magnificent fish and everything it represents.

In the West, there is an adage that steelhead are easy to catch, it's finding them that is difficult. Though there is some truth to this statement, there are circumstances that continually affect an angler's ability to take steelhead even when they are present, whether it be on the West Coast or Great Lakes region. Catching steelhead depends upon not only knowing when some fish are available but also where to find them and what to do in any given situation to hook one.

In this chapter, we will look at some common behavioral traits of Great Lakes steelhead and how they will impact fly fishing strategy. This sounds straightforward. Most exhibit similar behavior, but many individuals or small groups of individuals seem to play by their own set of rules. While these common traits can provide significant guidelines for our fly fishing approach, we must always realize that there are probably a few individual steelhead that will not react in the manner we anticipate. Their personalities are as wide and varied as the anglers who pursue them. It is one of the reasons they are such a special fish.

Timing the Run

Each year, mature steelhead get the urge to return to their water of origin. The signs that tell the fish that "it is time" are as predictable as the amount of sunlight in the day or as widely variable as water temperature and flow. The sunlight factor gives some stability to the basic time frame of when steelhead move close to shore and then ascend the streams and rivers. Other conditions create flexibility within the basic range. Understanding and monitoring the variables can pay big dividends. Timing can be critical.

Great Lakes steelhead spawn in the spring. Most strains of fish existing in the Great Lakes are winter-run fish beginning their runs the preceding fall. While some of these fish will begin to run as early as late August and the beginning weeks of September, October and November are the peak months across a good portion of the region. In some rivers, provided that water conditions remain agreeable, steelhead that have moved in during the fall will stay throughout the winter months. Others will filter in during December, January, and February. Some tributaries do not provide suitable winter habitat for steelhead. Those that freeze over, or that commonly have very little winter flow will hold few fish at this time, and steelhead that had previously entered may drop back to the lake. These fish will find a more favorable river or wait for the spring thaw and rains to try again. Dropping out of the river during the run is a trait that will normally be found only in Great Lakes steelhead since there is no transition between fresh and salt water as on rivers of the Pacific Ocean.

March, April, and early May are the peak months for spawning activity. This equates to an increase in the number of steelhead that will be found in the rivers at this time. In some areas, winter-run fish will be found into June.

A commonly asked question is why do steelhead enter rivers in the fall if they do not spawn until the following spring? One basic reason would seem to be their genetic connection to Pacific coast fish. Pacific coast rivers are generally much longer than the typical Great Lakes tributary. It may be hundreds of miles to suitable spawning areas. Varied river conditions can make the journey arduous and prolong it for months. Starting the trip in the fall allows fish to arrive with time to spare. This trait has been genetically programmed over thousands of years. However, all winter-run fish do not begin their run at one time. Some enter in the fall, some in the winter and others in the spring. Theories suggest a method to this madness. It may be nature's way of spreading out risk. At any one point in time, fish of a similar strain will be found in various sections of the river and some still in the lake or ocean as the case may be. This could create a defense against an adverse event at one particular time causing significant harm to the entire run.

Other theories suggest that there are vanguard steelhead which may lead the way and investigate the river. If conditions are not favorable they may drop back prematurely, signaling to others that the run be put on hold for a while. This may sound a little far-fetched. Such suspected behavior has been observed on Pacific coast rivers and, because of the genetic link, is a characteristic that is most likely present in Great Lakes fish. We observed possible evidence of this a few seasons ago. Low water in a New York river kept steelhead schooled in deep pools for weeks. There was very little apparent movement. Somehow these fish seemed to know that the water upriver was so low that passage would have been nearly impossible. The steelhead waited patiently until rains raised the level. Maybe it was simply an instinctive reaction, but these events seemed to suggest something more.

In recent years, the timing of runs has extended itself through the summer months with the introduction of the summer-run Skamania strain steelhead, which has established consistent runs in some rivers. While many steelhead managers see such a strain that has not developed itself in the Great Lakes as a detriment to wild fish management, it can provide year-round fishing opportunity. These fish will enter the rivers throughout the summer if conditions are favorable. Skamania runs are largely supported through stocking programs.

Within the basic framework of the peak steelhead months, there can be extreme fluctuations between particular regions and their individual rivers. Runs on some tributaries can be strong by the middle of September. This can be especially true of some of the northern tributaries in Michigan and Ontario. This is in dramatic contrast to other rivers where good numbers do not exist until November. An example of this is the Niagara River. Sporadic steelhead can be found as early as September and throughout October, but the brunt of the run traditionally occurs later and continues throughout the winter months.

Such timing variations can be tied to the peculiarities of a particular river or region. The various wild Great Lakes strains that have developed in the last one hundred years have done so in reaction to the environmental factors they encounter. The harsh weather conditions of the north shore of Lake Superior has created strong, hearty strains of fish that have genetically "learned" to survive and thrive under such conditions. These fish are programmed to run earlier in the fall and later in the spring. This seems to be a characteristic common to many of the rivers in the northern part of the Great Lakes region.

Water temperature can also be a key factor in the seasonal variations of the run in a particular river. The optimum water temperature range for steelhead seems to be 42 to 58 degree F. This will vary slightly, but it is a good guide. Steelhead activity will most likely occur within the parameters of these temperatures. This probably explains the later runs on such rivers as the Niagara. It receives almost all of its water from Lake Erie. The large body of the lake takes much longer to reach the prime temperature. Water temperature can also be the reason for variations in spring runs. We have witnessed times where the peak of spring fishing has varied by as much as a month on the same river from one year to the next. A close analysis of thermometer readings confirmed our suspicions. When the mercury hit the 40 to 42 degrees F. range there was an obvious increase in the number of available, active steelhead. Rivers that feed from impoundments will normally take longer to warm up in the spring than surrounding tributaries that run free from their headwaters.

It should be noted that the nature of many Great Lakes tributaries contributes to wide temperature swings throughout the day. Some drainages are both short and somewhat shallow. These can be greatly influenced by the extremes between nighttime and daytime air temperatures, particularly during late fall. Five degree fluctuations daily are not uncommon. Slate-bottomed tributaries with no groundwater influence are particularly sensitive. A slight rise in water temperature from 40 to 41 degrees F., for example, can trigger fish activity. After a cold night, steelhead activity may be at its highest in the afternoon when water temperatures commonly rise. On the other hand, late in the day, the temperature may drop *down* to 41 degrees F. and activity may cease. Same temperature, but now the mercury is moving in a negative direction. Suffice to say that nothing has a more dramatic impact on fall fishing for steelhead in the Great Lakes than swings in water temperature. A river can be alive when the temperatures are in the 40 degree F. range. However, when the cold air sweeps down from the north and water temperatures plummet, you are left with the impression that there are no fish present. This fluctuation and the impact on fish activity can result in a small window for consistent fishing on some rivers and is one of the main differences between Great Lakes and Pacific coast steelhead fly fishing.

Rivers that contain a high degree of groundwater, like Michigan's Pere Marquette, will often create a neutralizing effect on water temperature fluctuations. Such drainages will not experience the same sensitivity to changes in the air temperature. They will also tend to run slightly warmer in the winter and cooler in the late spring, summer, and early fall.

Steelhead movement does not cease once water temperatures drop below 40 degrees F. But due to a lowered metabolism, activity is greatly reduced. Fish will spend more time in one place, sometimes for days or possibly weeks if not harassed. However, some individuals or groups will decide that it is their time, even in the height of winter conditions. This is evidenced by the regular presence of fresh-run fish in some rivers during the winter months. An example of this is New York's Salmon River. Steelhead fresh from the lake can be found all winter. It could be that even though a particular river is carrying a temperature in the mid 30 degree range, it may be higher than the lake temperature. This could draw fish. It is important to realize that the temperature of a river can rise noticeably if the sky is bright and the air is warm. If the river has a dam and a reservoir, it may stay a little warmer later into the winter.

Some theorize that if a tributary is colder than the lake, this may delay or slow down run activity. Likewise, if the lake is colder than the streams or rivers, the fish will be more inspired to enter the tributary. This seems especially true for some spring fish as mentioned above. Despite the urgency to spawn, until the temperature of its desired drainage is presumably conducive, a fish may wait until the last possible moment to move. At times, the window of opportunity is so restrictive that a fish may only be in the river for a few days. Some fish may even abort the mission if water temperatures do not cooperate.

The steelhead's mood also sours in water that exceeds the 62 to 65 degree range. Major movements of fish would not be expected when a river is running temperatures greater than this range. This would be a key consideration when anticipating late summer and early fall migrations of winter-run fish. It is also a prominent factor in the timing of summer-run fish. Rivers that receive runs of Skamania may have fish positioned near them for a good portion of the summer. A cool rain or lower than average nighttime air temperatures can quickly drop water temperatures and bring fish into the river. Those rivers that are fed by many springs will help keep summer temperatures moderate. This creates a good environment for summer-run returns. However, summer-run fish in some areas like Indiana routinely enter tributaries that have temperature readings into the 70 degree F. range.

Water flow is the one factor that most directly affects the timing of the steelhead run in a particular river on a day-to-day basis. Rain or snowmelt that raises the water level will often trigger good movements of fish. Steelhead prefer to travel as the water is on the rise. Some rivers rise quickly and dirty fast with heavy rains. In these instances, the fishing will often be good until visibility is dramatically reduced. Good fishing will normally resume when the water begins to clear and drop as this can condense large numbers of still-active fish into a small area. While the phenomenon of rising water will have a positive effect on most tributaries, it is especially true of the many small spate rivers found throughout the Great Lakes region. This is the case with a handful of the streams on the southern coast of Lake Erie in Ohio and Pennsylvania. They depend on rain or snowmelt for most of their flow. When the water is low and a heavy rain raises the water significantly, these streams can become chock full of steelhead. As the water rises or begins to clear, everyone catches fish. The water can return to the very clear stage in just a few days if there is no additional rain. The fishing then becomes much more difficult. This sequence occurs on most of the steelhead rivers in the Great Lakes region. It is usually not as extreme elsewhere as it is with these Lake Erie tributaries.

To hit the timing of a steelhead movement head-on is one of the main objectives of this great pursuit. Much of the time it takes plain luck—being in the right place at the right time. But sometimes one can make his or her own luck. As serious steelhead anglers, we are always planning, trying to anticipate

Water flow is the most important factor controlling steelhead migration on a day-to-day basis.

good fishing opportunities. We watch weather forecasts as far as a week in advance. Strategy is planned based on expected moisture or lack thereof. We hope that the right conditions will exist on the days we can make it to the river, or we feverishly rearrange schedules to be there when it should be prime. Plans are constantly amended based on changes in the forecast. Much goes into the strategy of where and when to fish. Many times success or failure is determined before you wet a line. Sometimes you are left guessing which river to try as you leave the driveway. Things commonly do not work out as planned, but when they do, the feeling is sweet.

It is important to learn all you can about a few rivers. Learn their habits—their subtleties and nuances. It is of critical importance to know the best time periods for a particular river as well as understanding how much rain a river can withstand before becoming unfishable and how long it will take to clear after becoming muddy. It is equally important to have a basic understanding of that river's water temperatures at specific times of the year. All this will assist in choosing the right river for a given time of year or conditions. Of course there always is the intangible aspect of just plain liking one river the most because it is a beautiful place—a few are even magical.

It should not be misunderstood that steelhead fishing in the Great Lakes is solely a hit-or-miss proposition. In fact, it is quite the contrary. Many rivers will have at least some fish present at all times from early fall through the following spring. In such rivers, rain or snowmelt can draw more fish into the river or cause the fish that are present to be more active. Normally, good fishing can exist in the periods between wet-weather systems, although some fish may drop back as the water level declines. And while there is always the desire to be on the river when the conditions are at their best, many hours will be spent on water that is something less than perfect. This is an integral part of the sport, and it is an important aspect of the challenge.

"Fishable conditions" is a fairly subjective term. Each angler seems to have a tolerable limit of high and dirty water. Steelhead will take a fly in dirty water, but action seems to be severely limited in water that has visibility of less than three to six inches. This is especially true of water on the rise. We have witnessed numerous instances where water that clouds up quickly will shut the steelhead activity right down. Also, water that rises too high can result in a dramatic reduction of defined holding water. The fish can be anywhere. This, combined with low visibility, can make the effort futile. It is then time to go to another river that may be in better condition or just go home and tie flies. Some rivers seem to fish much better in dirty conditions than others. We have had some good days on New York's Oak Orchard Creek in water that looked like mud. There are others where we have never taken a fish in dirty conditions. Again it is important to know your rivers.

There are those rivers that receive such high numbers of stocked fish that there is almost always a number of fish present. This is common of Elk and Walnut Creeks in Pennsylvania. In these rivers, some of the true mystique of steelhead fishing is lost since the sheer abundance of fish, at times, makes it more like fishing an inland trout stream for big fish. Rains are then needed to make the fish that are already present more active as well as to bring in new fish.

At times, there are no defined indicators that signal the movement of fish. For reasons undetectable to the human senses, a group of fish may just decide it's time. That is why it is always worth being on the water, even during mediocre conditions.

One final observation on the increase in water flow. Warm rains in the winter and especially in the spring will normally attract more fish than snow runoff because the melting snow may actually lower the water temperature. While the rising water is important, low water temperature can slow down activity.

Positioning

Steelhead will be found in various types of water throughout the year. Numerous factors play a role in the positioning of fish in the tributaries. Possibly the most prominent is the desire for security. The confinement of a stream or river represents a dramatic change from the open expanse of the lake. It forces the migrating fish to seek out water with certain qualities which provide this comfort level. In general, under normal conditions, fish will be found in water that has a minimum depth of two to three feet. A broken surface also gives steelhead a sense of confidence. They will be found in shallower water if there is a disturbance on top, such as a heavy riffle.

Under varying water conditions, the security considerations begin to change. As the water begins to drop and clear, comfortable holds become more difficult to find. This may force fish to drop back down. They may condense into deeper pools. In low, clear water, steelhead will utilize the available structure to their advantage. They will use overhanging brush, logjams, deeper depressions, and sharp drop-offs or crevices in the bottom. The latter is common of many of the Great Lakes rivers that have a floor consisting mainly of shale.

Because of tributary size, Great Lakes steelhead utilize a wide array of holding water and lies, all of which can be important to the angler. West Coast steelhead can afford to be more choosy because of the greater volume of water associated with rivers of the Pacific. In this situation, there are only certain types of water where steelhead and angler have the opportunity to meet.

High and dirty water creates the opposite effect. Because of the lack of visibility, steelhead can find easy security. Additionally, the off-color water seems to disorient the fish to a degree. They can be found in water that is a foot or less in depth. It is always wise to fish before you wade under such conditions. Steelhead seem to have an aversion to stained water since the sediment can irritate their gills. They will often take advantage of clearer water such as that provided by a feeder stream that is running clean. We have seen evidence of this on a number of occasions. The water level presents its own considerations. High water usually equates to an increased current flow. Steelhead will avoid the heaviest flows if possible. For this reason, in high water, fish will tend to concentrate in areas that break off from the main current. Back eddies, quiet water along the bank, or the inside of the main current are all such places.

Sunlight seems to have a similar effect as water clarity. Under normal water conditions, bright sunlight can have a significant impact on positioning. It does not seem as though it bothers the fish, it just provides a decrease in the security level. At these times, they seem to react more to human presence. The low light of early morning may find fish in the shallow tailout of a pool or in the riffles at the head of a run. Sunlight and angling pressure can quickly force fish out of such lies in search of cover. This should not imply that fishing will be poor under sunlit skies. We have had some great days under these conditions and, in fact, sunlight can be an ally when the water is stained. However, with low, clear water conditions, the first couple hours of the day can be some of the most productive fishing. If the activity slows during the day because of intense sunlight, there will normally be a point towards evening and nightfall which will prompt fish movement. Overcast skies allow steelhead to feel secure in a wide variety of water types—even shallow runs. If it rains, all the better. Security is combined with increased activity caused by rising water. These are the conditions of which dreams are made.

During their migration upriver, steelhead will normally select the path of least resistance in an effort to conserve energy. Travel lanes will be determined by a combination of security and gentler flows. Many fish will use the same lane. Look for the softer sides of the current to determine likely travel routes. Keep in mind that surface currents will be greater than those along the bottom. Steelhead may be able to find agreeable travel in deeper runs that have a heavy surface current.

Water temperature can be a major factor in a steelhead's choice of holding water. In the optimum range of 42 to 58 degrees, fish can be found in a wide range of water. Riffles, runs, and pools that provide security can hold fish under agreeable temperatures. As temperatures move toward the extremes, steelhead move toward water with more defined specifications. Water that drops below 40 degrees will normally find fish in deep pools with a minimum of current. Their slowed metabolism forces them to seek areas where less energy is expended. For water that exceeds the 62 to 65 degree range, dissolved oxygen becomes the issue. Steelhead will seek out the heads of riffles where the moving, churning flow aerates the water. Also, in both the low and high extremes of the temperature range, fish will gravitate toward any spring seeps providing a consistent temperature year-round. Locating these areas can be quite advantageous from a fishing standpoint.

One last positioning factor is determined by the actual spawning activity, both of the steelhead and other species. As some steelhead enter the rivers in October, many of these waters can be densely active with the spawning rituals of Chinook salmon and lake-run browns. Many times steelhead will be found positioned below the redds of the salmon and browns, feeding on drifting eggs. In the spring, the steelhead's behavior is dictated by its own instinct to propagate the species. Fish will often be positioned near spawning gravel. Large concentrations can be found in the pockets, depressions, and drop-offs below spawning areas as they wait for something to happen. Also, fish will be readily spotted on the spawning gravel. The urge to spawn often places steelhead in open areas where they would not normally be found. Spawning fish represent poor angling targets and should be left alone to do their duty.

Condition of the Steelhead

The ultimate objective of Great Lakes steelhead fly fishing is to intercept fish fresh from the lake. Fresh-run fish will normally have a very bright, silvery appearance. They are firm and strong, capable of the exciting fights that have made steelhead famous. Fresh-run fish are typically aggressive. They will take a fly very well as they enter the tributary and for days afterward. These fish will be more likely to quickly chase a fly or to move great distances to take. They will also be more likely to rise off the bottom for a fly. What this means is that fresh fish make good targets for the more traditional techniques—those that incorporate a fly fished under tension and off the bottom.

Steelhead that have spent a fair time in the river become less aggressive. During this period, these fish have probably felt the pressure of human presence. In addition, their strength has most likely been diminished from the lack of a regular eating routine and their general appearance has darkened while possibly showing signs of weight loss. Males will be darker than females. Darker fish will typically be found higher in the river system since more days in the river also allows for greater advancement. But these fish can still be quite cooperative. Their eagerness to move to a fly seems to go in spurts. When older fish make up the bulk of the population of a particular river, it is quite common that a series of hookups will be experienced in short periods of time. This leaves one to conclude that the fish simply "turned on." There is usually no clear sign as to when this is going to happen. Being on the river for extended periods of time improves the odds. Steelhead that have been in for a while tend to react to a fly more consistently in lower light. The first few hours and last few of the day can make all the difference. This is especially true of heavily pressured rivers and clear water conditions.

It is difficult to predict when fish within a river will "turn on" during a given day. Fish movement usually equates to activity for the angler. Fresh fish may encourage older fish to move to a fly. Water temperature, angle of the sun, and many other variables play an important role, eventually inspiring steelhead to take. The persistent fly fisher is often rewarded. Over the years, we have hooked a large number of steelhead during the 11:00 A.M. to 1:00 P.M. time period, possibly due to the gradual warming of the day. Many fish are also taken very early in the morning, but this may have to do with positioning as fish usually settle into the obvious "moving lies" during the night. Because steelhead usually begin to move late in the evening, this can also provide an active period before dark. For whatever reasons, there are a few high-percentage times that fish do turn on and these times can even follow a predictable pattern.

Fish that have been in a river for an extended time can become stale or dour. Such fish tend to be only slightly active. Stale steelhead will normally possess a very dark look and show clear signs of weight loss. They will not readily move to a fly. Much of the time, only a dead-drifted presentation will be successful. It may take a number of casts with a variety of flies to entice a take. Most often, they will not take at all. This situation is amplified if the river is heavily pressured. The fight of a stale fish will typically be much less spirited than that of a fresh steelhead. Stale fish are not the preferred target.

Steelhead seem to become stale faster in short or smaller tributaries. In those that drop and clear quickly, even fairly fresh fish will begin to act dour. Larger concentrations of stale fish will be found in the upper parts of longer river systems. On shorter tributaries, there is a greater tendency for fish to drop back to the lake as the water clears and recedes.

There can be a significant difference between steelhead entering in the fall compared to those present in the spring. Fall fish are likely to be more aggressive and in prime physical condition. Some spring fish have already spent many days in the river. Their bodies can show significant wear from the winter months. Spring water temperatures will just be reaching the active range. Even fish that are just ascending the river for the first time in the spring seem to act quite differently than fall fish. It seems to be in their attitude. Spawning activity now dictates their movement and actions. Some individuals at this stage will simply not be interested in taking a fly. Others will be active for short periods of time. Occasionally, very active spring fish can be encountered. This usually involves a combination of fish on the move and rising water temperatures. If the fish are fresh from the lake, all the better.

The attitude of spring steelhead tends to create tougher fishing. Fish that are entirely preoccupied with spawning can be frustrating. As discussed, we feel that fishing to those on their beds is not true sport. This occasionally leaves us with the feeling that spring fishing can be a little overrated. Some of the best opportunity for spring fish is to concentrate on the areas near the spawning gravel. Pockets, depressions, runs and pools, above and below gravel bars, will collect fish on the move. Under these circumstances, spring fish exhibit an aggressive side and can take a fly well. When you hit it right, the action is amazing. We were given clear evidence of just how explosive spring fishing can be one day on Michigan's Manistee River. Conditions were right, fish were on the move and many paused to hold in the water in which we worked our flies. We had many hookups and did battle with strong fish. But it was also typical for the spring, as we spent the previous days on other rivers casting to fish that were generally uncooperative.

Post-spawn steelhead dropping back to the lake can be in surprisingly good condition. Once the spawn has concluded, fish go back on the feed. They can build their strength up quickly. This is especially true of females, since males will remain in the spawning mode for a longer period of time. In some rivers, drop-back males will also be in good shape. On rivers such as Ontario's Ganaraska River, healthy steelhead dropping back to Lake Ontario can be found until June. Since the open season on this river occurs on the last

Saturday of April, a good portion of the opportunity is for drop-backs. As May water temperatures climb toward optimum levels, steelhead become active and are again susceptible to more traditional techniques.

Feeding

Some discussion has always existed as to whether Great Lakes steelhead actually feed during their spawning migration. We have heard speculation over the years that they only take a fly for other reasons. And while aggression, instinct, and curiosity all seem to prompt a steelhead to move to a fly, there is no doubt that at times it is the result of active feeding. We have witnessed fresh steelhead chasing baitfish at the surface, others collecting eggs drifting free from salmon spawning beds, and even a few taking flies off the surface. Studies and observations have turned up large concentrations of caddis larvae, stonefly, and mayfly nymphs in the stomachs of steelhead returning to those rivers rich in aquatic insect life. It is also clear that in some rivers where a concentration of a particular food source exists, fish will key in on this item. This feeding tendency may require that the fly being used imitate the natural food available and that it be presented in a realistic manner.

It only makes sense that the steelhead, which may spend in excess of six months in the river, would need to feed to maintain at least a minimum energy level. Such feeding patterns will typically be quite different than when in the lake. No longer will there be readily available schools of baitfish at their disposal. They need to adapt. Wild fish probably do a better job, since they spent one to two years in the river as juveniles, thus allowing them to learn the ways of the river. It is usually not clear what triggers feeding activity. But as trout, steelhead are opportunists, and they will take advantage of what presents itself. It is normally not clear whether a steelhead is actively feeding or just on the take for other reasons. Most of the time it will not be critical to make a distinction. Other times it can directly affect fly selection.

The behavioral traits of steelhead in the Great Lakes follow many consistent patterns. However, the only hard-and-fast rule is that there is no hard-and-fast rule. Variations will be caused by how factors relate to one another in a particular river system, with each river possessing its own unique qualities. It is important to keep aware and make observations of the rivers that you frequent. Keep notes and refer to them, and then plan a strategy based on all available information.

Most avid steelheaders do their homework. Based on acquired knowledge and an instinct that evolves from a committed passion, they head to a location believed to hold the greatest potential for a given time. Sometimes it all comes together, sometimes it doesn't—therein lies the intriguing challenge of the pursuit. Finding a fish that actually takes a fly based upon consideration of all the facts available can be the greatest thrill in the world of fishing.

8

Reading Water

Determining the qualities required of a particular piece of water to attract or hold fish is an important aspect of any type of fishing. The importance of this understanding is magnified when it comes to fly fishing for steelhead. In larger rivers, a few fish can be spread out over miles of water or can be concentrated into limited sections. In smaller streams, steelhead will often be found in unconventional holds. In each situation, the keen ability to determine likely holding water will directly impact one's success.

Being able to properly read the water is a function of understanding the quarry combined with the experience gained by spending time on the streams and rivers. The learning curve can be shortened by acute observation. When a steelhead is encountered in a particular spot, you should try to understand why. For us, it simply provides the ability to fish with confidence. The experienced steelhead angler is always in search of water that, at a minimum, has a reasonable chance of containing some fish. It is this confidence factor that leads us to certain water and away from others. In the end, making the proper decision on what water to fish equates to more than just success, it lends itself to a greater enjoyment and satisfaction.

In this chapter, we will examine some of the key aspects of reading steelhead water in the Great Lakes region. We will see that some characteristics are quite obvious, while others are subtle. We must look at the big picture as well as the details, especially on longer watersheds. With experience, reading and selecting the water to fish almost becomes second nature. However, there is always something to learn no matter how intimately familiar one is with a particular river.

Basic Characteristics

One of the defining elements of the basic approach to steelhead fly fishing in the Great Lakes relates to the makeup of the typical stream or river of the region. It is another main difference between steelheading in the Great Lakes and that of the Pacific coast. And while genetic makeup and learned characteristics play an important role in the way steelhead react when they enter a river, so does the type of water in which they are found.

In general, a typical Great Lakes river has a greater gradient than we find on steelhead drainages of the Pacific coast or salmon rivers of the Atlantic. This causes a faster, heavier flow throughout their course. Many consist of a more narrow or channelized flow. This is true also of some of the region's rivers that are considered classic steelhead waters. Most Great Lakes watersheds are shorter than the average coastal river. They are typically smaller and some are lined with brush creating tighter, confined conditions. One other factor that is unfortunately a part of some rivers is angling pressure. Those that are located in proximity to large population centers can draw crowds. Although this isn't a physical characteristic of the water itself, it is an element which can directly affect the behavior of the steelhead and where they will be found.

Great Lakes rivers vary widely and not all are defined solely by the above characteristics. Many contain more traditional lies, and some are even dominated by classic runs and pools. However, the typical river usually contains some combination. This combination can come in the form of various stretches of one river containing traditional water where other sections do not, or, more commonly, where certain elements of both traditional and typical Great Lakes water are present in each run or pool. Making a distinction between the two can be a moot point, but it can also be the reason behind steelhead location and the fly fishing technique to be employed. We will first take a look at traditional holding water and then contrast this with the more unconventional lies commonly found in Great Lakes waters.

Traditional Water

The basic concept of traditional steelhead holding water is a series of riffles flowing into runs or pools. Typically, the current flow is greater at the head of the pool and becomes gentler toward the tail. This is caused by the flow moving through a more shallow, channeled area which results in the riffles. As the flow continues through the run or pool, there is normally greater depth and the river channel widens. At the tail, there is less depth as the river bottom rises to meet the next set of riffles.

Steelhead can be found anywhere from the faster water, just as it begins to deepen, through the tailout. Within this area, there are certain signs that may give some insight on the preferred lies, and you can bet that there will be one or more holds favored by steelhead. If a steelhead is in the area, it normally will be occupying one of these choice spots. If there are a number of steelhead located in a run or pool, they may be spread out or positioned in secondary lies. Steelhead seem to aggressively attempt to gain the preferred lies, and more fish present in and around these areas tend to create a greater degree of activity for the steelhead and the angler. Keep in mind that steelhead follow and seek the softer currents, and these often define the prime areas. Traditional water is usually best fished on the inside or slack side of the current. Anywhere that the main current breaks into slower water along the edge can be a potential holding lie. This break is commonly quite visible and will be evidenced by a seam on the water's surface. Sometimes this seam can be quite distinct as a faster current butts up against a decidedly slower flow. Others are more subtle as a faster current feathers into the slower movement.

Fish toward the head of the pool will place heavy emphasis on the seam water. The closer to the tail, the more evenly spread the current flow will become. Fish will be more likely found across the width of the river. Fishing pressure can spread fish across the head of a pool. In most traditional runs or pools, there is a transition area where the flow goes from the quicker confined head to the wider tail. This transition zone can be the sweet spot. It normally occurs about a third of the way down from the beginning of the run or pool and will commonly be characterized by a gentle, wide seam and gradually increasing depth. The transition zone requires special attention from the fly fishing steelheader.

Some of the factors that create preferred lies will not be obvious on the water's surface. Depressions, drop-offs, and troughs in the river's floor can create softer currents and only be determined by a concentrated and meticulous coverage of the water. Once discovered, this could be a prime hold for future outings. Sometimes these less obvious structures can be anticipated by careful consideration of the river's surrounding features or by looking into the water. Where the head of a run moves through tight confines, often the water in the transition zone can be quite deep, creating a soft flow near the bottom. Also, deeper water has a darker, greener appearance than surrounding shallow water and can be a clue to a drop-off or trough. Large boulders can also provide current breaks that attract steelhead. Sometimes they are not visible and will often be discovered by the terminal end of the fly fishing rig. Losing a few flies on a hidden obstruction serves as a clear indicator and reminder that it is there. However, careful presentation of the fly near the boulder can yield satisfying results. Sometimes boulders will leave their mark on the surface in the form of a disturbance or slick. This is very common in the tailouts of pools.

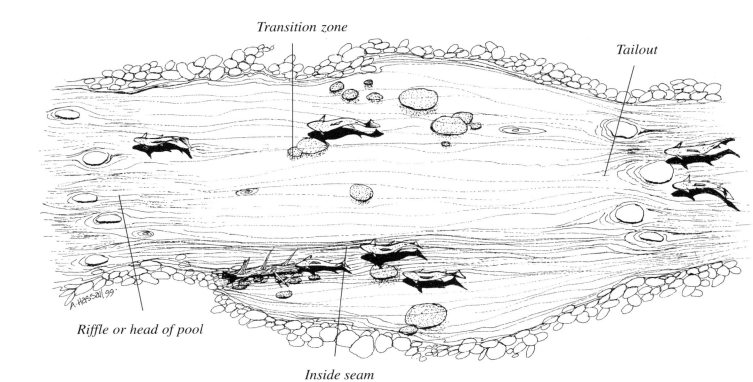

Transition zone

Tailout

Riffle or head of pool

Inside seam

The holding potential for a particular piece of traditional water is often directly impacted by the makeup of the water both up and down stream. This also impacts upon the prime holding areas of a run or pool. When migrating through long sections of heavy water, steelhead will often rest in the first current break with a dramatically slower flow. Sometimes the riffles leading into the next pool are long and rough. If there is very little water for fish to stop and rest within the riffles, good numbers can be found in the tail of the pool above, especially where boulders provide additional breaks in the current. The head of a run or pool can also accumulate steelhead. If the riffles above a pool are extremely thin or are very heavy, steelhead on the move may congregate at the top of the run or pool and wait until they are ready to migrate. In the case of thin or shallow water, movement is commonly confined to the low light periods or at night. At first light, steelhead can be found in the shallow water at the head of runs and pools. It is important to fish the water before wading if nobody else has fished through.

Many of the basic principles of approaching traditional water are similar to those utilized in West Coast steelheading. As we will see in the next chapter some of the techniques will be similar as well.

Using More than Traditional Lies

This type of water would encompass all the lies that were not discussed above. In other words, those that do not entail a riffle running into a run or pool with a moderating current speed.

The most common type of Great Lakes water is a fast, quick run or a deep slot which is created by a high gradient combined with a channeled flow. This is commonly found on small- to medium-sized rivers and can be very common on large rivers as well. This type of water will normally be at least two feet deep and sometimes much deeper. It is characterized by a quick uniform flow. It is common for the water at the head of the run or slot to be similar in character to the lower portion. The run or slot can be the width of the river or a narrow band caused by a lengthwise depression or trough. It is common for the run or slot to be pushed up against a bank. The run or slot can contain large rocks, boulders, or a drop-off which creates structure. The flow will often be fast and forceful, especially on top. The surface will generally show riffles or swirling currents.

On the surface, some rivers appear to have a uniform flow, but beneath can be hidden bottom structure such as drop-offs and rises in the gravel which create holding water similar to traditional runs. As the depth increases, softer currents can be found similar to the transition zone of an obvious run or pool. A rise in the bottom can create similar holds as a tailout. There can be very little visible sign. Possibly darker water will signify the drop-off. Fishing the water and becoming familiar with the bottom structure will be necessary to identify and effectively fish this type of water. Because of their lack of obvious characteristics, these uniform flows are occasionally overlooked by other anglers.

In many rivers, this will be the most productive water as it provides security. Some runs may look too fast or forceful to hold fish. However, keep in mind that currents will be heaviest on the surface. This does pose a challenge to the fly fisher in that the fly must be presented in a manner that will allow it to cut through the surface tension and get to the bottom quickly. Some specialized techniques have been developed to accomplish this task. Sometimes subtle or even distinct seams will be found along the edge of a fast run. For reasons discussed earlier, always pay attention to seam water.

Pocket water is also quite common on many Great Lakes rivers and streams. This water is of great importance to the fly fishing steelheader. Pockets are created by large boulders, a series of rocks, or even fallen timber and can show themselves as visible slicks in the main current. The obstruction creating the pocket may even protrude through the water's surface. The heavy currents of Great Lakes tributaries create significant areas of pocket water. The slack flow of the pocket invites a steelhead to rest for a while during its migration. Some pockets will not be visible on the surface so it is important to look through the water's surface to find hidden boulders which can provide security and resting areas to steelhead.

In some rivers, especially those of the Midwest, small to quite large-sized pockets can be found downstream from shallow patches of gravel or rocky flats. Where the bottom drops off from visible gravel to the dark unknown, pockets are created that will hold fish. As discussed in the previous chapter, this can be prime water in the spring as steelhead position themselves near gravel in anticipation of spawning activity. Sometimes concentrations of fish will accumulate in such pockets resulting in aggressive behavior and forceful takes.

Abrupt drop-offs will often create a soft current near the bottom and provide perfect resting water for steelhead.

The inside currents of a bend in the river often provide the softer flow sought by steelhead. This is especially true of sharp turns common to the many Great Lakes rivers that wind through the countryside. A number of Michigan rivers possess this characteristic. Even if the water is fairly shallow, inside bends can hold fish, particularly in the first and last light of the day. Steelhead will slide to the greater depths with fishing pressure and increased light exposure.

In smaller rivers and streams, many of the runs and pools will be condensed and effectively be very similar in character to pocket water on larger rivers. Certain sections of other rivers are made up entirely of a long series of pockets.

The bottom composition of some Great Lakes rivers and streams also creates holding areas that would not be considered traditional holds. Slate and shale dominate the floor of some tributaries. The slate often prevents a run from reaching a proper depth to comfortably hold steelhead. But cuts,

Pocket water represents prime holding areas on some rivers.

slots and drops in the shale can create optimum holding areas. Sometimes the cuts and slots are very obvious, especially on small rivers. By looking through the water's surface, shallow shale bottoms will normally show up as tan or brown flats. Evidence of a cut or slot will show as greener, darker water. The area of deeper water can be quite small or considerably large, and if the surrounding water is fairly thin, the cut can be a prime lie. In deeper pools and runs that possess a shale bottom, the cuts or slots may not be easy to decipher. And even in this deeper water, steelhead may lie in the comfort zone of a cut in the shale. Some of this will be discovered through the experience of fishing a particular piece of water. However, scouting out a river during lower water periods may provide useful insight on holding structure. A pair of polarized sunglasses are essential in the process of determining cuts and slots.

Occasionally the current flow runs perpendicular to a cut in the slate and creates a dramatic drop-off. The drop-off can create security as well as a soft current. Sometimes the drop-off is nearly a right angle. Even if the flow is heavy on the surface, most of the flow can be condensed in the top of the water column and the current along the bottom may be nonexistent. It may be important to roll the fly off the shelf into the deeper water. Many times such a drop-off is small and fast, and overlooked by most anglers.

Another type of overlooked water found in most rivers of the Great Lakes are riffles at the head of a pool or a thin, fast run with a broken surface. Rivers that receive moderate to heavy fishing pressure do so in many of the obvious pools and runs during the height of the fall and spring migrations. This approach often results in hookups in the early morning, but the continued pressure can push steelhead into more secure holds. This is mainly the case when water temperatures exceed 40 degrees F. The fast water provides the perfect sanctuary as most anglers do not fish or wade such heavy flows. The results can be very surprising. Always keep in mind that if steelhead are present in a river and angling pressure is high, the fish will put a greater emphasis on self-preservation and will seek out the most secure areas of the river.

Fast gravelly runs and flats are especially important in the spring. Fresh fish on the move will often congregate in these areas in anticipation of the spawn. This is a key factor on larger rivers as steelhead concentrations into these gravelly areas help in narrowing down the prime fishing sections. This is a key consideration since some of the more traditional lies may be lacking of fish during the spring.

It is not necessary to label each type of water being fished. Some sections will be comprised of a combination of various types. However, it is important to note similarities and differences since it will have an impact on the approach and techniques utilized.

When fishing big water, it is sometimes necessary to break the large flow down into manageable areas or quadrants. Try to identify the important characteristics of each to determine if it is likely holding water and what would be the most effective approach. We have a preference for medium to large rivers. Many anglers are intimidated by such water, but it is critical to not be overwhelmed by a water's vastness. It is equally critical to methodically identify those areas that are likely to concentrate fish at a particular time of the year. Ironically, large rivers may have a relatively small percentage of fishable water. Current edges and consistent flows over gravel or rocky bottoms will be likely holding areas. It will take trial and error to find consistently

Big rivers require a methodical approach to determine high-percentage areas. Here Jim Johnson fishes a gravel bar on the Muskegon River.

producing water, and it may require years of concentrated effort to identify those areas.

Reading the water involves factors that are observed on a particular day along with the knowledge that may have been gained on previous visits to the river. It is ongoing education. What is learned one year is often put to use in following seasons. With experience, certain "honey holes" will develop. These are spots which seem to hold fish throughout the season, year after year. In fact, if any fish are present, they are likely to be in these areas and almost act as a barometer of the numbers and aggressiveness of the steelhead on a particular day. Occasionally after striking out on the prime lies of a particular river, we have concluded that our chances were poor and formed the basis for moving to a different section or river.

Normally the "honey hole" is just a small part of a larger section of holding water. It can be any one of the characteristics or pieces of structure that were discussed above. It is commonly a soft spot in the current, a boulder, or a cut in the bottom. Sometimes it is an exact spot. After catching a few fish on different days in the same area, it becomes a potential "honey hole." After catching fish in that spot nearly every time out, it is confirmed. Success in fly fishing for Great Lakes steelhead is often defined by how well you know your water.

Proper reading of the water leaves very little room for complacency. While cumulative knowledge is important, things do tend to change from year to year or even from one week to the next. Spring runoff or high water can have a dramatic impact on a river. New runs and pools may be dug out and others filled. Downed trees and washed-out banks can push the flow to the opposite side of the river or even move the main channel. Some rivers are more susceptible to change than others. It is important to always observe and note the changes that may impact the water's potential to hold steelhead.

Variables

Certain factors will affect the way we look at water. During the course of a season, it is quite common to see a river at various water levels. The virtue of fishing a river after levels have risen was discussed in the previous chapter. A stream or river will have an entirely different look at high levels as opposed to low flow. A pool, run, or pocket that holds fish in high water may be too thin to comfortably hold fish in normal or low conditions. Other lies may become too deep and fast to cover with a fly rod. Water level is a key consideration when selecting likely holds.

There are a number of rivers in the Great Lakes region where water level changes play a critical role. Some of these are short drainages that rise and lower quickly with rainfall or runoff. Dramatic changes can often be experienced on one of the many rivers in the region that have a dam interrupting their free-flowing nature. One of the best examples of this is New York's Salmon River. Common flow ranges from 375 cubic feet per second (cfs) to 1,500 cfs. The river has an entirely different look at one end of this range as opposed to the other, and becomes more difficult to fly fish when running at 1,500 cfs or above. For this reason, it is best to check water flow in advance of a trip on any river where the levels fluctuate widely.

Water that is dirty as well as high becomes difficult to read, and such conditions allow the fish to spread out. Experience is often the best guide, especially in the spring. Steelhead may be located on or near the same gravel bars that have attracted fish under normal, clear flows. This can also be true of typical fall holds. The angler that is intimately familiar with a section of river always has the advantage, especially in high, dirty conditions. Conversely, when fishing a stream or river for the first time, it is very difficult and frustrating when confronted with high, stained water.

The other end of the spectrum is represented by low, clear conditions where available holding water becomes limited. The deeper, darker pools and pockets clearly show themselves as the obvious lies. Distinguishing the less than obvious holds can be the key to success. Look for any depression or broken water that can hide a fish. Explore even the smallest of pockets. Fresh-run fish are very light in color and can be almost invisible against a rocky bottom. They can stay fairly well hidden in thin pockets if good holding water is at a minimum. Approach such areas with stealth.

Reading More than the Water

In addition to just reading the physical characteristics of the water, it is equally important to recognize the clues of fish migration. The reality of fly fishing for steelhead is that success is greatly dependent on working water where fish are present. It is fruitless to fish even the nicest holding water when nobody is home. Determining whether steelhead are present or not will allow the angler to fish with confidence or to decide on some different water.

Information and observation will normally serve as the key indicators. Good information can be as simple as what is gained from a reputable fly shop or an acquaintance that has recently fished the river. However, such news must be recent. To know that a movement of fish occurred through a certain section of river a few days prior will normally be dated information. The best information comes from someone who was on the water earlier in the day. Developing a network of reliable contacts where information can be shared and exchanged will go a long way. Reports of steelhead movement or the anticipation of the water conditions and timing "being right" are what commonly draws us to the rivers. Observations of the presence of fish will keep us there. The clues can be obvious, such as witnessing angler success or steelhead rolling or boiling in a pool. Other times it will be the sighting of fish as they move through thin water or while positioned on or near spawning gravel. Commonly, one's own success early in an outing will verify the presence of steelhead and provide firsthand information.

On larger rivers, it is possible to actually follow the migration of fish. You may hear of reports that steelhead were being caught near the river mouth one day and a few miles up the river the next. Such information may allow the angler to head off the movement by fishing areas where fresh fish are anticipated. It is commonly felt that steelhead in the Great Lakes may move five miles or so in a twenty-four hour period. Obviously, this can vary dramatically based upon conditions. By staying in touch with the river, placing oneself in the right section becomes a calculated strategy, one that often pays off. Some rivers that have dams with ladders or fish ways that allow for migration actually have fish count stations. This can provide very accurate data on how many steelhead are in a certain section, and this will help the angler chart out the migration as well as determine if a certain section is worth fishing.

As fly fishing steelheaders, we seemingly develop a sixth sense in determining the presence of fish. Through experience we are able to anticipate certain occurrences at specific times of year. This allows us to fish with confidence even if there are no visible signs. Maybe the signs are there, but only available to the subconscious. Others may only be noticed by the seasoned fly fisher. Possibly one lone fish showing itself or the angler on the opposite side of the pool with a brief hookup will be the encouragement needed to forge onward until pleasantly and almost expectedly the section of water or specific pool turns on with steelhead activity—a reward that is often reserved for the observant and persistent.

9

Fly Fishing Strategy

Our pursuit of the steelhead pushes and pulls us toward a balance. Involved are many key elements—river selection, type of water, equipment, fly patterns, presentation—which, when synchronized, define the very essence of the sport. To some, success is found simply in the number of fish hooked or landed. But to an increasing number of seasoned anglers how a fish was caught is more important than how many. Some rivers, techniques and fly patterns are more pleasing to fish than others. And while not always the most productive for a given situation, "success" is measured in the quality of the experience and not only in the quantity of the catch. This is an axiom that has existed among Atlantic salmon and Pacific coast steelhead fly fishers for years. Its roots are just beginning to take hold in the Great Lakes region.

In this chapter, we will take a close look at the proper balance of a complete fly fishing system. We must read the signs and evaluate the conditions. The strategy and approach will be impacted by many physical characteristics as well as our own personal preferences. There should be a purpose for all that we do when it comes to fly fishing for steelhead. Each decision should be based on cumulative knowledge and current information. Sometimes our choices, even when based on the best of information, can result in frustration. Let this be a lesson for a future outing.

Equipment

A complete discussion of any type of fly fishing must include at least a background of the required equipment. This is especially true of fly fishing for steelhead in the Great Lakes. Proper equipment forms the very foundation for many of the techniques utilized. Current technology and manufacturers' attempts to create products for more specific means has resulted in a wide range of equipment that is geared toward this type of fly fishing. Some equipment that is even designed specifically for Great Lakes steelhead is beginning to appear. There are certain key elements which determine whether a piece of equipment will be functional for Great Lakes steelhead, and a closer examination can be critical to success and enjoyment.

Rods

Except for very tight, brushy streams, the longer the better. Length translates into greater line and fly control. It also allows for longer leaders with floating lines, more efficient line pickup, and easier roll casting. For single-handed rods, nine to nine and a half feet is a minimum. Our preference is for ten or even ten and a half feet. The benefits of length are amplified by the use of two-handed rods which vary from eleven to sixteen feet in length.

They provide the ultimate in line control. Two-handed rods will undoubtedly become more popular in the Great Lakes in the near future.

A range of line sizes are applicable to Great Lakes steelhead fishing. The size of the fish, length of the cast, amount of weight on the leader, and strength of the tippet will all have an impact on the selection of the proper rod. For one-handed rods, the most versatile would be a seven weight as it provides adequate fish-fighting capability, has the ability to turn over weighted leaders, and can cast the distances required by most Great Lakes rivers. The extra fighting strength of an eight weight can be useful when fishing rivers with a heavy current flow and where big steelhead abound. The eight weight will also punch into the wind more efficiently and allow for the casting of large bushy flies. There occasionally is the need for lighter rods. Six and even five weight outfits can be a good match for smaller strains of fish. The smaller steelhead of the northern latitudes of the Great Lakes are a prime example as the lighter rods allow for maximum enjoyment. One of the main functions of rods built for lighter line weights is the ability to facilitate the finest of tippets. Since six and five weight rods are softer than a comparable eight or seven weight, more of the fight of a steelhead will be absorbed by the rod, creating less strain on the tippet. Also, the lighter line weights which balance these rods can result in delicate presentations for timid steelhead. The disadvantage is that lighter rods may not provide the proper leverage on larger fish. The result can be fighting the fish to near exhaustion and making a successful release difficult or near impossible. For two-handed rods, a seven through a nine weight each have their application in the Great Lakes region. A further discussion of two-handed rods is included later in this chapter.

Faster action rods have casting benefits in some situations. Windy conditions, heavy sink-tips, and large amounts of weight on the leader or fly are common circumstances where a faster action rod may be preferred. However, a fast rod may not be as forgiving during the fight, possibly resulting in lost fish or broken tippets. A good Great Lakes steelhead rod consists of balance, creating sufficient line speed for distance and turning over weight, yet having a smooth fighting point that cushions the battle of a steelhead throughout the rod.

There are a number of rods that will generally meet the criteria of the Great Lakes region which can be found in a wide range of prices. Winston, Thomas & Thomas, Sage, Scott, Orvis, Diamondback, and St. Croix are names associated with rods that are time-tested in the Great Lakes.

<u>Reels</u>

Opinions vary on the importance of the fly reel. One school of thought would place a lower significance in this area. Many feel that a click-style drag with an exposed rim is sufficient for the fight of a steelhead. In some cases this is true. However, in addition to their energetic and erratic fighting style, Great Lakes steelhead are often fought in confined areas and on light tippets.

A quality single-action, disk-drag reel is a major advantage. Smooth is the key. There should be no hesitation when a fish begins its run, and the drag should remain smooth throughout. When properly utilized, a quality disk-drag reel can be the difference between a landed steelhead and disappointment. The drag should be adjustable and is best positioned on the lighter settings unless a lack of room to fight a fish dictates otherwise. The lever or knob which controls the drag setting should be easy to maneuver while fighting a fish. An exposed rim allows for added drag by the palm of the reel hand. A good steelhead reel for a one-handed rod should be simple, light, and require very little maintenance. Spool changes should be easy and quick with no additional tools required. Capacity to hold at least one hundred to one hundred and fifty yards of twenty-pound backing is adequate. Reels for two-handed rods will normally need more capacity to hold the thick diameter of a spey line. Also, it should weigh enough to properly balance the rod. Great advancements have been accomplished in recent years in the area of smooth disk drags in the moderate price range.

Lamson, Hardy, Harris, Ross, and Ryall reels each combine quality with being quite affordable. Abel, Islander, and Billy Pate reels are known for their quality and durability with a slightly higher sticker price. Large arbor reels are becoming quite popular among steelheaders for their fast line pick up and greater line-holding capacity. Bauer, Tibor, and Sage each produce a quality large arbor reel. Of course, some traditional anglers are at home with a simple single-action reel devoid of today's cutting-edge technology. They opt for the beautiful song of the Hardy Marquis or Orvis CFO as a steelhead strips line from the spool. This is a joy that is lost on some of the reels currently being produced.

Lines

Fly lines for steelhead fishing in Great Lakes waters generally fall into two groups: floaters and sink-tips. Within these two basic types are wide variations to satisfy the requirements of the full range of rivers and techniques of the region. Serious steelheaders may carry a handful of extra spools filled with lines for specific situations.

In general, the most common floating lines consist of weight forward tapers and level running lines. While double taper lines are able to easily roll cast a leader with weight added to it, this type of line seems to lack the versatility required for steelhead fishing.

A wide range of weight forward lines are available, and many are designed for a specific purpose. They vary in the length of the head which consists of the front taper, the belly and the rear taper. Some also have special coatings. A standard weight forward configuration with a head of approximately 45 feet on a seven or eight weight line is sufficient in most situations. A good all-round weight forward line is the Scientific Anglers GPX. Scientific Anglers also produces two other lines that match very well with Great Lakes steelhead fishing. The first is the nymph taper which has an exaggerated front taper combined with a hard coating. The result is a line that more easily handles weighted flies and leaders with weight added while either roll casting or standard casting. This line is most useful in shorter to moderate casting distances and currently is only produced in line weights five through seven. The second is the steelhead taper. This line has a long rear taper resulting in a 65-foot head which is approximately 20 feet longer than a standard weight forward line. The longer head lends itself to greater distance casting which is ideal for larger rivers. The long head also makes for easier roll casting, especially longer casts, and provides for good line control and mending abilities. Rio Products also produces a steelhead and Atlantic salmon line which features a long belly and a bullet-style front taper for delivering large flies. The Wulff triangle taper is also a useful floating line for Great Lakes fly fishing. The strength of this line is that it casts weighted braided leaders or lightly weighted flies in a smooth and effortless fashion. It does tend to break down somewhat when casting weight added to a monofilament leader. Airflo, Cortland, and Rio also produce a wide range of weight forward lines.

A running line is a small diameter level line. They are available in low memory monofilament or as a level floating fly line. The common diameter is .029 to .031 inches and is the equivalent to a level two or three weight fly line. Running lines serve two useful purposes in Great Lakes steelhead fishing. First, as the running portion of a shooting head combination. In this set up, a head is added through a loop-to-loop connection. Running lines can also be utilized as the main fly line with a long monofilament leader. This arrangement can be cast with a moderate action five to six weight rod.

The one area where double taper floating lines are functional is when spey casting with a two-handed rod. Lines engineered specifically for spey rods are offered by some manufacturers and are discussed later in this chapter.

Sink-tip lines are gaining in popularity in the Great Lakes region. A sink-tip functions as its name implies, the front section sinks taking the fly with it, the rear section floats for mending and line control. Standard manufactured sink-tips normally consist of a ten to fifteen foot sinking section and a weight forward design. Sink rates range from one to seven inches per second. Those with a sink rate in the range of three to six inches per second are the most useful for this type of fishing. Scientific Anglers, Airflo, Cortland, Rio, and Orvis each produce a full range of sink-tip lines. Rio's density compensated sink-tip, which allows the very tip of the line to sink faster than the thicker sinking belly, may have the widest application in the Great Lakes. The Teeny Nymph Company produces two lines that are useful for steelhead fishing. Their mini-tip line has a five-foot, fast-sinking tip. The Teeny T Series lines are a combination sink-tip and shooting head. This line consists of a 24-foot sinking section varying in weight from 130 to 500 grains. The extra-fast sinking tip of these lines can attain sink rates approaching ten inches per second and can be used to cover a wide range of water. The floating portion is actually a running line which can be a little difficult to mend. The 24-foot sinking section is a little long for most Great Lakes steelhead applications and functions best if cut back by five to eight feet.

The most versatile arrangement for sink-tip lines are homemade versions utilizing loop-to-loop connections. Tips can be changed easily and quickly to accommodate the water being fished. Tip lengths will vary with the type of water and technique, and some will be as long as ten to twelve feet. However, mini-tips of eight feet or less tend to be the most effective. Mini-tips can be utilized in two ways. Connected to a standard floating line, a sink-tip is created. Mini-tips can also be added to a conventional sink-tip to increase its sink rate. Homemade sink-tip lines which use a short tip of five to eight feet, capable of attaining the desired depth and looped to a floating line, represent one of the more effective approaches to Great Lakes steelheading. The mini-tips can hinge somewhat when attached to the end of a standard weight forward line. Cutting back the first four to eight feet of the line will provide smoother turnover with mini-tips.

There are some commercially produced mini-tip lines on the market. Both Beartooth and Orvis offer a mini-head selection complete with loops attached. They are level tips with the ability to reach useful depths. Airflo has recently introduced two interesting products. The PolyLeader and PolyTip are added to a floating line using a prepackaged loop connector. Both taper gradually from the tip diameter of the fly line to that of a level tippet material. PolyLeaders are five feet in length. While offering great casting performance, the fast sink and extra-fast sink varieties create an effective mini-tip that handles much better than a tip of uniform diameter. Taking this a step further is the PolyTip. It is described as the first effective fly line extension. The basic concept is to provide a smoothness of casting and turnover. Sink rates range from one and a half to six inches per second. Rio also offers a seven-foot PolyLeader.

Homemade mini-tips create the most versatility for fishing a wide range of water. The easiest and most effective way to create a mini-tip is to add braided loops to each end of a piece of fly line of the desired length and sink rate. Heavy nylon that can stand up to the abuse and wear of abrasive rocks and boulders is preferred. Beartooth, Cortland, and Umpqua each market dependable nylon loops. The connections should be examined frequently. Any that show signs of wear should be replaced.

Attaching a loop connector is quite simple. First the nylon is "inchwormed" into place using the thumb and forefinger of one hand while the line is held in the other. Once into place, a drop of Permabond or Zap-A-Gap is added at the end of the nylon to create a bond between the loop connector and the line.

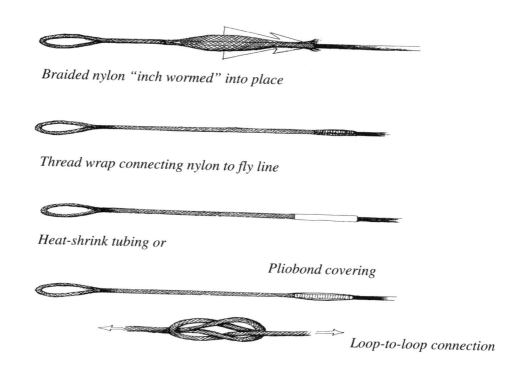

Braided nylon "inch wormed" into place

Thread wrap connecting nylon to fly line

Heat-shrink tubing or

Pliobond covering

Loop-to-loop connection

A strong, low diameter tying thread is used with a bobbin to lash the end of the nylon down to the line. The wraps should be tight enough to actually bite into the coating of the line. A short piece of shrink tubing is added and heated into place. The tubing completes a smooth, strong connection that will easily run through the guides. A coating of Pliobond is a good substitute for the tubing.

With an efficient mini-tip system, tips can be easily exchanged for various depths and current speeds. Utilizing lines with various lengths and sink rates, a combination can be created for nearly every situation. In general, the shorter four- to five-foot tips will be utilized in fast runs and pocket water. Longer tips of six to eight feet will be a good match for pools and runs with a moderate to slower current speed. Pools and runs on medium to larger rivers may be covered with the standard manufactured sink-tip discussed earlier. Very short tips of one to three feet will commonly be added to a conventional sink-tip or another mini-tip to increase its sink rate. The sink rate of the tip must be selected based on the depth of the water and current speed. Experience will be the best guide in selecting the proper tip.

For constructing custom homemade tips, three types of lines will provide the raw materials for just about every tip required for Great Lakes steelhead fishing. The first are standard 30-foot manufactured shooting heads cut into lengths of four to eight feet. The front taper portion is best utilized on the longer tips. Sink rates of standard shooting heads range from one to six and a half inches per second. Those on the faster end of the scale are most useful for Great Lakes fishing. Scientific Anglers, Rio, and Airflo each produce shooting heads that are appropriate for this purpose. Rio produces a density compensated full sinking line which results in an effective mini-tip. They also offer a fifteen-foot tip with the loop already attached. Rio loops are stiff, designed to minimize the hinging effect. Their Versitip fly line is designed to cast this fifteen-foot tip, but can be matched with other lines as well.

For heavy currents or substantial depths, greater sink rates are required. Scientific Anglers produces a very fast sinking line called Deep Water Express. Thirty-foot sections are available in weights of 550, 700, and 850 grains with sink rates ranging from seven to ten inches per second. These are typically cut into sections of four to eight feet. These lines have a taper at each end. The tapered sections are best used for the longer heads. A chart within the packaging provides a guide as to the grains per foot of each foot of the entire head which acts as a guide to create tips for a specific purpose. Due to their weight, a hinging effect will commonly be felt when cast. With their greater length and leverage, two-handed rods tend to handle these heavier tips more efficiently. Tips made from the 550 and 700 grain heads combine the ability to attain great depth while still being able to reasonably handle its weight.

Another type of very fast sinking line is a vinyl-coated lead-core line produced by Cortland called LC-13. It has a weight of 13 grains per foot. This weight combined with a low diameter results in a sink rate in excess of

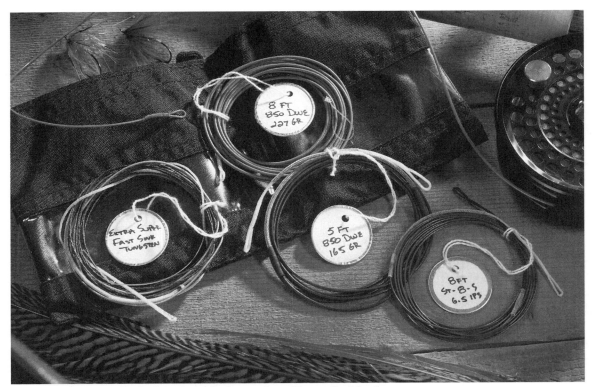

Various mini-tips marked and ready for action. Shaun Smith photo.

ten inches per second. LC-13 tips in lengths of one to five feet in one-foot intervals help create a complete tip system. LC-13 tips are most commonly added to the front end of a conventional sink-tip or mini-tip to increase overall sink rate. From a tactical standpoint, this creates another advantage. With the fastest sink rate at the end of the line, the end of the tip will reach the greatest depths and reduce the amount of sag in the portion of the line beneath the water's surface. Longer sections of LC-13 can be used as a sink-tip for attaining great depths.

Mini-tips can also be added to a monofilament leader using loops. This rig would begin with an eight- to ten-foot heavy-butt tapered leader. A two- to three-foot piece of mini-tip is looped in and then the tippet is looped to the tip. This rig forms an innovative arrangement that casts very well and is used for getting down quickly in moderate to fast current speeds.

Leaders

Leaders for Great Lakes steelhead can be split into those designed for floating lines and those for sink-tips. Leaders for floating lines will be required to perform various functions depending on the circumstances. In general, manufactured knotless or knotted leaders designed for steelhead fishing will be sufficient in many situations. However, custom-tied leaders create an advantage when designed specifically for a purpose. Two basic configurations of custom leaders for floating lines will cover a wide range of water and techniques. A constructed leader with a more conventional configuration will turn over heavily weighted flies and carry weight added to the leader. Such a leader would consist of approximately a 60% butt section of .021 to .019 inch diameter stiff leader material, 20% middle section of .017 to .013 inch material, and 20% tippet. This leader will normally be tied in lengths of nine to twelve feet. Scientific Anglers produces a heavy-butt (.027 inch) knotless, tapered leader which works well for this purpose. An opposite approach is a leader with a short butt and a long middle section of low diameter material. While not built for efficient casting, this leader allows for effectively cutting through the surface tension of the water. This configuration is best utilized when dead drifting a fly or when fishing heavy currents. A typical low diameter leader would consist of approximately 20% butt section of .021 to .019 inch material, 60% middle section of .013 to .011 inch material, and 20% tippet. Ten to fourteen feet is a common length for this leader. Various combinations of these two extremes can be created to meet specific situations. Key to this process is understanding the mechanics of the leader and the effect certain modifications have on casting and presentation. If fishing a technique where weight is added to the leader, it is normally placed above the knot of the middle and tippet sections. Adding the weight to a dropper created by the tag end of this knot seems to have some technical presentation advantages, but attaching it directly to the leader facilitates casting. Added weight usually is in the form of split shot or twist-on strips. Two sizes of split shot—BB and 3/0—are the most useful and versatile. However, Airflo recently began marketing a tungsten putty that is dense, versatile and, when spread out and rolled onto the leader, is quite easy to cast.

Leaders attached to the business end of a sink-tip or mini-tip are normally quite simple and short since the fly should be kept relatively close to the sink source. Lengths of two to four feet are common. Anglers new to the sink-tip game are normally surprised to find that the sink-tip leader is so short. Most of the time, water clarity will impact length with four footers the choice for clearer conditions. A leader for sink-tips and mini-tips can be constructed of one or two sections. Commonly a one-foot butt section of .017 inch material is looped to the tip, and the tippet of desired length is knotted to the butt. In some specific situations, such as fishing a fairly deep, quick slot with a sink-tip and a weighted fly, a leader of five to six feet may perform best as the weight of the fly will maintain the desired depth. Umpqua produces a four-foot leader designed for sink-tip fishing.

There is one other type of leader which is very useful in Great Lakes steelhead fishing and is helping to form some successful techniques new to the region. Actually, this one product will most likely become very popular throughout the Great Lakes over the years. It is a tapered leader made of braided nylon and weighted with tungsten. Its advantages are quite simple. When looped to a weight forward floating line, it casts beautifully, similar to an unweighted nylon leader. And because of a low diameter compared to the weight, it sinks extremely well. Airflo's Salmon Tapered Braided Leader is produced in six sink rates. The two fastest sink rates have the greatest application to Great Lakes fishing and each are available in lengths of seven feet and ten feet. Normally two feet of tippet is added to the leader. The fastest sink rate, which is the extra super-fast sinking, is an incredible 13.1 inches per second! Rio also markets a tungsten braided leader with the fastest sink rate of 5.6 inches per second.

The proper tippet size for Great Lakes steelhead can be a debated issue. There are many situations when tippet size does not matter at all. When fresh fish are available, especially in water that is slightly stained, they will normally not be tippet shy. This is also true when using techniques that add tension to the fly and where the fish takes from the side or behind. We have both witnessed times when steelhead have been so aggressive that they probably would take a fly tied to the end of the fly line. We hate to break off any steelhead and use the heaviest tippet for the given situation. 1x or 0x with a breaking strength of ten to fourteen pounds is desired. This allows us to enjoy the fight knowing there is sufficient strength, even in heavy water, and to end the fight in an efficient manner for a successful release.

There is no doubt that tippet size is very important under certain circumstances. Low, clear water and dour fish on smaller rivers and streams would be the most common. This is often the case in winter and early spring. Lighter tippets will work best under these conditions, especially when dead drifting a fly. While the lighter tippet reduces the steelhead's ability to see the monofilament attached to the offering, its true advantage lies in the fact that its lower diameter facilitates a more natural drift. 2x or 3x with a breaking strength of six to eight pounds is commonly used under these conditions. 4x will further increase the ability to hook fish but also increase the possibility of break off. Some Great Lakes steelheaders are known to fish 5x or even 6x for steelhead! One has to question the ethics behind hooking a steelhead on tippet that most likely is not capable of landing the fish. The key seems to be perfecting one's technique so that a dead drift can be obtained with a tippet of sufficient strength.

The properties of leader and tippet material must be considered. Abrasion resistance is quite important. The fly will frequently drag along the river's floor, occasionally scuffing the surface of the leader. How well the material maintains its strength after an abrasion can be critical. Actually, one of the greatest tests of the leader's abrasion resistance can come at the hands of a fresh steelhead hooked in a pool full of large rocks. While many fish will jump and fight near the top of the water column, others will search for security, often in the form of a boulder, while dragging the leader along its surface. The leader should always be inspected after a battle and the knot to the fly retied frequently.

Fluorocarbon tippet material, which reflects very little light, is nearly invisible to a fish. It does seem to provide for a greater rate of steelhead hooked than conventional monofilament. This is normally the case in low, clear water conditions when the fish are not overly aggressive. Fluorocarbon material also seems to be more abrasion resistant.

Knots

The knots used in the complete system of steelhead fly fishing in the Great Lakes are quite limited and simple. Leaders are attached using a loop-to-loop connection. We have found a braided loop connector added in the same manner as described for creating a homemade tip to be the strongest and slides through the guides very well. The loop at the butt end of the leader is created with either a surgeon's loop or a perfection loop. The surgeon's loop is slightly easier to tie, but the perfection loop results in a smaller knot and less likely to hang up in the guides.

For constructing a leader or adding tippet, either a surgeon's knot or a blood knot is sufficient. The surgeon's knot is simpler and possibly stronger. However, the blood knot results in a nice straight connection which is a preferred knot when tying leaders. The surgeon's knot is useful for quickly adding tippet or repairing a leader when on the river. The improved clinch knot is our preferred knot for attaching the fly to the tippet. The turle knot is another choice and may be stronger. This knot is best used with heavier tippets.

Presentation

The presentation of the fly is at the heart of successful steelhead fishing. It is also the element of the process that consumes us as fly fishers. It is interactive, mentally and physically, as the fly is presented through cast and calculated manipulation of the line. An enjoyment is derived from presenting the fly in a desired manner that is nearly separate yet central to successfully hooking a steelhead. The rod, reel, and line are the medium for our art form, and the steelhead is our ultimate reward.

This fishery is still in its infancy from a sportfishing standpoint and is one that has been built on an abundance of big fish. It has created high expectations and pressure to catch many fish to have a "good day." For those reasons, techniques that provide for the absolute greatest degree of success in terms of fish hooked have been the most popular, even if they compromised enjoyment or the true essence of fly fishing. This is not to imply that certain techniques represent a lower class of fishing, but that others present a greater challenge, enjoyment, and reward when done successfully. When selecting a technique in which to present a fly for Great Lakes steelhead, the choice will be made both on its anticipated success as well as its level of enjoyment. Beginning and less-experienced steelhead fly fishers will normally select a technique which is weighted toward mere success in terms of hookups. This may be preferred at this level as it provides the opportunity to experience the thrill of a steelhead while practicing the manner in which to handle one on a fly rod. As a fly fisher matures, the tendency is to increase the level of challenge and the overall fly fishing experience. As for ourselves, we employ a wide range of techniques and each provides a level of challenge for the particular river being fished.

Most of the time, the type of water, conditions and the availability of fresh-run steelhead will determine the possible riggings and techniques for a given situation. Great Lakes streams and rivers have some specific characteristics which were discussed in an earlier chapter. Certain techniques and adaptations have been developed to meet the challenges that they provide. Some of these techniques have clearly been developed from the requirements of the water and fish behavior, and would be considered Great Lakes steelhead techniques. Other presentations would be more appropriately considered traditional techniques as they have been employed in the pursuit of Atlantic salmon and West Coast steelhead for many years. With an ever-increasing frequency, traditional techniques are finding a home on Great Lakes waters. Much of the time, determining the right water and conditions is important for reasonable success. Many of the traditional techniques have been modified to match the needs of the water. These innovative, hybridized riggings and methods create a middle ground between success and enjoyment. We will take a close look at the combination of line, leader, and presentation.

<u>Floating line and long leaders</u>

   This may be the most versatile setup for Great Lakes steelhead. There are many variations along this theme. Leaders will commonly be nine to twelve feet. The techniques in this section represent those that would mainly be considered traditional angling methods for migratory fish. Some have been modified to meet the specifics of Great Lakes rivers and steelhead.

Wet fly and no additional weight

   Some techniques used in the Great Lakes require the right conditions and type of water. This is certainly a prime example and is a standard manner of rigging for Atlantic salmon and West Coast steelhead. The fly will present itself within a foot of the surface. Water temperatures will normally need to be in the 45 to 60 degree F. range in order for Great Lakes fish to take in the upper portion of the water column. Clear water and fresh fish will be important. The best type of water in which to employ this approach is the moderate to slower currents found in the middle to tails of pools where water depths are two to five feet. Rocks and boulders are a big plus for attracting and holding steelhead. Fresh-run fish react better to this presentation and, because of the temperature constraints, will work best in late summer, early fall, and mid spring. The softer light periods in both the morning and evening will commonly represent the best time of day.

   Great Lakes fish seem to be quite bottom oriented when compared to certain strains of West Coast steelhead. This clearly impacts upon whether a fish will take in the top of the water column. One theory concerns hatchery fish which dominate the runs in many rivers. Since they are not raised naturally, they do not develope a full range of feeding instincts. The same may hold true for wild fish which are comprised of various strains. Their instinctive signals could be somewhat mixed. Once again, there are never any definite rules when it comes to steelhead. However, our experience shows that rivers which have runs comprised at least partially of wild fish provide a greater opportunity. The degree of opportunity seems to increase with the number of wild fish and the purity of the strain. It is well accepted that wild Atlantic salmon and many West Coast steelhead strains which take a fly very well in the top of the water column are most likely reacting out of an instinctive response left over from its younger days of opportunistic feeding. One major exception to this theory seems to exist with Skamania-strain steelhead which seem to be more aggressive than other hatchery fish and even other wild strains. Being a summer-run fish, they are commonly encountered when water temperatures are warmer. But Skamania seem to retain this aggressive behavior into colder temperatures as well. Along with this aggressive behavior is a tendency to chase or take a fly in the upper portions of the water column. This is a common occurrence on some rivers in Wisconsin, Michigan, and Indiana.

Another factor which may contribute to bottom orientation is the seasonal activity which occurs in most rivers. Chinook salmon thrive in many steelhead rivers. Their fall spawning stirs aquatic insects and deposits drifting spawn. Both draw the attention of steelhead as a consistent food source. In the spring, its own spawning activity occupies most of the steelheads' effort until they begin their descent to the lake.

There are two main presentations to be utilized when using a wet fly and no additional weight. The first is the greased line technique and the other, the wet fly swing. The former presents the fly across and down while the latter is down and across. Let's take a closer look at the distinction.

The greased line technique was developed by A.E.H. Wood in the early 1900's. It was named as such because the silk line used at the time was greased with animal fat in order for it to float. Greased line fishing may be one of the most misused terms in salmon and steelhead angling. This is, in part, from being overused to describe any technique which uses a floating line and a long leader, and also, in part, from the fact that what exactly Wood meant by greased line fishing was left to interpretation and its true meaning to some debate. Wood himself never wrote a book on the subject, but an accumulation of his writings were published in one entitled *Greased Line Fishing for Salmon* written by Jock Scott, the pen name of Donald Rudd. We will make no attempt at any further interpretation and simply concentrate on those elements of the presentation that seem to comprise greased line fishing.

Earlier, a reference was made to across and down. This relates to the manner in which the fly is presented. In the case of greased line fishing, it is broadside to the current and fish. The area that has resulted in much discussion is the amount of tension, if any, on the fly. Some schools of thought lean toward a drag-free presentation and others toward a tight leader and tight tension. *Greased Line Fishing for Salmon* seems to clearly describe a drag-free imitation even though the word "drag," in the context it is used, has been debated. Without advancing the debate any further, greased line fishing represents fishing a wet fly near the surface, in a broadside presentation with little or no tension. Whether the exact interpretation or not, this approach has worked under the right conditions.

The cast is made across stream with a stop cast to add slack to the leader and reduce or eliminate drag. Mends are made upstream in a manner which repositions the line without moving or straightening the leader. The fly drifts freely under the surface with the varying currents creating an undulating, breathing effect. The last few feet of fly line before the leader can act as a guide to the proper amount of mend. An effective mend places the belly of the line upstream, tending toward parallel with the current as the last few feet remain perpendicular. In effect an "L" is shaped at the end of the line. This position of the line is maintained by leading with the rod tip and pointing it downstream. Additional mends are made as necessary. The most effective mends are performed by pushing the arm forward as the mend is made and will work best if some slack line exists on the water's surface from the cast. This is in contrast to the common mend where the line is actually pulled back slightly, which will have a tendency to tighten the line and reduce the drift.

Slack in leader

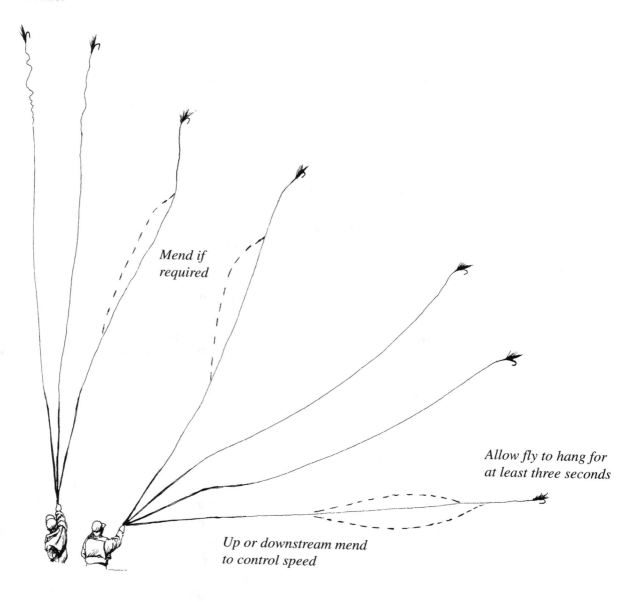

Mend if required

Allow fly to hang for at least three seconds

Up or downstream mend to control speed

All the traditional techniques are fished with just the rod hand and the fly line pinched between the forefinger and cork of the rod. The rod is positioned at an angle that is somewhat less than 45 degrees to the water. The line hand remains free of duties during the presentation of the fly but is quickly moved to the reel when a fish is hooked. The line hand is used mainly in stripping the line to pick it off the water and for control when casting. During the presentation, there should be a couple feet of loose line between the reel and where it is pinched against the cork. Ideally when a steelhead takes the fly, it is given the loose line, allowing the fish to turn on the fly and create a solid hook set. During the presentation, five feet or more of line can hang loose. This can be added to the line on the water, extending the drift. This works best in slower current flows. The slack is added by raising the rod tip which pulls the slack line and places it beyond the rod tip. The new line is added to the water by placing the tip to its original position and is manipulated accordingly. A mend up or down may be required to maintain the drift as reading the current flows becomes extremely important. By utilizing these techniques, the slow broadside presentation can be maintained for a considerable distance.

There will be a point in every greased line presentation where the broadside drift will no longer be maintained and the fly begins to move across current. At this point, the fly begins the wet fly swing or what was referred to earlier as down and across. The wet fly swing can be used as the completion of a greased line approach or can be employed separately. When used in conjunction with greased line fishing, the wet fly swing usually begins when the fly is at an approximate 45 degree angle downstream. When utilized by itself, the cast is made angling downstream.

Instead of broadside, the fly will swing through the various current lanes at an angle to the flow. The fly will show its butt to the fish as the swing is controlled through line manipulation. Large downstream bellies in the line will normally be avoided since this will speed up the fly. A slow swing seems preferable as the fly is made more accessible to the steelhead. During the swing, the line is kept straight to the fly with a slight downstream belly to encourage the undulating movement. The line may need continual manipulation through large or small mends. The wet fly swing will most effectively be fished in runs and pools on the inside of the main current. Actually, the best water will be where the current flow gently tapers from a moderate or fast speed down to a slow flow in the current lane of the casting position. In some pools, this situation may exist on each side. When the fly approaches this softer inside water, a slightly larger downstream belly will help swing the fly through what is often the most productive part of the presentation. At the end of the swing, the fly should be allowed to hang in the current for at least three seconds. Many takes will occur at this point either from fish that are resting in the soft current or by those that followed the fly from the faster currents.

Both the greased line technique and the wet fly swing are designed to be fished by rotating through, starting from the head of the run or pool down to the tail. A step or two is made downstream after the water has been covered from one position. For a meticulous coverage, four or five casts are made from one position starting with a short line and lengthening the cast by five feet each time. A few steps are taken after this process is complete. Maintaining one length of line allows for faster coverage, which is a good approach when in search of aggressive steelhead. To ensure reasonable coverage of the water, the distance between positions should be less when using one length of line. The important factor seems to be employing a systematic approach. Making a mental grid of the water and evenly applying the selected approach will lead to a greater opportunity of a hookup. Spending a little extra time on the prime lies is a good idea when no other anglers are following through the pool. In dirty water, a slow, careful coverage seems to have its advantages.

For both the greased line technique and wet fly swing fished with a floating line and no weight added to the leader or fly, certain conditions must exist as previously discussed. It will be helpful to be the first angler through a pool in the morning and to fish water that has been rested in the evening. Fly fishing in this manner is a pleasurable way to catch a steelhead. One must realize that this approach relies on a fish moving quite a distance for a fly, a trait more common to summer and early fall steelhead. Because of this, expectations have to be adjusted accordingly.

Traditional techniques are somewhat new to the Great Lakes as is the idea of rotating through a run or pool. This presents certain ethical and esthetic considerations. Many bait and spin fishermen will work one area for long periods of time without moving. Fly fishers may do the same when using dead drift or bottom-bouncing techniques, and this approach can be quite effective when steelhead are on the move. A clash in style exists when traditional techniques are employed in water that is being fished by stationary anglers. If there is only one or two, it is possible to work around the other anglers in larger pools. One approach that has resulted in some success is to encourage and invite others to rotate. Probably the most frustrating situation is when someone jumps in and begins fishing downstream before having the opportunity to fish through. Kindly explaining one's intentions of working downstream has been respected by some anglers, providing a perfect opportunity to invite a fellow steelheader into the rotation and creating the belief that traditional fishing may take hold in the Great Lakes someday. Such kind explanations have also witnessed reactions of belligerent ignorance by the "you can't tell me what to do—this is my river too" crowd. Hogging a spot and not allowing others to work through is just plain poor sportsmanship. The best way to pursue traditional fishing is to find water not being fished by anyone else. On one of the handful of very popular rivers in the region this might be difficult, at least on the most well-known pools. But some of the better Great Lakes rivers for using traditional methods are big with miles to fish. It is almost always possible to find your own water. A little creativity can go a long way.

Each of the two floating line techniques as described have their limitations in the Great Lakes fishery. However, certain modifications have been made to these purest forms of traditional methods by steelheaders in the Great Lakes, as well as those on the West Coast, to adapt to the varying conditions of steelhead fishing. Many rivers in the Great Lakes receive the bulk of their steelhead run in October and November when, commonly, water temperatures drop through the 40's. Somewhere around 42 to 44 degrees F. seems to be the lower end of the temperature range for Great Lakes fish taking a fly near the surface. Also for reasons related most likely to hatchery fish or the type of water characterizing a river's flow, the surface opportunities may be limited even under the proper water temperatures. Enter the modified or hybrid floating line techniques that have proven so successful on streams and rivers of the region.

Wet fly and weight added

If a steelhead won't come to the fly, it is necessary to take the fly to the steelhead. Adding weight to the leader or the fly provides an effective means for sinking the fly and maintaining good sensitivity. To some traditional anglers of migratory fish, this concept borders on heresy. We find no need to defend these techniques. Anyone who has spent time on a wide range of Great Lakes rivers throughout an entire year will find significant benefit from being able to efficiently sink a fly in quick slots, pockets, or runs. This is certainly the case in the colder water of late fall, winter, and early spring. As previously mentioned, this type of water and temperature fluctuations is what separates Great Lakes fishing from West Coast steelheading or, for that matter, Atlantic salmon fishing. Fly fishing traditions in the Great Lakes are only being established today. We are searching for techniques which combine sport and challenge with a reasonable chance of hooking a steelhead. Many of the traditions that we follow in West Coast steelheading were only established within the last sixty or seventy years. Certain technological changes have enabled us to take a new look at the challenges that we face as fly fishers. Had tungsten putty and dumbbell eyes existed for sixty years, would they have worked their way into West Coast steelheading tradition? It is quite common to fish some of the tight, fast-flowing steelhead streams of Alaska with weight on the leader since the water dictates this type of an approach. Casting weight certainly should be no deterrent. With the proper rod, line, and leader, it is no problem and, with practice, you will forget that it is part of your system. We view the use of weight on the leader or fly as an innovative approach to a situation. It is a personal decision. One very good friend of ours scoffs at weight on the leader but finds a weighted fly as completely

Fishing the deep broadside approach on a short line.

acceptable. A line in a recent magazine article seemed to sum it up: "if you feel uncomfortable with weight on the leader or fly, then don't do it."

Adding weight to the leader was discussed earlier in the chapter. Adding it to the fly is normally accomplished through wire wrapped under the body or one of the various means for weighting the head such as beads, cones, or dumbbell eyes. Weighting a fly will be explored further in the next chapter. The two basic techniques when using weight mirror the greased line and wet fly swing. The first is really a deep broadside swimming technique and the second is the wet fly swing fished deeper in the water column. Much of the time, they are fished in combination.

The deep broadside approach can be utilized in a very wide range of water types. In reality, just about any water that might hold a steelhead. The cast is made across stream angling slightly up. An immediate upstream mend relieves tension from the leader and fly and allows it to sink quickly. Depth can also be controlled by the angle of the cast. A 45 degree angle upstream will provide the maximum depth. The amount of weight will also control depth. There should be enough to provide for effective fishing but not so much as to create cumbersome casting or compromise fly casting integrity to the point where it is merely a case of launching weight as opposed to casting the fly line. The fly should be fishing effectively by the time it is directly in front of the casting position. The line should be perpendicular to the current and the fly traveling broadside and seductively in the lower reaches of the water column. Additional upstream mends will eliminate a downstream belly. Such a belly will accelerate the fly and pull it from the depths. The rod tip leads the fly downstream. Actually pointing the rod directly downstream and even extending the arm in that direction will assist in maintaining a broadside presentation. Additional line can be added to the water by releasing slack beyond the rod tip. As with greased line fishing, once the fly reaches a point approximately 45 degrees downstream, the presentation will be completed using a wet fly swing.

This technique takes great concentration as the take of a steelhead may be subtle. The fly will normally be fished under slight tension, and a take will be transmitted by the line tightening up with a very slight give of the fish being moved toward the angler's position. This sensation should be met with a sweeping downstream hook set which will improve the chances of an effective side of the mouth hookup.

When the wet fly swing is utilized with weight on the leader or fly as the main presentation, the cast is commonly made across and slightly downstream. The fly essentially leads the rod tip as it is pointed directly at the fly's position in the water. The fly presents itself at an angle to the current. The wet fly swing, even with weight added, will perform best in runs and pools of moderate to slower flows and fished from the inside of the current. Upstream mends will eliminate a belly in the line. The rod should be positioned at an angle to the water to cushion the take of a steelhead. A fish will often hook itself when using this presentation as it takes and turns on the fly all in one motion. Many takes will come at the end of the swing. Stripping the line back slowly at the end of the swing before picking up for the next cast can also produce takes. The deep swimming broadside presentation fished in combination with the wet fly swing can be a very effective combination on many Great Lakes rivers.

Dry fly

As we are beginning to discover, there are some opportunities for steelhead on a dry fly in the Great Lakes region. What has often been viewed as a waste of time has now taken on the stature of a real possibility when conditions are just right. This is an approach that takes considerable persistence even when the conditions are favorable, and raising a fish or even two during a day's fishing would be considered very good. But at the end of the greatest challenges are the deepest rewards. The opportunities seem to be much more substantial on rivers with runs of wild fish and with a great degree of conducive water. It is a difficult subject to approach. We do not want to give the impression that if you drag a dry fly around long enough a steelhead will take. It may not happen on some rivers. Many of the first dry fly stories we experienced were steelhead taken while the fly fisher was in pursuit of another species. Little is probably known as to the full extent of dry fly possibilities since very few have pursued this manner of fishing. The reality is that the opportunity exists, and it may even be better on some rivers than anyone has ever thought. Only time will tell.

Good opportunities exist on fresh, aggressive summer and early fall steelhead. Possibly the most consistent situation is in mid to late spring for those fish that have completed their spawning and are dropping back to the lake. They will commonly stage in pools on their descent and feed actively in an attempt to build their strength, which is often left weakened from the rigors of spawning. In rivers that have consistent spring hatches, steelhead can be found plucking mayflies and caddis off the surface. This occurrence is common on some rivers in Ontario.

There are mainly two dry fly approaches for Great Lakes steelhead. The first is most applicable to summer and early fall fish. This entails waking a fly across the surface. Finding good dry fly water is the first step. For waking a fly, the mid sections to tailout of pools and runs with a moderate to slow current flow will normally comprise the most sought-after water. Larger rivers will possess more flows with these characteristics than smaller streams. Water depth is very important with two to three feet seeming to be the optimum. Steelhead normally require some cover to feel comfortable, being positioned in the otherwise-exposed water of a tailout, and will prefer those that are filled with various-sized rocks and boulders.

The waking fly is fished on a leader with a heavy butt and tippet. A straight line cast is made angling down and across. The objective is to intentionally create drag upon the fly so that it produces a slight wake as it crosses the various current lanes. The key is to wake the fly slowly—enough movement to result in the slight disturbance on the water but not so much as to speed the

This steelhead took a waking bomber on the surface.

fly across the current lanes. Active participation and line manipulation are critical. The rod tip will be pointed in the direction of the fly and will normally lead the fly similar to greased line fishing. In some instances, the rod tip will follow in order to slow the fly. An upstream mend will also slow the speed of the fly. A downstream mend is often required to create a small belly which will wake the fly into the quiet water below the angler's position. Speed can also be controlled by raising and lowering the rod tip. Raising collects slack from the water's surface and increases speed while lowering the rod tip has an opposite effect.

A riffle hitch added to the dry fly will allow it to effectively wake on the surface. This is also the case for thinly dressed wet flies. For this reason, flies that are tied to be fished on the surface should be placed on hooks with an upturned eye. Morning and evenings will represent the best opportunities, particularly on rivers that receive a fair amount of angling pressure. Overcast days extend the possibilities. A steelhead is more likely to show for the fly than to actually take. A take can come in the form of a considerable disturbance on the water's surface, but always be intently looking for the subtle clues of a short rise such as the slight disturbance behind the fly or even the flash of a fish. If an interested fish is located, it should be worked over intently. If the same pattern brings no result, try a smaller dry or a riffle hitched wet over the exact same area. When a fish takes, it is imperative that it be allowed to turn on the fly. This requires great constraint. The steelhead should actually be allowed to take the one to two feet of slack pinched off by the index finger before the hook is set.

The key to prospecting with a waking dry fly in the summer and early fall is to find a river and the right water where rising a fish is a likely event. Work the water confidently and consistently with a dry. Bouncing back and forth between surface and subsurface is not efficient. One of the reasons that dry fly fishing has been largely ineffective on Great Lakes rivers is that such techniques are normally only experimented with during low percentage times of the day. Those that have the persistence and do not cave in to the temptation of fishing the fly deep will be much more likely to reach the ultimate reward.

Dead drifting a dry fly is the other effective technique and is most applicable to the drop-back feeders of the spring. During hatches and spinner falls, these fish can occasionally be seen feeding in the mid section through the tails of pools. The steelhead will not rise as consistently as a feeding trout but will commonly maintain their position so that a cast can be made to the same area. The best approach is to take position slightly up from the suspected lie. The fly should represent the insect comprising the hatch. It is commonly a Hendrickson hatch or an early season tan caddis. The fly is fished on a dry fly leader with a long tippet to encourage a drag-free float. A stop or dump cast is made to create slack in the leader. The fly should land a couple feet above the suspected position and be allowed to float for four to five feet. Repeated casts may be required to rise a fish and periodically resting the area may encourage the fish to rise. The take will be similar to the manner in which a stream trout feeds. After the hook set, be prepared—it is amazing how well a drop-back steelhead can fight. Dead drifting a dry can also be used on summer-run fish during hatches or prospecting with terrestrials.

Sink-tips and short leaders

For purposes of the discussion of techniques, the term "sink-tip" takes on a rather broad meaning. We will expand it to encompass not only conventional commercial sink-tips but also mini-tips and weighted leaders. All these setups are aimed at a common goal—sinking the fly. The various sink-tip arrangements provide an effective yet versatile system that allows for the enjoyment of casting a fly line not hampered by additional weight, an attractive feature for many fly fishers. The sink-tip techniques themselves have considerable similarities with those previously discussed. But with this approach comes the challenge of selecting the proper sink-tip system for the situation and of casting, handling, and manipulating the line in a manner that will offer an effective presentation.

To fully understand sink-tip fishing, it may be useful to look at a comparison to a floating line, long leader, and weight added. A sink-tip will generally be of a thicker diameter than a monofilament leader. This creates a greater surface area. River currents can make a slow to medium sink rate tip almost buoyant and can make faster rate tips sink much slower than what they are rated. When choosing a tip, it must not only have a fast enough sink rate to reach the desired depth but also to punch through the surface currents of heavy water. Also, the sink-tip line does not have the same sensitivity as a monofilament leader. It may be difficult to decipher when the fly is traveling along the bottom or to determine the take of a steelhead. A sinking braided leader does provide more sensitivity than a tip. Fishing a sink-tip often requires a greater degree of concentration, but certain steps or modifications will make the process more effective.

Deep broadside

This technique can be adapted to a wide range of water. The most common will be runs and pools of three to six feet in depth from fast to slow current speeds. The deep broadside technique is a good match for less active steelhead or when water temperatures drop into the low 40 degree range and even into the 30's but is an effective approach under a wide range of conditions. The cast is made up and across stream with a large upstream mend added immediately after the line hits the water. This takes tension off the tip and allows it to sink at a greater rate. As the fly drifts to just below the casting position, it should be traveling at the desired depth, all slack line should be collected, and the fly line should be straight to the fly. The rod should be at an angle which is less than 45 degrees to the water. At this point, the fly is being fished under tension. A slight upstream mend without moving the fly will place the floating portion of the line up from the sink-tip. This will encourage a presentation where the fly is downstream of the leader and tip, avoiding the belly of the line from arriving at the steelhead's location before the fly. This control is the key aspect of shorter tips. The broadside presentation is maintained by following the fly with the rod and arm as the tip of the rod is pointed directly downstream. Additional slack added to the surface of the water will extend the presentation well below the casting position without the fly cutting across the current.

Depth will be controlled in various ways. Initially, the sink rate of the tip will be the main consideration. When fishing quick runs where a deep trough is cut along a bank or logjam, a weighted fly may be required as well to quickly reach the proper depth and maintain the presentation through the deeper area. Depth can also be controlled by the angle of the upstream cast— the further upstream, the greater depths that can be obtained by the fly. This rule is good to about a 45 degree angle with the current. Greater than this will bring the fly too close to the casting position and not allow for the proper line control.

The take of a steelhead might come at any time and can be in the form of a violent strike or, more commonly, a subtle interception of the fly's path. It is important to concentrate on the movement of the line and fly, and be ready to react to those which seem contrary to what is anticipated. A downstream sweeping hook set works well at placing the fly in the corner of the steelhead's mouth. The hook set can be quite important with this technique as there may be time for the fish to reject the fly on slow, subtle takes. Steelhead may even take as the fly is sinking into place in front of the casting position. Most will occur at the point or just after where the fly has come under tension.

Wet Fly Swing

The wet fly swing technique can then be used as an extension of the broadside presentation or can be used alone beginning with a down and across cast. If used by itself, a mend should be made to allow the fly to attain the desired depth by the time it is at a 45 degree angle downstream. The line should be straight with a slight upstream mend helping to slow the swing of the fly. We attempt to swing the fly across the current lanes so that the fly is still in a semi-broadside position until the end of the swing. As the fly approaches the softer currents below the casting position, a downstream mend may actually be required to complete the swing. The fly should be allowed to hang in the current for at least three seconds. It can also be stripped slowly to entice a timid steelhead.

The fly hanging in the current can lead into a separate technique. While the fly is in the hang phase, if mends are thrown into the line toward either bank, a swimming motion will be imparted upon the fly. This lifelike movement occasionally will enrage or intrigue a sulking steelhead into taking. Changing the angle of the rod tip while the fly is hanging from pointing downstream to pointing toward the far or near bank will also allow the fly to swim and change position while possibly showing itself to another fish. Actually walking the fly down a few steps can also be productive, especially for lethargic fish. This can be effective in the winter and early spring. With one cast, effective line control, and utilizing one or all of the above steps, a fly can be fished for quite some time as it is carefully worked through suspected holds.

Much of the time, the fly should ride near the bottom; however, we have experienced times where aggressive fish will move to a fly fished on a sink-tip that takes the fly only halfway down the water column. This mainly occurs in slow tailouts. Modifications can also be made to fish small rivers and pocket water with this technique using the proper tips with short casts and swings.

Always let the fly hang at the end of the swing as a steelhead will often follow until the fly stops.

During the wet fly swing, the speed of the fly can also be controlled by the angle of the rod. To this point, the technique that has been described points the line at the fly as it leads the rod. The speed of the swing can be slowed slightly by pointing the rod across stream. This angle holds up the swing by creating less of an arc. This allows the fly to move across the current lanes much more slowly than the standard presentation. Once the fly is located in the same current lane as the rod tip, the rod is slowly led to a position pointing directly downstream to complete the swing. The key consideration when using this approach is depth. The angle of the rod is actually holding back the swing, which creates more tension and tends to raise the fly off the bottom. This approach will normally work best in slower flows and may require a heavier head than when fished with the standard wet fly swing.

Sink-tip techniques may require persistence. The key to success is to gain an intimate understanding of a few pieces of water in your favorite river that seem conducive to sink-tip fishing. It may be only two or three runs. Determine which tip is required to effectively cover each portion of each piece. Discover the casts, mends, and manipulations which place the fly in the likely zone at a slow speed. Learn the variations in technique and tips required by different water levels. This type of commitment is certain to be rewarded.

It is important to emphasize that understanding the differences between the presentation properties of a sink-tip versus the monofilament leader with weight added is critical. The larger diameter of a sink-tip, no matter how great the sink rate, will result in a certain buoyancy when heavy currents are involved. This will cause the fly to not reach desired depths. In addition, as the fly reaches a point approximately 45 degrees down, the heavier currents may accelerate the swing speed of the fly to a point which is too fast for effective presentation. We would refer to this effect as a sweep of the fly. Conversely, proper weighting on a monofilament leader can sink a fly effectively in heavy currents and maintain this depth even as the fly begins its swing at the 45 degree angle. With this arrangement, there exists what we refer to as turnover, meaning the lower diameter of the monofilament cuts through the heavy current and allows the fly to swing at a speed which can result in a take. Adding weight to the leader in the form of split shot also provides for a good feel of the bottom which can assist in determining its contour. This arrangement also seems to spook less fish under clear water conditions. As much as we enjoy fishing with sink-tips, there are certain types of water, mainly deeper runs with fast, heavy current, where weight added to a monofilament leader may be the best way to find a combination of fly fishing and a reasonable opportunity for a hookup. The in-line system of adding a mini-tip to a monofilament leader, as described earlier in this chapter, provides for a versatile arrangement which possesses the turnover advantages of a monfilament leader combined with the casting ease of a sink-tip. A one or two foot tip added to a short tungsten braided leader has also proven to be quite effective.

Dead-drift techniques

The dead-drift approach is designed to present a fly in a natural drift with the current. The techniques used for steelhead are quite similar to those employed when nymph fishing for trout. Dead-drift fishing has a wide application throughout the Great Lakes steelhead waters and can be used during the fall, winter, or spring. Our preference is for the more traditional techniques that require longer casts and acute line control; however, there are situations throughout the year which may dictate dead drifting as the most reasonable approach. One such situation is cold water temperatures. Once the water drops below 40 degrees, a steelhead's activity tends to slow, especially as the water approaches the freezing mark. And while fresh, energetic fish can be found in any water temperature, the likelihood of a Great Lakes fish chasing a fly more than a foot when the water is cold is quite limited. A naturally drifted fly presents itself potentially right in the fish's face in a slow and accessible manner. Even an inactive fish may be unable to let such an opportunity pass. Other prime situations for a dead-drifted fly are fast, deep slots, pockets, or short runs. These types of water are common on smaller streams or rivers with high gradients and may be difficult or near impossible to fish with other techniques, especially if the fish are fairly inactive. A dead-drifted fly can quickly reach significant depths, making it a perfect combination for fishing small pieces of water.

There are times in the fall and spring when steelhead may feed selectively on an abundant food source. Fishing a pattern that is a reasonable representation of the food being keyed on and presenting it in a natural manner may be the only way to take a steelhead where such conditions exist. The dead-drift technique is the ideal approach for presenting a fly that drifts naturally with the flow of the water. Dead drifting is also a good approach for beginning fly fishing steelheaders to become accustomed to reading the water and hooking and playing fish. This will build a solid foundation to mature into more traditional techniques.

Floating weight forward line

The basic setup for dead-drift fly fishing for steelhead involves a weight forward line, a leader of ten to fifteen feet, and either a weighted fly or weight added to the leader. Leader length will be determined by water depth and current speed. Casts will generally be quite short, 20 feet or less, and careful wading and positioning are very important. Tippets will normally consist of 2x to 4x material of 24 to 48 inches in length. Weight can be added directly to the leader or to the unclipped tag end of the knot between the leader and tippet. An aid in the detection of the often subtle take of an inactive fish can be quite helpful. Strike indicators of foam or yarn are the most popular and are commonly placed near or on the butt section of the leader. Using a brightly colored butt section can substitute for the typical strike indicator and represents

By keeping the rod tip high, the amount of line resting on the water's surface is minimized.

a more creative alternative in addition to being easier to cast. The most challenging approach to dead drifting is to combine a long leader with a weighted fly and no indicator. A combination of feel and observation of the point where the fly line and leader butt section meet the water is used to detect a take.

The basic approach begins by taking a position across from the suspected holding area. The cast is made up and across stream. It is common of smaller streams that backcasting room may be limited, and roll casts are required. Becoming proficient with the roll cast can be the key to success. A good roll cast is simply one half of a standard cast. The line on the water creates the tension to load the rod and the forward stroke should cast the line toward the horizon, parallel to the water in a similar manner as a standard cast.

A good cast for dead drifting allows the fly and any weight added to hit the water's surface prior to the fly line. This is accomplished with a tuck cast, which is performed by slightly overpowering the forward stroke. When this extra energy is transmitted to the end of the line, it forces the fly to tuck downward in the direction of the water. The key to casting weight on the leader is to allow the leader to fully straighten before beginning a more deliberate forward cast. An upstream belly should exist on the water's surface just after the line rests on the water's surface. This can be accomplished by concluding the cast with an upstream reach or by making an upstream mend immediately after the line hits the water. The tuck and the reach allow the fly to attain the greatest depth in as short a time as possible. Modifying the weight of the fly or on the leader will also affect sink rate.

After the cast, all unnecessary slack line is gathered by stripping in line. The rod tip starts low and is raised as the fly drifts directly in front of the casting position. At this point, the fly should be fishing at the desired depth. With the rod at an approximate 45 degree angle to the water and the arm extended, only a few feet of fly line should rest on the water's surface, which greatly reduces drag. All slack has been eliminated. The drift continues to a point quartering downstream and is prolonged by again lowering the rod tip and following the drift downstream. Throughout the drift, the indicator or butt of the leader is studied closely for the subtle sign that the drifting fly has been sucked in by a steelhead. Any unnatural movement should be met with a quick hook set. If the rig hangs up on the bottom, an adjustment to the weighting or angle of the cast should be made.

Solid corner-of-the-mouth hookups are uncommon with this approach. With inactive fish in cold water, most often the fly hooks the fish on the edge of the upper part of the mouth. This can result in many lost steelhead, to a point of sheer frustration. There does not seem to be any solution to this problem but rather one of the downsides of dead-drift fishing when compared to more traditional techniques. Chemically sharpened hooks, confidently identifying takes, and firm hook sets can minimize the problem.

Running line

This is a somewhat controversial fly fishing technique that has become quite popular in certain parts of the Great Lakes. With this approach, the standard fly line is substituted with a level floating running line and a leader with a total length of ten to fourteen feet. It results in a precise, delicate, and effective manner of presentation. The advantages of this approach are the ability of a truly natural drift and the use of lighter tippets protected by softer, lower-weight rods. The leader is rigged with weight attached, normally to a dropper, just above the tippet to sink the fly and efficiently work it along the bottom. Weight can be in the form of split shot or a slinky—parachute cord filled with buckshot. A swivel rig is used to attach the slinky. It is common to use a barrel swivel and allow the slinky, which is attached to a snap swivel and the leader threaded through its eye, to slide on the leader above the barrel swivel. Leaders are commonly constructed of straight .011 or .013 inch diameter material with a tippet of three to four feet in length.

The cast is made up and across stream and slack is immediately gathered. The fly should quickly be near the bottom. Since the lighter running line carries less weight beyond the rod tip, there is less sag in the line from tip to water. This allows for good line control and reduced drag when utilizing casts which are longer than what is normally comfortable with a standard fly line. The rod tip is held high through most of the presentation until the end of the drift as the fly is allowed to slowly swing on a tight line. The take of a steelhead will be detected by feel and sight as the point where the line touches the water is used as an indicator. Actually, a brightly colored butt section can assist in this as well. The hook should be set when a movement contrary to the current is experienced or when it feels as though the drift of the fly has been impeded.

This approach can be an important part of the steelhead repertoire when utilized in the situations that dictate its use. Since the line is so light, it can be cast with softer five- and six-weight rods which can better protect lighter tippets. This technique has proven itself on dour steelhead in low, clear water where small flies and light tippets were important. This is also true of winter and early spring conditions. Additionally, it is an efficient means for covering fast deep slots, particularly those where a wading obstruction prohibits the possibility of close positioning to the desired water.

With adequate backcasting room, the running line can be fly cast in a standard manner. Slow, open loops are critical as is allowing the line to straighten completely on the backcast. A pendulum motion may result in the most efficient backcast. The line is lifted off the water and kept tight in a 180 degree motion off to the same side of the body as the casting arm until it is straight behind. The forward cast follows with an open loop. A three- or four-weight line such as a Wulff Triangle Taper is a good alternative to the running line. It casts much better yet, since it is light, can be controlled in a similar manner to the running line.

The controversy of this technique has provoked many discussions. First is the consideration of light tippets and rods which may not be able to sufficiently tire a fish in time for a successful release. More commonly is the cast. Many anglers choose to slip cast when using this technique as the weight added to the leader is simply used to pull and shoot loose line peeled from the reel. The debate exists over whether this is truly fly fishing. We will make no attempt at that definition here as this is the personal determination of each individual angler. We do acknowledge that traditions are often derived from necessity. This technique has existed in the Great Lakes for nearly twenty years and is an integral part of the evolution of the fishery. It can be the only reasonable manner to cover some types of water under certain conditions. Manistee River guide Ray Schmidt, who is also an advocate of traditional techniques, can be credited with devising this innovation and now sees second-generation clients using this technique while developing new fly fishing traditions. However, for our own purposes, we feel more comfortable and challenged by those techniques where the weight of the fly line is being cast and carries the fly and leader as opposed to the weight on the leader carrying the fly line. Unfortunately, there is an aspect of this technique that has really soured us. We have witnessed it in use in some rivers where some so-called fly anglers using this approach with overly weighted rigs have so badly shortcutted the fly fishing learning curve as to make a sheer mockery of the sport. We certainly agree that the running line technique is an innovation designed to effectively fish certain types of water under certain conditions. Given this, it can be an enjoyable and challenging method in which to hook a fish. And while it may be the best approach at times, it has been our experience throughout the region that it is certainly not required on most rivers in order to catch steelhead.

Two-handed rods

There are a few tactical advantages gained by the use of two-handed rods. The techniques employed with these rods will be very similar or identical to those already described, but their use in some situations so greatly improves the opportunity for success, and even the overall experience, that some special attention is required. To this point, two-handed rods have had very limited use in Great Lakes steelhead fishing, partly due to the fact that some rivers are quite small while others that receive heavy pressure may not provide adequate room to properly utilize the rod. Probably the main reason for this lack of use lies in the equipment itself. In the past, most two-handed rods were long, heavy, and built for line weights of nine to eleven. Such rods were engineered for large salmon and steelhead rivers. They were too much for most rivers in terms of length and in enjoying the fight of smaller fish. In recent years, a number of lighter two-handed rods have appeared that are perfect for Great Lakes fly fishing. Most are 11 to 14 feet in length and accommodate line weights of seven to nine. They provide the advantages of a two-handed rod and fit the smaller river situations found on many of the region's waters.

The proper rod for a given situation will be determined by a few factors. The size of the river and the steelhead are certainly important considerations. An eight-weight or even one of the lighter seven-weight rods in eleven to thirteen feet have proven to be a good match for many rivers. Longer eight to nine weights seem to be the answer on larger rivers, but more importantly, the leverage and lifting power gained by rods of this size is critical when using heavy sink-tips.

Two-handed rods can be spey casted, overhead casted or even roll casted. Learning to spey cast maximizes the versatility of a two-handed rod. A few good instructional books and videos currently exist on this subject. Actually learning the spey casting motion is not difficult, but mastering the cast given the various river positions and wind conditions takes some time and experience.

One of the advantages of two-handed rods is the ability to cover water that would otherwise be difficult to fish. Spey casting was developed on the River Spey in Scotland to allow for long casts where backcasting room is at a minimum. This situation often exists on Great Lakes rivers. A spey cast can then allow for an efficient cast on rivers that are channelized and lined with brush and trees since the line only goes behind the casting position by a few feet. The spey cast can be used to set up a greased line, deep broadside or wet fly swing presentation. This is even the case on smaller rivers that may only be thirty to forty feet wide. It may be difficult to truly spey cast when using short lengths of line as the casting loop doesn't really develop, with the result being more of a roll cast. However, the leverage of the rod can still play an important part. The greater length over that of a one-handed rod makes picking up the line, even a heavy sink-tip, and laying it down almost effortless. This really seems to be a desired approach on tight rivers for those in search of a more traditional angling experience. It is important, however, to at least learn the basics of the single spey. Although the single spey is traditionally used only when fishing the right-side bank (if facing upriver), many Great Lakes

The length of two-handed rods lends itself to greater line control which results in more precise presentation.

rivers are too small for an effective double spey cast. A single spey then works well from either side of the river.

Another important advantage of two-handed rods is line control. It is simple—length equals line control in steelhead fishing. Mending is much easier and to a degree reduced as mends will be replaced by a simple movement of the rod tip. The line control aspect also seems to lend itself to depth control. A fly can be fished deeper with less weight in terms of the sink-tip or fly than with a single-handed rod since less line rides on the water.

A number of manufactured spey lines are available. Rio Products offers the most extensive standard spey lines in line weights six through twelve. The lines are available in two series and include a floater, a sink-tip and an interchangeable tip. Scientific Anglers and Wulff also offer a quality spey line. The standard spey lines work well on larger rivers and longer casts. However, on smaller rivers the casts are reduced to the point that there is not enough fly line past the tip of the rod to reach the belly of the line. This makes spey casting difficult. A solution for short spey casting is to use a line with an exaggerated weight forward design such as a pike taper. This design can quickly build up line speed to make short casts and accelerate a heavy tip. We are in the process of designing a fly line system for short spey casts. We are also working with Sage to assist in developing a rod that will comfortably handle short lines and heavy tips while being smooth, sensitive, and provide for full enjoyment of the fight of the size steelhead common to the Great Lakes. The early prototype of this rod, a 12½ foot, eight weight seems right on the mark.

Custom-made tips or sinking leaders looped to the end of a floating spey line provide the most versatile setup for fishing a two-handed rod for Great Lakes steelhead. The typical setup is similar to that when using a one-handed rod except that the two-hander can handle a heavier tip with less effort because of its leverage. Monofilament leaders of fourteen to eighteen feet can easily be used with a two-handed rod. This can easily facilitate a heavily weighted fly or weight added to the leader to effectively cover deep, heavy slots or even as an effective dead-drift tool when using natural patterns.

While the techniques are basically the same as those used with the one-handed rod, the extra rod length advantage seems to translate into a more direct management of the presentation of the fly. The greatest example can be seen by pointing the rod downriver when using the broadside presentation in combination with the wet fly swing. A slow broadside presentation can be maintained for an extended distance. Using the two-handed rod to its potential simply results in more hookups when using traditional techniques.

Two-handed rods reduce fatigue. While the casting stroke may look cumbersome and that much effort is being used, the leverage of the longer rod allows it to do more of the work—basic physics. It can help protect against the wear and tear on the wrist, elbow, and shoulder of day-long casting of a one hander. We have only been using two-handed rods for the last few years ourselves. However, it is obvious that two-handed rods will be the rod of choice for a number of rivers.

Fighting a Steelhead

The hookup sets the tone for any battle with a steelhead, and a solid one dramatically increases the chance of bringing the fish to hand. The fly fishing method employed and the reaction of the angler will directly impact the quality of the connection with the fish. The best hookups are those where the point of the fly comes to rest in the corner of the steelhead's jaw. Techniques which present the fly in a manner broadside to the current combined with a downstream sweeping set motion will improve the odds. In contrast, dead-drift techniques will normally rely on a decisive determination of the take and a quick reaction. Other approaches such as greased line and dry fly fishing will benefit from a delayed response, one that gives the steelhead an opportunity to turn on the fly.

While it is the many facets of steelhead fly fishing that captivates us, it is often the sheer exhilaration of a mighty chrome-bright fish that makes the deepest mark on our memories. When a fish is hooked, it's time to hold on and enjoy. In water without any serious obstructions, a steelhead can be allowed to dance freely and tire itself. Enough drag should be provided to force the fish to fight some tension as it takes line from the spool. In areas confined by obstacles which may prove terminal to a battle with a steelhead, a tighter drag will force the fish to fight for each foot of line with the objective of tiring it before it reaches trouble. It is wise to preview a pool or run before it is fished to determine if there are any obvious areas to direct a steelhead away from if hooked.

When a steelhead is hooked, it will quite often run out and downstream. Occasionally one will make an upstream run which normally favors the angler. Others, particularly stale fish, may stay put and not run at all. When a fish runs out and down, there are two schools of thought as to the proper reaction— chase or hold your ground. When the hookup is good and the tippet strength sufficient, a strong case can be made for holding tight. This is especially the case when a long stretch of heavy water or an impassable obstruction is apparent downstream. Dropping the rod tip seems to provide more control for working a fish back upriver. Actually placing the tip of the rod so that it literally touches the water and by maintaining the lightest tension possible on the fish has allowed us to walk many a steelhead upriver away from danger. The low tension seems to eliminate the fish's urge to fight away from the pressure. This technique works best when the fish is beginning to tire. However, when a sufficient amount of water exists below in which the fish can be played, there does seem to be some significant advantages of following. Keeping a steelhead on as short a line as possible tends to reduce the opportunity for trouble. We carefully follow when the situation dictates to maintain control over the fish.

Normally the steelhead will dictate the beginning of the fight. Its initial runs are often powerful which can use a good portion of its energy. Once the tables begin to turn, the angler needs to actively fight the fish as not to play it to exhaustion. Staying even with a fish and applying pressure from the side with the rod parallel to the water will commonly provide maximum control. Pressure should be kept constant and the line tight with a significant bow in the rod which will cushion against the erratic movements of the fish. If it runs toward the fighting position, be prepared to gather line and keep it tight. Raising the rod and rapidly backing up will gather line more efficiently than revolutions of the reel or stripping the line. For this reason, and the agility that it provides, fighting a steelhead from the shore as opposed to standing in the water is preferred when possible.

Fast current and in-water obstacles such as logjams cause more lost steelhead than anything else. The key to fast water is to attempt to keep a steelhead away from its power. After that opportunity has passed, it is best to stay with the fish. A steelhead in a powerful current below the fighting position can use that flow to such an advantage that it may never be seen again if given too much latitude. Ideally, if the fighting position can be changed to one below the fish, it will normally force it back upstream since steelhead generally will move away from the source of the pressure. This is often the best position to finish a fight with a steelhead. It should be led to shore with sturdy and constant pressure, taking line at every opportunity. Even a tired fish may have enough energy for another short run or two. Always be prepared.

One little trick that has worked on a few occasions on fish hopelessly running downstream is to throw slack into the line. The theory is that once the tension is removed the fish will stop fighting and often seek some quiet refuge area. In the past, this has fooled a runaway fish long enough to catch up and resume the fight on a level playing field. This technique requires that the steelhead be well hooked or the fly will drop out once the tension is removed. Another pitfall of fast, heavy water is that the surface area of the standard fly line can create significant resistance which can cause the fly to pull from the fish's mouth. One idea for small- to medium-size rivers is to use just the front end of the fly line, as much as normally required to fish that river. The back end is cut and attached to a much thinner running line. The reduction in diameter decreases the resistance.

When it comes to in-water obstructions, a balance is often required between finesse and power. When playing a fish in tight quarters, it must fight for everything it gets. Much of the time, by standing your ground, the fish can be coaxed away from trouble. Steelhead do not tend to use structure as well as a streambred trout. And while coming very close to danger, they can be directed away by a decisive and forceful movement of the rod. Again, side pressure will usually work best.

When landing a fish, it is best kept in the water. In slower currents, a tired steelhead can be easily corralled, hook removed, and revived for release. For pictures, grab the steelhead at the wrist of the tail with one hand and lightly cradle the other on its belly just below the head. Keeping the fish out of water as little as possible will increase its chance of survival. If a net is used, it should have a soft cloth bag which will not damage the fish. Catch and release is the only way for wild steelhead—any steelhead for that matter. They are much too special.

Additional Thoughts

Paying close attention to details can be the difference between satisfaction and sheer disappointment. Careful wading habits are closely related to the pursuit of trout in small streams. We don't often realize that these same principles may help on steelhead rivers as well. Be careful not to scuff feet and stumble over rocks, especially when the proper positioning is close to the expected lie of a steelhead. In the situation of being the first person through a pool or run in the morning, care should be given to not wade too deeply at first. Sometimes steelhead will be positioned in very shallow water at first light. It is a good idea to drift a fly through any water before wading in it during these morning hours. This is also a good rule of thumb when the water is off-color.

More than a few fish have been lost by careless leader maintenance. Make sure all knots are good. Use moisture on the knot when tightening and utilize both a pull on the line and your fingernails to properly seat all knots. With heavy leader or tippet material, it is quite common for a loosely tied knot to back itself out. Check the leader for abrasion caused by contact with rocks or possibly trees and take the time to change heavily abraded leaders as they can be quite weak. Retie the knot to the fly periodically as this will commonly be the weakest link. It is a somewhat tedious task but, considering that the fish of a lifetime could possibly take on the next cast, it is well worth the effort.

10

Flies

Flies for steelhead seem mystical or even enchanting, grabbing an angler's fascination like no other aspect of the pursuit. Sometimes this focus even goes beyond its relative importance. Such items as reading the water and proper presentation cannot be substituted by the magic powers of a particular pattern. Confidence is the word that should be closely associated with the fly selected for a particular situation. The faith placed in a reliable pattern allows the angler to experience the harmony of a steelhead river.

Patterns that will catch a steelhead in the Great Lakes region extend to each end of the spectrum and everything in between. An infinite combination of fur, feather and synthetic. Some combinations catch more steelhead than others. Some are elegant or even artistic, their creation a pastime within itself. Others are incredibly simple. The selection process of which fly to fish can be based on numerous factors, and one or all can figure into the equation. Feeding habits, water temperature and clarity, type of water, and the technique employed are the most common considerations. Advanced anglers may make their selection based on their own preference toward a certain pattern which possesses a style that is pleasing on its own and is further complimented by bringing a steelhead to its take.

Many anglers are in search of some rules or set of principles as a guide to fly selection. There really are none. However, there are a few things that we have observed. Small flies normally produce more takes in low, clear water—especially when water temperatures are in the 30 degree F. range. Large flies will work quite well in cold water, but normally on larger rivers. Both dark and very bright patterns can produce in dirty water and experience on a particular river will be the guide to determine which is preferred.

In this chapter, we will look at the flies used to catch Great Lakes steelhead along with some basic guidelines for selection. Many of the specific patterns have been born during the evolution of the Great Lakes steelhead fishery. We will also pay particular attention to the various materials required, examine reasonable substitutes, and explore some of the key tying steps of specific patterns or fly types.

Egg Patterns

Eggs deposited by spawning fish, mainly migratory salmonids, which are washed away from spawning redds create a significant food source on many rivers. Despite this obvious connection, various egg patterns are often looked down upon by those anglers in search of a more traditional approach. But selectivity coupled with certain types of water, such as quick runs, pockets, and deeper slots, may dictate egg patterns as the most reasonable approach. Through the years, we have observed numerous occasions where the selectivity toward eggs has been quite strong. Since some of these experiences have occurred on shorter rivers with a heavy hatchery influence, the natural progression of these occurrences seemed altered. This, combined with the simplicity of the tie, is the main reason that egg patterns are scorned by traditionalists. However, a recent Alaskan adventure for native trout and salmon species put things into perspective. Our trip was timed for the end of the summer. The river was rich with rainbow trout that had fed vigorously through the summer on drifting spawn of the various returning salmon species. We fished numerous patterns but found a certain egg pattern of a specific size and color to be the most interesting to the fish. It was the ultimate example of selective egg feeding and the importance of this natural process for the fish inhabiting and migrating to this river.

Beginning steelhead fly fishers can often benefit from starting with egg patterns since confidence can easily be gained in such a natural offering. For many, egg patterns represent a stepping stone to more advanced patterns and techniques. They also are useful when plying new or unfished waters as a locator since even timid steelhead will often take a dead-drifted egg. We prefer to bring steelhead to beautifully prepared flies fished in a traditional manner. But when the situation dictates, an egg pattern it is. We have both hooked and landed a number of exciting and extremely satisfying steelhead that took a well-presented egg pattern. Some are our most memorable fish. We do not consider these any less "fly caught" than those taken on elegant speys or soft hackles.

Egg patterns are synonymous with simplicity, making them a favorite of novice tyers. The simplicity aspect allows for rapid production which can result in a wide variety of sizes and colors with minimal effort. There seems to be a couple rules of thumb when selecting an egg fly for a particular situation. The first is that low, clear water seems to dictate a much smaller pattern than does water of the opposite condition. The second is that brighter patterns are more closely related with fresher natural eggs. When the abundance of naturally drifting spawn has a washed-out appearance, drab color egg patterns may be more effective.

We tend to favor a handful of very uncomplicated egg patterns that have proven extremely successful across the Great Lakes region. They are mainly tied from a handful of materials including various yarns, chenille, marabou, and flashier synthetics such as Estaz or Cactus Chenille. Most are tied on stout egg style or 2x strong nymph hooks. Thin-point, razor-sharp hooks are a must when using egg patterns as takes are often subtle, making it difficult for a firm hook set. Certainly the standard when it comes to egg patterns is the basic Glo Bug. Made from dense Glo Bug yarn, it creates the most realistic hand-tied egg pattern which can be trimmed to all sizes and produced in just about every color imaginable.

Nymph Patterns

Nymph patterns are useful and even necessary for many of the same reasons discussed for egg patterns. Late summer, fall, and early spring hatches often create active insects at times when rivers are visited by returning mature steelhead. This occurrence is quite common on rivers rich with aquatic insect activity. Both Michigan and Ontario contain rivers which fall into this category. Selective feeding on a specific insect can be normal. When low, clear water conditions persist on these rivers, dead drifting nymphs can be by far the most logical approach.

Nymphs and caddis larvae will also be dislodged from rocks and gravel by spawning activity of trout and salmon. Steelhead positioned below active salmon redds may be more likely to feed on a drifting nymph unrooted by a female fanning a redd as it will eggs that have escaped from the nest. In either case, active insects or those dislodged by spawning, it is important to have some basic knowledge of the dominant aquatic insects of a particular river. On water of lesser quality which contains only moderate or even little aquatic insect activity, nymph patterns may be of significantly less importance.

Those rivers containing rich insect life commonly host runs of wild steelhead which seem to quickly adapt to feeding on nymphs from their seasons of gorging on bait in the lake. Their reaction to nymphs most likely is a left over instinctive response from their juvenile years when aquatic insects comprised the balance of their diets. It may take a few weeks or more before a fish will demonstrate a strict selectivity to nymph patterns, even in those rivers crawling with insect life. Our preference is for fresh fish that will move readily to a more traditional pattern. But when a steelhead has become set in its ways, nymph patterns can be of great importance.

Nymph patterns have seemed to reach a greater degree of acceptance in the realm of steelhead fly fishing in the Great Lakes than have egg patterns. Possibly because of their closer relationship to fishing for streambred trout or that nymph patterns generally entail greater tying skills. Also, most nymph patterns incorporate some type of weight. This commonly is accomplished with lead strips or bead heads. This aspect of weighting the fly seems more appealing to some anglers as opposed to weighting the leader.

Most nymph patterns are tied using fairly traditional materials such as fur dubbing, hackle, turkey and pheasant feathers, peacock and ostrich herl, tinsels, and wire. Some include synthetic materials designed for realism or flash. Hooks need to be sharp, strong, and the approximate size of the natural insect. Innovative weighting techniques can be used that will allow the fly to drift hook point up, making it less likely to hang up on the bottom. The most common manner for accomplishing this task would be to line the top of the hook shank with enough lead wire affixed with tying thread, which would turn the hook up. Another method would be to include small dumbbell eyes on the top of the hook shank at the head of the fly. Of course the fly would need to be tied so that the top of the pattern is built on the underneath of the hook shank.

Again, our selection of nymphs is pretty basic. Enough to give an impressionistic view of popular aquatic insects found in the Great Lakes region. Old standby patterns such as the Pheasant Tail and Hare's Ear in various shades are a good representation of a variety of mayfly nymphs as well as other insects. The most common regional patterns have been tied to mimic various stonefly, caddis, and the famous Hexagenia Limbata mayfly of the Midwest. A number of such patterns have been created by Great Lakes tiers and proven on their local waters. Those listed here represent a mere fraction of the nymph patterns used to fool steelhead in the Great Lakes.

Leech Patterns

Lumped into the category of leech patterns are those tied with soft materials that undulate with river currents creating a lifelike appearance when fished under tension. Rabbit strips, marabou, and long, soft hackle are the most common components. Some are dashed with sparkle from Krystal Flash or

Flashabou. Along with this enticing movement, leech patterns generally cast a full silhouette in the water which can be a significant advantage in low light periods or when the water is stained. Leech patterns fish best with the deep broadside technique or the wet fly swing. The most consistent approach is to utilize the two in combination.

Simplicity is among the advantages of leech patterns. Since most of the tying steps are quite basic, even novice tiers can construct some that are sure to catch steelhead. Over the years we have developed a significant confidence in a variety of leech patterns. A confidence that has allowed us to successfully use these patterns on a wide array of steelhead waters. It is a confidence that can easily be gained and creates a starting point for anglers new to traditional techniques. Along with representing leeches which can be found in many steelhead rivers, leech patterns can be tied to mimic various aquatic life including chubs and sculpins. Rabbit strip leeches in white have proven to be a perfect representation of baitfish that inhabit or migrate to certain river systems. Modifications can be made to some of the standard leech patterns that give them more of a traditional steelhead fly appearance.

Another advantage of leech patterns is that weight can easily be added to the fly in the form of cone heads, bead heads, or dumbbell eyes. Since each of these manners of adding weight are visible, it is easy to determine how heavy each particular weighted fly is when selecting one from your box. This allows one to build a system of flies for many different situations. Weighted flies have their greatest benefit in faster currents, especially when fishing pockets or deep slots and drop-offs. Weighted leech patterns can often be fished on a monofilament leader and a floating line or in conjunction with a mini-tip system if greater depth is required. With a heavy butt leader, weighted leech patterns are easy to cast. With the weight added to the front of the fly, its action is enhanced as the fly will now move vertically when its speed is increased or decreased. A stripping retrieve will exaggerate this type of movement.

Our preference is for dumbbell eyes. Dumbbells offer the greatest range of weight, which is critical when building an inventory of flies to cover the greatest degree of circumstances. Also, when a dumbbell eye is added to the top of the hook shank, it will normally force the hook point to ride up, with the exception of a light eye and heavy hook combination. With the hook point up, it will remain sharper and less likely to hang on the bottom or hook into a log while scouring the floor for stubborn steelhead. Dumbbell eyes can easily be added to the top of the hook shank with a heavy tying thread using a figure eight wrap. A few drops of head cement is a good idea.

Unweighted leech patterns are normally tied on standard up eye black salmon hooks or on 2X strong bronze streamer hooks. For weighted flies, a loop eye salmon hook provides a flat surface which allows dumbbell eyes to be added quickly and securely. We often use a straight eye hook for those tied with dumbbells.

Wet Flies/Soft Hackles

Wet fly patterns represent the traditional side of steelhead fishing with a fly. They normally encompass a soft hackle or throat, a wing, and a dubbed body. Many are tied with a tail. Most combine elements of subtle movement, silhouette, and style to form a fly which is tied not to mimic a certain aquatic life but rather to suggest. Wet flies can be tied in colors natural to the underwater world such as black, brown, or olive or in bright colors such as orange, red, or chartreuse which could be taken for their likeness to drifting spawn but more likely from the steelhead's instinctive or inquisitive response.

We tie most of our wet fly patterns on standard up eye black salmon hooks. Heavy wire hooks have their advantages for those flies designed to fish deep; however, the lighter wire styles provide for more efficient hook penetration. The up eye design is required if the pattern is to be fished with a riffle hitch. A vast laundry list of materials is used to tie the wide and varied wet flies used to catch steelhead. One of the most important ingredients of the fly is the hackle. A soft, wispy hackle wraps nicely into place and undulates lifelike in the subtle undercurrents of a pool, pocket, or run. Soft natural hen necks are perfect for tying small wet flies that are handsome yet represent aquatic insect life. The soft hackles from a Hoffman Chickabou neck are ideal for small- to medium-size wets. Chickabou is available in a wide variety of colors which are perfect for steelhead flies. Soft Web Hackles marketed by Wapsi make nice larger-sized wet flies. Some saddle hackles, provided they are not too stiff, can make attractive and effective wet flies. It is also important that the hackle not be so webby that the fibers stick together and not evenly separate when wrapped.

There are a variety of dubbing materials available which provide a wide range of colors combined with a certain element of lifelike sheen. Hareline Steelhead & Salmon Dubbin combines natural rabbit fur with fine, short strands of a synthetic material similar to flashabou. It is very easy to work with and creates a nice body. Spirit River Psuedo Seal and SLF distributed by Hareline are a good seal substitute. Seal fur is called for on the traditional ties of certain steelhead and salmon patterns but is now illegal to possess in the United States. Each is coarse like seal and, because they are synthetics, are more difficult to work with. A bushy body seems to make a more effective fly. A bushy effect can be obtained with each of these dubbing materials. The simplest way to obtain this is to dub extra material on the thread and, after the body is formed, pick out some of the fibers with a dubbing brush. Utilizing a dubbing loop will create more durable bushy bodies and will make it easier to work with coarse materials. Using a dubbing loop may be awkward at first, but with a quality dubbing loop tool and a little practice, the dubbing loop becomes second nature.

Most wets are completed with a wing which provides movement and silhouette. Calf tail appears on many traditional steelhead wet flies and in a wide range of colors is quite useful on some patterns utilized in the Great Lakes region. Squirrel tail and fine bucktail also complete a wet fly quite nicely. Softer materials such as arctic fox tail and even marabou provide more movement in the water. Some synthetics like SLF in long hanks come in a wide range of colors and possess just the right amount of glimmer to add to a fly's appearance and its fish-enticing qualities, especially in stained water. The SLF provides a good substitute for polar bear which is called for on some original steelhead patterns but which is also illegal to possess in the United States. However, some tiers believe that the natural sheen of polar bear can be copied but not duplicated.

Adding the hackle may be the most important step of tying a wet fly. There are two tying techniques which will encourage the hackle to lay back toward the rear of the hook. The first is to fold the hackle. The most efficient way to fold is while the hackle is being wound onto the hook. The hackle is tied in at the tip. For right-handed tyers, the hackle fibers are stroked back with the left hand as the hackle is wound by the right. Each wrap is made toward the eye of the hook, right at the base of the previous wrap. This process will take some practice but in time becomes quite easy. The softer the hackle fibers and stem, the easier it will be to fold.

The second technique involves stripping one side of the hackle. It is easier and creates a nice result, especially on small flies. This technique begins by grasping the tip of the hackle with the thumb and forefinger. For right-handed tyers, the tip is held with the right hand, and the face or brighter side of the hackle is showing in your direction. With the thumb and forefinger of the left hand, the hackle fibers from just below the tip are stripped away from the stem. The hackle is then tied in at the tip with the fibers pointing to the rear of the hook. The hackle is then wrapped at an angle that allows the fibers to lay back. Make sure that, before each wrap, the hackle fibers from the previous one are laying back, out of the way. The wraps should be made forward with the stem positioned tightly against itself with each wrap. A few wraps of the thread in front of and even onto the hackle will assure that the fibers will point to the rear of the hook.

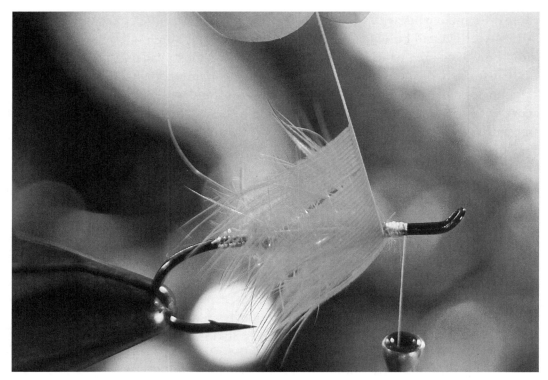

Wrapping a hackle that has been stripped down one side. Shaun Smith photo.

Wet flies are the most versatile of Great Lakes steelhead patterns and can be fished using a variety of techniques. The greased line technique, the deep broadside approach, or wet fly swing are commonly fished with wet fly patterns. However, some can also be effectively dead drifted near the bottom or used with a riffle hitch to coax a steelhead that has shown for a dry fly.

Spey Flies

In his classic book *Atlantic Salmon Flies & Fishing*, Joseph D. Bates, Jr. writes:

> One idea that North American anglers should find valuable is the adoption of the British method of using flies with long, flowing hackles such as black and gray heron, used chiefly in Spey flies. A leading exponent of this is the famous English angler, Geoffey Bucknall. In an article in the August, 1969, *Trout and Salmon* he says: "It would be a mistake to assume that Spey flies should be confined to the river that gives them their name."

Mr. Bucknall's reference is to Scotland's River Spey, the birth river of spey flies as well as spey fishing. And indeed it would be a mistake to not consider these beautiful creations for steelhead fishing. Spey flies first became popular in North America with Atlantic salmon anglers, then Pacific coast steelhead fly fishers. Now the popularity of spey-type flies is increasing in the Great Lakes region.

Although many of the patterns used in the Great Lakes deviate dramatically from the original ties and one could argue that such a pattern is not truly a spey fly unless fished on the river bearing its name, the general concept of the long flowing hackles seems to be the main characteristic which carries on this tying concept. Heron, which is now illegal to possess in the United States, was the original hackle of the spey fly. For this reason, a number of substitutes are used to complete the modern versions, pushing these patterns further from the original.

Spey patterns begin with the proper hook which adds to its appearance and allows the fly to track upright without spinning as it travels through the water. The Alec Jackson spey hook distributed by Daiichi or the Partridge Bartleet Traditional are both fine hooks for this purpose. A combination of tinsel, floss, and dubbing commonly comprise the body. Natural dubbings such as seal, wool, badger, or angora goat are still used, but so are a number of other synthetics and natural/synthetic blends. The dubbing described in the previous section can all be incorporated into the spey fly design. Most dubbing on successful patterns contain a lifelike sheen. Some are even shiny like Spirit River Lite Brite or Arizona Diamondbraid distributed by Umpqua. The wings on traditional ties are mainly comprised of matching pairs of mallard, teal, or turkey. However, we have had considerable success with wings of natural furs such as arctic fox, rabbit, or badger.

Aside from heron hackle that has somehow been legally secured, there are a number of substitutes capable of creating very elegant flies. The key element of a substitute is suitable length of the hackle and a stem which is thin and soft which will not build excessive bulk. Blue-eared pheasant may come closest to heron in terms of general appearance and results. It is similar also in color to heron, possessing a bluish/slate hue. Blue-eared pheasant is the most expensive of the substitutes. Pheasant rump also creates a nice spey fly. To a limited degree, it accepts a dye so that a few colors are available. The natural has a reddish/brown appearance and dyed colors are available in about eight variations. However, many of the natural colors show through on the dyed feathers. The size and quality of the pheasant rump varies dramatically within a package and requires sifting through to find the right hackle. Turkey rump can also be utilized as hackle.

There are a few options when it comes to a wide variety of colors. One of the most common is schlappen. This is a long, soft hackle that is quite easy to tie with and available in nearly every color imaginable. The down side is that schlappen tends to be quite webby which restricts its ability to evenly hackle the hook as bunches of fibers can stick together. Also, some of the hackles in a package of schlappen may not be long enough for larger flies. Still a very useful component for Great Lakes spey flies. Some of the most common heron substitutes are those distributed by Hareline and Spirit River. The hackle is burned goose feather which has a soft curve, making it suitable for spey flies. This heron substitute is available in all the colors needed for a full repertoire of steelhead speys. It is capable of tying beautiful flies, although successful use of this material does take some practice. A disadvantage of this type of hackle is that the quality within a package can vary greatly. Also, the stems can become very thick and even brittle near the butt, making it difficult to work with. Soaking the hackles before tying with them will soften the texture. With practice, it will become fairly easy to determine which feathers in a package will perform properly and those which do not make the grade.

One other hackle which creates gorgeous flies that are very productive is marabou. Wrapped in at the head of the fly and swept back, marabou adds the enticing action that readily brings a steelhead to a fly. Marabou can be found in all colors. It is important to use those with long straight fibers as opposed to thick and bushy. Hareline distributes selected marabou spey hackles which are perfect for tying marabou spey flies. The only disadvantage of this product is that they tend to be just a little small for tying extra large size flies. Good spey hackle can be found in some standard marabou packages. We see marabou speys as playing an important role in the development of traditional fly fishing in the Great Lakes region.

Traditionally, the hackle of a spey fly is added at the third wrap of tinsel and is round through the front portion of the body. Some of the successful patterns of the Great Lakes rivers place the hackle at the front of the fly. This is the main practice for marabou spey flies. The procedure for adding the hackle is similar to that above for wet flies. We have found that stripping down one side and tying the hackle in at the tip produces a nice, neat pattern. The key with every wrap of the stripped hackle is to slightly rotate the stem down and away so that it lays back toward the rear of the hook. The traditional approach is to tie the hackle in at the butt of the stem and fold the hackle instead of stripping it down. This can be effectively accomplished with softer materials. In the same above referenced article, Geoffrey Bucknall states:

> A minor problem is doubling the hackle, but heron folds over easily once the butt has been tied down firmly to the hook. Moisten the long fibers and they can be stroked into the doubled position. As in all salmon flies, stripping one side of the stalk denudes the fly of its share of working parts, and it is a sloppy expedient.

We tend to agree. Using both sides of the hackle creates a fuller, more enticing fly. For this reason folding the hackle is recommended if the material allows for this technique.

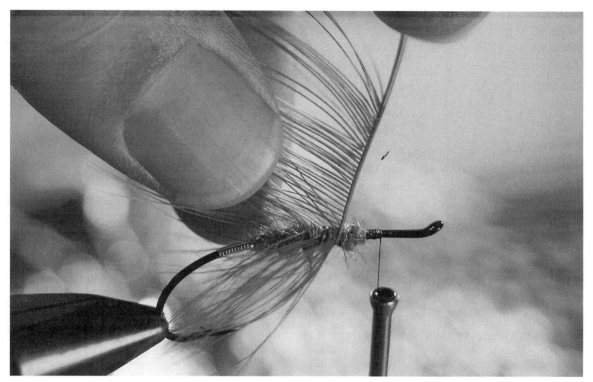

Folding and wrapping a spey hackle. Shaun Smith photo.

Spey flies are commonly fished in the Great Lakes region with the greased line technique or the deep broadside approach in combination with the wet fly swing.

Dry Flies

There are very few if any Great Lakes fly fishers that have wide experience with the steelhead of their region on a dry fly. Most dry fly situations that we have encountered or have discussed with other anglers fit into specific situations when conditions and timing were just so. However, the possibilities do show themselves with increasing frequency if knowledge of a certain river is combined with a more active pursuit of surface fishing. Some rivers will provide better opportunity than others, but to not miss out on an opportunity, it is wise to carry some dry flies.

In the Great Lakes, steelhead that take dries can be classified loosely into two groups: those taking out of an instinctive response to movement or opportunity and those that are actively feeding on drifting insect life. The former may be the most exciting way to fish a dry for steelhead while the latter appears to represent a more consistent opportunity. For drawing an instinctive response, larger flies that can be waked in the surface water are a good starting point. Bombers and Waller Wakers tied in white, orange, red, or some combination of these have produced rises either for us or anglers with whom we have spoken. Flies with muddler heads that create a surface disturbance but which ride in the film have also produced surface takes.

As first mentioned in the nymph pattern section, insect hatches often occur when steelhead are found in many rivers. When fishing rivers where such an intersection is possible, carrying some dries tied on hooks with enough strength to hold a steelhead and to represent the hatch of the day is a very good idea. The most common mayfly hatch which has shown its importance on both Michigan and Ontario rivers is *Ephemerella Subvaria*, commonly known as the Hendrickson. Both the hatch and spinner falls can create the occurrence of active feeders. Also a wide variety of caddis, mostly with dark tan bodies in a range of sizes, can be found on a number of Great Lakes rivers. Summer runs in the St. Joseph river are known to take individual caddis from blanket evening hatches. Basic caddis patterns have brought both fall and spring fish to the surface that were found holding in the tails of low, clear pools. Early spring stonefly hatches can also be found on many steelhead rivers. We have also heard tales of steelhead coming to hoppers and even beatles.

The Tyers and Fly Patterns

As Great Lakes steelhead fly fishing continues to develop, flies specific to the region are being created, tested, and refined. It is clear that fly patterns for Great Lakes steelhead are evolving from sheer simplicity to those with more elegance and functionality. Many that have more traditional lines, similar to those used for centuries for Atlantic salmon, are proving to be very effective. Also, as our understanding of a steelhead's feeding habits or selectivity has increased, so, too, have the flies that imitate or represent food sources found in a particular river. Tying flies and developing ideas for new patterns, or improving upon those already existing, is an integral part of what we call Great Lakes steelheading.

We have attempted to identify the region's most influential tyers and patterns. What follows is a brief profile of these tyers along with a variety of flies tied by them, as well as other Great Lakes anglers. The patterns selected for the book were compiled to show the entire spectrum of flies used throughout the Great Lakes, with an emphasis toward the more eye-pleasing patterns which are changing the way we view the fishery. Certainly our own favorites are part of the mix, including a series of flies that have been created or adapted by Rick. These flies are designed to have eye-appeal, but each has proven to be especially effective. This series was designed to cover all the techniques described in the previous chapter.

The fly patterns are loosely grouped by fly type and by tyer. A tying recipe is given for each fly pictured in the fly plates in the same order as it appears. There are two items to note. The first is that the style of hook and a guideline for size is given for each pattern. There are basically four styles of hooks used for most of the patterns. They are an up eye black salmon hook, a streamer hook, an egg-style hook, and a nymph hook (usually 3x long.) We strongly believe in quality, chemically sharpened hooks that are razor sharp right out of the package. Two of the highest-quality hooks on the market are Tiemco and Daiichi. Some recommendations for each style of hook available from each of these manufacturers are as follows: up eye salmon – Tiemco 7999 (heavy wire) or 7989 (light wire), Daiichi 2441 (heavy wire) or 2421 (light wire); streamer – Tiemco 9395 or Daiichi 1750; egg hook – Tiemco 105 or Daiichi 4250; and standard nymph hook – Tiemco 3761. We use the Daiichi Alec Jackson spey hook for most of our spey flies in either black 2051 or gold 2055. Any other specific hook requirements are addressed in the fly recipe.

The second is that we prefer a low diameter tying thread to keep the head small and neat. Uni-thread in size 8/0 is perfect for this purpose. It has tremendous strength for its low diameter and is available in a range of colors. For those patterns where a large, colorful head adds to the fly's appeal, a larger diameter thread such as Uni-thread 3/0 may be preferred.

The Tyers

Jeff "Bear" Andrews – Grand Ledge, Michigan. Jeff is a well-known and award-winning professional fly tyer whose tying and fishing adventures take him all over the world. He has become synonymous with the Federation of Fly Fishers Conclave where each year he ties for 24 straight hours to raise funds for education and conservation programs. He has also released his first of three videos on tying Great Lakes steelhead flies.

Dave Barber – Altmar, New York. Dave owns and operates the Fish Inn Post on the banks of the Salmon River. He is also a knowledeable, full-time fly fishing guide.

Bob Blumreich – Janesville, Wisconsin. Bob is one of the most sought-after steelhead and trout guides in the Great Lakes region. His Silver Doctor Fly Fishing instruction and guide service covers a number of Wisconsin steelhead rivers with an emphasis on traditional techniques, beautifully crafted flies, and the highest of ethical standards.

Mark Conway – Amherst, New York. Mark's passion for Victorian-style flies has led to his use of these elegant patterns for Great Lakes steelhead. He is a very good tyer with a keen eye for detail.

Tom Cornell – Tonawanda, New York. Tom is a year-round guide in Great Lakes waters, a dedicated steelhead fly fisher, and has given valued volunteer hours to local wild steelhead projects.

Charlie Dickson – Tonawanda, New York. Charlie is an award-winning tyer who ties for style and function. He has perfected his patterns on the steelhead waters of Western New York.

Kelly Galloup – Traverse City, Michigan. Kelly is the owner of The Troutsman, a complete fly fishing shop in Traverse City. He has been a professional guide and tyer for more than twenty years, has written several magazine articles, and is co-author with Bob Linsenman of the book entitled *Modern Streamer Tactics for Trophy Trout*.

Walt Grau – Branch, Michigan. Walt is a well-known guide on the Pere Marquette River. His rather abstract fly designs are found in many steelheaders' fly boxes.

Greg Liu – Pulaski, New York. Greg is a full-time guide and operates his Oswego Outfitters guide service throughout the fall, winter, and spring on New York's Salmon River and other area streams and rivers. He has acquired a sincere interest in swinging flies for steelhead when the conditions allow for such an approach. He has developed a series of simple tube flies which steelhead have found enticing.

Rob "Bucky" McCormick – Tonawanda, New York. Rob is a fly shop manager and guide who enjoys the solitude of stalking steelhead on less-popular waters. Many of his flies are designed for a swinging presentation in clear water.

Bob Morrissey – Angola, New York. Bob is part owner of the Oak Orchard Fly Shop. He enjoys pursuing steelhead using a wet fly swing and his well-tied patterns are effective as well as realistic.

Joe Penich – Hamilton, Ontario. Joe ties professionally and is simply one of the best all-around tyers in the Great Lakes region. His flies are beautiful. Joe has the ability to combine an understanding of available fly tying materials with a desire to design effective, realistic fly patterns.

Nick Pionessa – Cheektowaga, New York. Logging more days fishing than just about anyone else we know, Nick keeps the mystique of the true fly fishing bum alive and well. His flies are built for effectiveness. Nick is also a steelhead guide.

Ray Schmidt – Wellston, Michigan. Ray has been deeply involved in the Great Lakes steelhead fishery since the 1970's as an angler, guide, and shop and lodge owner. His shop is near the banks of the Big Manistee. Ray has developed many patterns to match the various techniques required to hook steelhead on his river throughout the season. Here we feature some of the patterns he uses for swinging flies to aggressive steelhead.

Brian Slavinski – Cheektowaga, New York. Brian is a professional guide, tyer, and avid steelheader. He is always experimenting with new materials to design effective patterns.

Scott Smith – Thunder Bay, Ontario. Scott is a knowledgeable angler, writer, instructor, and dedicated guide on the rivers of the north shore of Lake Superior. His flies are designed to fish the pockets and quick runs that are common to many of his rivers.

Troy Standish – Williamsville, New York. Troy ties beautiful married wing flies for steelhead. Those featured in the fly plate combine elegance with effective color combinations and the enticing movement of marabou.

Matt Supinski – Newaygo, Michigan. Along with his wife Laurie, Matt owns and operates the Gray Drake on the banks of the Muskegon. Matt's flair for both exploration and for constantly taking a fresh look at his approach to steelhead is reflected in the offbeat style of many of his patterns.

John Valk – Waterdown, Ontario. John owns and operates Grindstone Angling in Waterdown. As an angler and guide, John has explored more fly water in southern Ontario than anyone else we have met. John has designed a series of wet flies to meet the various conditions he encounters across the region.

Rick Whorwood – Stoney Creek, Ontario. Rick has been a fly tyer for over twenty years and has spent the last five becoming an accomplished classic tyer. He has worked with the best classic tyers to learn the secrets of Dee style, speys, and full-dressed classics. The flies featured demonstrate the variations of these styles. Rick's work has been featured in national magazines.

Glo Bug
Hook: Egg style, size 6-12
Thread: Kevlar
Body: Assorted Glo Bug yarn trimmed to size

Nuclear Roe Bug
Hook: Daiichi 1530, size 6-10
Thread: Color to match body
Body: Assorted chenille or Glo Bug yarn cut and
      dubbed
Wing: White Glo Bug yarn tied sparsely to encase
      entire body

Cactus Fly (Scott Smith)
Hook: Egg style, size 6-10
Thread: Orange Uni-thread 6/0
Tail: Tuft of colored filoplume or marabou the
      length of the hook gap
Body: Cactus Chenille
Wing: Tuft of colored filoplume, marabou, or
      polypropylene

Estaz Egg (Dave Barber)
Hook: Egg style, size 6-10
Thread: Color to match body
Body: Assorted Estaz

Frammus
Hook: Daiichi 1530, size 6-12
Thread: Color to match body
Body: Assorted chenille
Wing: Assorted Glo Bug yarn
NOTE: Combinations of chartreuse and orange
      have been very effective.

Salmon Flea
Hook: Daiichi 1530, size 6-12
Thread: Color to match body
Tail: Front and rear, white Glo Bug yarn
Body: Assorted small chenille

Carpet Fly (Mark Stothard)
Hook: Daiichi 1530, size 6-10
Thread: Kevlar
Body: Mix of yellow, gold, orange, pink, and white
      knitting yarn tied in Glo Bug fashion

Sucker Spawn
Hook: Egg style or Daiichi 1530, size 8-14
Thread: Color to match yarn
Body: Angora yarn tied to give appearance of egg
      cluster—chartreuse, orange, yellow, cream,
      and pink are all effective colors

Halo Egg (Kelly Galloup)
Hook: Egg style, size 10-12
Thread: To match wing
Underwing: Very short length of Glo Bug yarn
      approximately one-quarter width of a strand
      of a bright color
Wing: Glo Bug yarn of a lighter color such as
      Oregon Cheese tied in around hook shank
      and cut twice as long as underwing

Egg Omelet (Matt Supinski)
Hook: Egg style, size 4-8
Thread: Kevlar
Tail: White rabbit strip with strands of pink and
      pearl Flashabou
Head: Pink Glo Bug yarn shaped as a large egg

Pom-Pom Stone (Matt Supinski)
Hook: Egg style, size 6-8
Thread: Black
Tail: Black biots
Abdomen: Black dubbing
Thorax: Purple Estaz
Wing case: Pearl Flashabou

Thugmeister Stone (Matt Supinski)
Hook: Nymph, size 8-10
Thread: Black
Tail: Black hackle fibers
Rib: Blue Flashabou
Body: Black wool
Throat: Black soft hackle

Caddis Larvae
Hook: Tiemco 2457, size 8-10
Thread: Black
Body: Green dubbing with black for head

Soft Hackle Caddis (James Empie)
Hook: Tiemco 2457, size 8-10
Thread: Olive
Body: Green yarn
Collar: Small natural hen or partridge

Reverse Caddis (Kelly Galloup)
Hook: 4x long nymph or streamer, size 10
Thread: Brown
Tail and butt: Black dubbing
Body: Green dubbing or sparkle yarn for rear
      portion and brown dubbing with two brown
      hackles wound through and clipped for
      the front

Nympho (Scott Smith)
Hook: Nymph, size 8-10
Thread: Orange Uni-thread 6/0
Tail: Golden pheasant crest
Rib: Gold oval tinsel
Body: Chartreuse Steelhead and Salmon Dubbin
Wing case: Six strands of peacock herl
Thorax: Orange or fuchsia Steelhead and Salmon
       Dubbin with fibers picked out to resemble legs

Steelhead Hare's Ear (Kelly Galloup)
Hook: Up eye salmon, size 8-12
Thread: Brown
Tail: Pheasant tail
Abdomen: Hare's ear dubbing
Thorax: Hare's mask dubbed full and picked out
Wing case: Turkey
Head: Black rabbit dubbing

Flashback Pheasant Tail Stone (Matt Supinski)
Hook: Short nymph hook or Daiichi 1530, size 8-10
Thread: Black
Tail: Stiff gray hackle fibers
Body: Black pheasant tail
Legs: Stiff black hackle

Claret Stone (Matt Supinski)
Hook: Short nymph hook or Daiichi 1530, size 8-10
Thread: Black
Tail: Black biots
Rib: Black vinyl round rib
Body: Claret Steelhead and Salmon Dubbin
Wing case: Black turkey
Hackle: Black soft hackle

Creepy Stone (Matt Supinski)
Hook: Nymph, size 8-10
Thread: Black
Body: Black dubbing
Rib: Fine oval tinsel followed by Pearl Flashabou
Hackle: Black wound through thorax
Head: Gold bead followed by black dubbing

Mike's Stone (Scott Smith)
Hook: Tiemco 5263, size 10-12
Thread: Black Uni-thread 6/0
Tail: Black goose biots
Rib: Black balloon strip
Body: Brown dubbing
Wing case: Turkey quill
Legs: Grouse
Thorax: Ostrich herl
Antennae: Black goose biots

Joe's Black Stonefly Nymph (Joe Penich)
Hook: Nymph, size 6-8
Thread: Black
Underbody: Lead strips parallel to body
Tail and antennae: Black goose biots
Body: Black SRC Pro Dub
Wing case: Copper or black Raffia
Eyes: Black plastic bead chain

Joe's Golden Stonefly Nymph (Joe Penich)
Hook: Nymph, size 6-8
Thread: Black
Underbody: Lead strips parallel to body
Tail and antennae: Gold goose biots
Body: Gold SRC Pro Dub
Wing case: Copper or black Raffia
Eyes: Black plastic bead chain

Walt's Flashback Stone (Walt Grau)
Hook: Nymph, size 6-8
Thread: Black
Tail: Black rubber legs (used for antennae as well)
Ribbing: Fine silver oval tinsel
Body: Black fur dubbing with thorax picked out for legs
Wing case: Pearl Krystal Flash
Hackle: Black

Gartside Sparrow – Green (Matt Supinski)
Hook: Short nymph, size 4-8
Thread: Brown or gray
Tail: Filoplume
Body: Green dubbing
Hackle: Pheasant rump
Head: Filoplume wrapped as a collar

Gartside Sparrow – Tan (Matt Supinski)
Hook: Short nymph, size 4-8
Thread: Brown or gray
Tail: Filoplume
Body: Tan dubbing
Hackle: Pheasant rump
Head: Filoplume wrapped as a collar

Hex Wiggle Nymph (Matt Supinski)
Hook: 2 hooks with nymph hook in rear and egg hook
       up front held together with monofilament loop
Thread: Brown
Tail: Pheasant tail
Rib: Fine oval silver tinsel
Body: Cream yarn or dubbing on rear hook
Gills: Filoplume tied on top
Legs and wing case: Pheasant tail
Head: Orange ostrich herl
Eyes: Black plastic

Filoplume Hex (Walt Grau)

Hook: 4x long nymph, size 4-8
Thread: Yellow
Tail: Brown hackle fibers
Rib: Fine gold oval tinsel
Gills: Filoplume tied in on top of abdomen
Body: Yellowish, cream dubbing
Wing case: Brown turkey
Hackle: Light brown hen
Eyes: Mono or plastic eyes

Squirrel Hex Nymph (Dave Roller)

Hook: 4x long nymph, size 4-8
Thread: Yellow
Tail: Pheasant tail fibers
Rib: Fine copper oval tinsel
Abdomen: Yellow dubbing
Wing case: Pheasant tail fibers, same as used for tail
Thorax: Squirrel guard hairs dubbed thick using a dubbing loop or dubbing tool
Head: Tan dubbing
Eyes: Mono or plastic eyes

Wigular Hex (James Empie)

Hook: Extra short nymph hook, size 6-8
Thread: Yellow
Tail: Pheasant tail
Extended body: Tan antron
Body: Light yellow dubbing
Wing case: Tan antron over length of hook shank
Hackle: Light hen wound through thorax
Eyes: Small mono or plastic eyes

Hex Nymph (Jason Frank)

Hook: 4x long nymph, size 4-8
Thread: Brown
Tail: Pheasant tail fibers
Body: Cream dubbing or yarn
Legs: Hen hackle wound through thorax starting with long filoplume fibers
Wing case: Brown Swiss Straw
Eyes: Mono or plastic eyes

Bear's Hex Nymph (Jeff Andrews)

Hook: 4x long nymph, size 4-8
Thread: Brown
Tail: Three strands of natural gray ostrich herl
Rib: Fine silver wire
Body: Cream or light yellow antron dubbing
Gills: Filoplume tied on top
Back and wing case: Pheasant tail
Hackle: Gray soft hackle palmered through thorax
Eyes: Black plastic

Winter's Midge (Matt Supinski)

Hook: Tiemco 2457, size 12-14
Thread: Black
Rib: Very small flat silver tinsel
Body: Black thread or floss
Wing: White Z-lon
Head: Gray dubbing

Orange-Throated Wooly Sculpin (Kelly Galloup)

Hook: Up eye salmon, size 2-8
Thread: Black
Tail: Black marabou
Body: Black marabou plume wrapped forward
Hackle: Black stripped down one side
Head: Black deer hair clipped to muddler style
Throat: Orange Glo Bug yarn

Turkey Bugger (Kelly Galloup)

Hook: Up eye salmon, size 2-8
Thread: Brown
Tail: Turkey marabou
Body: Turkey marabou wrapped forward
Hackle: Brown stripped down one side
Head: Black rabbit dubbing

Wooly Bugger

Hook: Up eye salmon, size 4-8
Thread: Color to match body
Tail: Black marabou
Body: Black chenille
Hackle: Black saddle hackle palmered the length of body
NOTE: Purple and olive have also been very effective colors.

Zonker

Hook: Up eye salmon, size 2-6
Thread: Black or red
Body: Gold mylar tubing
Wing: Natural rabbit strip tied in at bend and head
Collar: Natural grizzly hackle
NOTE: A wide variety of color combinations can be effective. White with pearl body has worked very well when baitfish populations are high.

Bunny Leech

Hook: Up eye salmon, size 2-6
Thread: Black
Tail: A portion of rabbit strip tied in for body that extends back of bend
Body: Rabbit strip tied in at bend and palmered forward
Eyes: Dumbbell style sized to reach desired depth
NOTE: Black, purple, or olive are effective colors.

Egg Sucking Leech

Hook: Up eye salmon, size 4-8
Thread: Color to match egg
Tail: Black or purple marabou
Body: Black or purple chenille
Hackle: Black or purple saddle hackle palmered the
      length of body
Head: Egg-colored chenille

Egg Sucking Bunny Leech

Hook: Up eye salmon, size 2-8
Thread: Orange or chartreuse
Body: Rainbow Lite Brite, cut and dubbed
Wing: Black or purple rabbit tied at bend and head
Head: Orange or chartreuse Steelhead and Salmon
      Dubbin in the shape of an egg

Estaz Egg Sucking Leech (Greg Liu)

Hook: Streamer hook, size 2-4
Thread: White
Body: Pearl Estaz
Wing: White rabbit strip
Head: Pink chenille wrapped to form egg

Super Chief (Charlie Dickson)

Hook: Tiemco 9395, size 6-8
Thread: Black
Tail: Purple marabou
Body: Orange chenille
Hackle: Purple palmered
Eyes: Orange painted dumbbell

Seneca Special (Charlie Dickson)

Hook: Daiichi 2055, size 1/0-3
Thread: Red 8/0
Rib: Oval gold tinsel
Body: Orange seal type dubbing
Wing: Purple rabbit strip fastened matuka-style
Hackle: Purple teal

Marabou Leech

Hook: Up eye salmon, size 1/0-4
Thread: To match color of marabou
Body: Four or five clumps of marabou tied in on
      top of hook shank

Steelhead Sculpin (Nick Pionessa)

Hook: Tiemco 9395, size 2
Rib: Red copper wire
Body: Purple angora goat, heavy lead wire wrapped
      around hook shank
Wing: Black rabbit strip
Head: Black deer hair spun and trimmed
Eyes: Dumbbell eyes tied in on bottom of hook shank

Starburst (Matt Supinski)

Hook: Daiichi 2050, size 3
Thread: Black
Body: A few wraps of red ostrich herl
Hackle: Mottled dyed orange turkey flank marabou

Chartreuse Tazmanian Devil (Matt Supinski)

Hook: Streamer, size 4-6
Thread: Chartreuse
Tail: Chartreuse rabbit strip with a few strands of
      green and gold Flashabou
Body: Chartreuse Estaz
Hackle: Chartreuse palmered through body
Legs: Hoola hoop legs
Head: Gold bead

Purple and Cerise Bunny Tube (Greg Liu)

Thread: Black
Tail: Cerise rabbit strip
Body: Purple rabbit strip palmered over tube
NOTE: Tube flies are tied on a hollow tube instead of
      the hook shank. To fish the tube fly, the leader is
      threaded through the tube and a short-shanked
      hook is tied to the end of the leader. The tube can
      be made of weightless plastic or heavily weighted
      copper, giving this style of fly great versatility.

Purple Bunny Tube (Greg Liu)

Thread: Black
Tail: Purple rabbit strip
Body: Purple rabbit strip palmered over tubing

White Marabou Tube (Greg Liu)

Thread: Red
Tail: Red Z-lon tied around tube
Rear Hackle: Two turns of white marabou
Body: Silver tinsel with more red Z-lon tied in
      around tube near head
Front Hackle: Three turns of white marabou
Collar: Red saddle hackle

Cerise and Black Bunny Tube (Greg Liu)

Thread: Black
Tail: Black rabbit strip
Body: Black rabbit strip
Collar: Two wraps of cerise rabbit strip

Orange Catnip (Rick Kustich)

Hook: Up eye salmon, size 6-10
Thread: Red 8/0
Tag: Silver tinsel
Body: Orange Steelhead and Salmon Dubbin
Hackle: Orange soft hackle
Wing: Yellow calf tail

Chartreuse Catnip (Rick Kustich)

Hook: Up eye salmon, size 6-10
Thread: Yellow 8/0
Tag: Silver tinsel
Body: Chartreuse Steelhead and Salmon Dubbin
Hackle: Chartreuse soft hackle
Wing: Orange calf tail

Citation (Rick Kustich)

Hook: Up eye salmon, size 6-10
Thread: Yellow 8/0
Tag: Natural hen neck fibers
Rib: small copper wire
Body: Summer duck SLF
Hackle: Natural hen neck
Wing: Filoplume from natural pheasant rump

Malinda

Hook: Up eye salmon, size 6-8
Thread: Tan 6/0
Tag: Flat gold tinsel
Tail: Purple hackle fibers
Rib: Three turns of oval or flat silver tinsel over floss
Body: Rear quarter chartreuse floss, middle quarter
        hot orange floss, front half purple chenille
Wing: Tan bucktail
Hackle: Purple webby saddle, collar style and tied
        with fibers extending to hook point

Night Dancer (Dave Barber)

Hook: Up eye salmon, size 10
Thread: Black
Tail: Black hackle fibers
Butt: Chartreuse wool
Body: Black antron/hare's ear blend
Hackle: Purple saddle

First Light (Rick Kustich)

Hook: Up eye salmon, size 4-8
Thread: Purple 8/0
Tag: Silver tinsel
Body: Purple Steelhead and Salmon Dubbin
Wing: Purple dyed teal feather tips
Hackle: Orange soft hackle

Orange Spade (Brian Slavinski)

Hook: Up eye salmon, size 6-10
Thread: Orange 8/0
Tag: Silver tinsel
Body: First yellow then orange ostrich herl tied in
        spade style
Hackle: A few turns of soft, short yellow over
        longer white

Chartreuse Spade (Brian Slavinski)

Hook: Up eye salmon, size 6-10
Thread: Pink 8/0
Tag: Silver tinsel
Body: Chartreuse ostrich herl tied in spade style
Hackle: A few turns of soft, longer white over
        shorter pink

The Petite Steelhead Series (John Valk)

Hook: Kamasan B220 black nymph hook or up eye
        salmon, size 6-10
Thread: Black or olive
Tag: Silver or gold flat tinsel
Rib: Silver or gold flat tinsel
Body: Uni-stretch body floss
Thorax: Peacock herl
Wing: 2 or 3 layers of spooled antron, dependent
        on hook size
Collar: 2 or 3 turns of grizzly hen hackle or
        Hoffman Chicabou hackle

Petite Black

Body: Black
Wing: Black

Petite Purple

Body: Purple
Wing: Purple

Petite Olive

Body: Olive
Wing: Chartreuse

Petite Orange

Body: Orange
Wing: Chartreuse

Petite Pink

Body: Pink
Wing: White

Petite Green

Body: Chartreuse
Wing: Chartreuse

Nick at Night (Nick Pionessa)

Hook: Up eye salmon, size 6-8
Thread: Purple
Tail: Purple hackle fibers
Rib: Silver tinsel
Body: Fuchsia angora goat dubbing
Hackle: Dark purple soft hackle
Wing: White calf tail

Row one: Glo Bug   Nuclear Roe Bug   Cactus Fly   Estaz Egg
Row two: Frammus   Salmon Flea   Carpet Fly   Sucker Spawn
Row three: Halo Egg   Egg Omelet   Pom-Pom Stone   Thugmeister Stone
Row four: Caddis Larvae   Soft Hackle Caddis   Reverse Caddis   Nympho
Row five: Steelhead Hare's Ear   Flashback Pheasant Tail Stone   Claret Stone   Creepy Stone

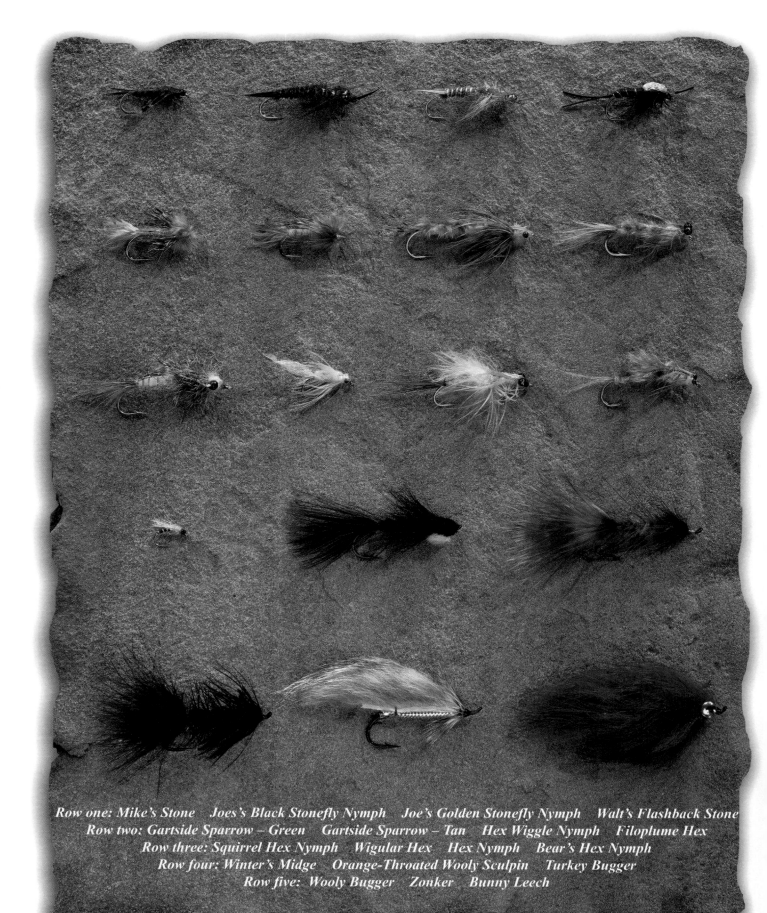

Row one: Mike's Stone   Joes's Black Stonefly Nymph   Joe's Golden Stonefly Nymph   Walt's Flashback Stone
Row two: Gartside Sparrow – Green   Gartside Sparrow – Tan   Hex Wiggle Nymph   Filoplume Hex
Row three: Squirrel Hex Nymph   Wigular Hex   Hex Nymph   Bear's Hex Nymph
Row four: Winter's Midge   Orange-Throated Wooly Sculpin   Turkey Bugger
Row five: Wooly Bugger   Zonker   Bunny Leech

Row one: Egg Sucking Leech   Egg Sucking Bunny Leech   Estaz Egg Sucking Leech
Row two: Super Chief   Seneca Special   Marabou Leech
Row three: Steelhead Sculpin   Starburst   Chartreuse Tazmanian Devil
Row four: Purple and Cerise Bunny Tube   Purple Bunny Tube
Row five: White Marabou Tube   Cerise and Black Bunny Tube

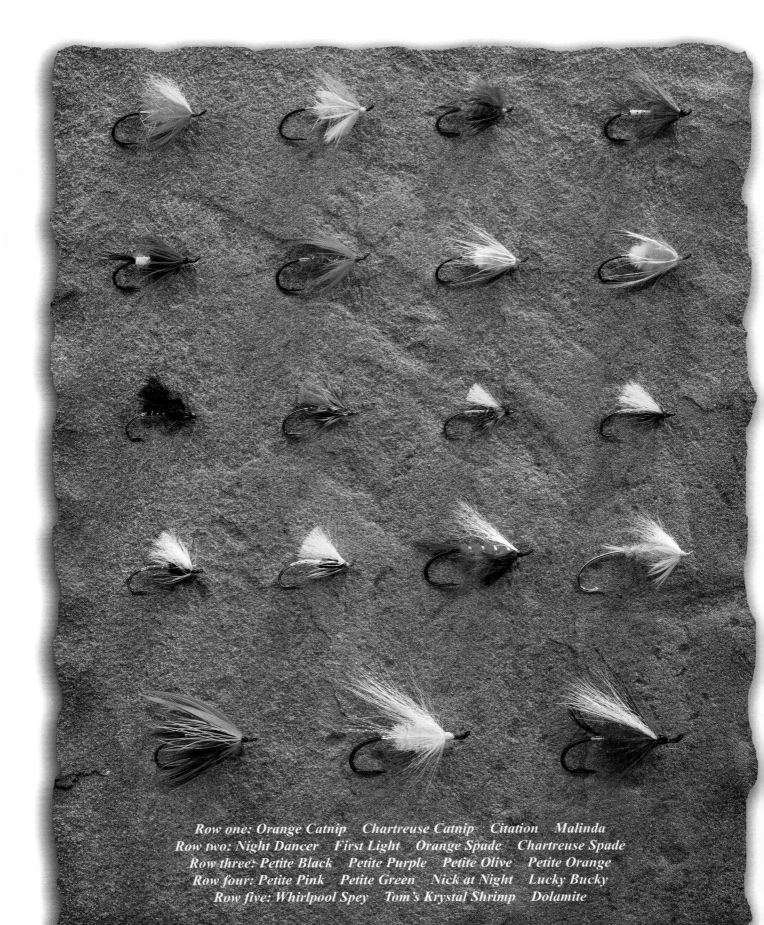

Row one: Orange Catnip   Chartreuse Catnip   Citation   Malinda
Row two: Night Dancer   First Light   Orange Spade   Chartreuse Spade
Row three: Petite Black   Petite Purple   Petite Olive   Petite Orange
Row four: Petite Pink   Petite Green   Nick at Night   Lucky Bucky
Row five: Whirlpool Spey   Tom's Krystal Shrimp   Dolamite

Row one: Joe's Perch   Joe's Niagara Shiner   Joe's Niagara Smelt
Row two: Old Nine Mile   Tyson Parr   The Tiger
Row three: Thugmeister   Thugmeister Spey   Small Orange Spey   Joe's Leech
Row four: Bear's Blue Guinea   Bush Weasel   Olive OTL   Purple OTL
Row five: Purple Bunny Spey   Black Bunny Spey   White Bunny Spey

Row one: Purple & Orange Marabou Spey   Black & Chartreuse Marabou Spey   Devil's Advocate
Row two: The Devil's Brother   P.P.   Bad Hair Day
Row three: Milwaukee Spey   Green Butt Skunk Spey   Winter's Hope Spey
Row four: Dark Water Spey   Orange and Red Spey   Chartreuse Kingfisher Spey
Row five: Purple Snow Spey   White Conehead Spey

Row one: Purple October   September Spey   Orange Spey
Row two: Olive Spey   Black Schmidt's Spey   Natural Schmidt's Spey
Row three: The Instigator   Nick's Purple Spey   Nick's Olive Spey
Row four: Muddy Waters   Sasa   Adam's Fancy
Row five: Niagara Sunrise (Three styles) – Spey Style   Simple Married Wing   Dee Style Strip Wing

Row one: Green Highlander   Gordon   Nighthawk
Row two: Sweep   Kate   Yellow Floodtide
Row three: Fuchsia Floodtide   Purple Floodtide   Gray Ghost Tube
Row four: Tommy's Hot Bee   Speed Skater   Bucky Bomber   Waller Waker
Row five: Black Surface Muddler   Muddler Caddis   Steelhead Red Quill   Rusty Steelhead Spinner

Luck Bucky (Rob McCormick)
Hook: Daiichi 2055, size 1½-7
Thread: Yellow 8/0 Uni-thread
Tail: Yellow hackle fibers
Body: Hot orange SLF
Rib: Gold oval tinsel
Hackle: Yellow soft hackle
Wing: White calf tail

Whirlpool Spey (Joe Penich)
Hook: Daiichi 2051, size 7
Thread: Black
Tag: Small flat silver tinsel
Body: Purple seal's fur or substitute
Wing: Orange goose shoulder
Hackle: Purple schlappen
Collar: Yellow schlappen

Tom's Krystal Shrimp (Tom Cornell)
Hook: Up eye salmon, size 2-8
Thread: Yellow 8/0
Tag: Silver tinsel
Tail: Lime green Krystal Flash
Body: Chartreuse Ice Chenille
Hackle: Yellow
Wing: Lime green Krystal Flash over white polar
    bear or white calf tail

Dolamite (Pat Dolan)
Hook: Up eye salmon, size 2-8
Thread: Black 8/0
Tag: Silver tinsel
Tail: Black hackle fibers
Body: Purple Ice Chenille
Hackle: Purple
Wing: Black Krystal Flash over white polar bear
    or white calf tail

Joe's Perch (Joe Penich)
Hook: Streamer hook, size 4-8
Thread: Black 8/0
Body: Metallic tape covered by gold mylar tubing
Throat: Orange CDC fiber puffs
Wing: White under yellow Gehrke's Fish Fuzz
    barred with green marker
Topping: Four strands of peacock herl
Eyes: Gold 3-D eyes

Joe's Niagara Shiner (Joe Penich)
Hook: Streamer hook, size 4-8
Thread: Black 8/0
Body: Metallic tape covered by small silver mylar
    tubing
Throat: White CDC oiler puffs

Wing: Four strands of peacock herl over white
    Gehrke's Fish Fuzz
Eyes: Gold 3-D eyes

Joe's Niagara Smelt (Joe Penich)
Hook: Streamer hook, size 4-8
Thread: Black 8/0
Body: Flat silver mylar tinsel
Throat: White Gehrke's Fish Fuzz
Wing: Four strands peacock herl over white Gehrke's
    Fish Fuzz
Eyes: Gold 3-D eyes

Old Nine Mile (Rob McCormick)
Hook: Streamer, size 6-8
Thread: Black
Body: Flat silver tinsel ribbed with oval silver
Wing: Peacock herl over fine gray bucktail over fine
    white bucktail
Eyes: Painted

Tyson Parr (Matt Supinski)
Hook: Short streamer, size 6-8
Thread: Black
Wing: Yellow barred saddle tips over pearl Flashabou
    over green Flashabou over white Fly Fur
Eyes: Painted

The Tiger (Walt Grau)
Hook: Up eye salmon, size 2-4
Thread: Red
Body: Pearl Poly Flash
Throat: Fine orange bucktail
Wing: Green bucktail over chartreuse barred saddle
    hackle over yellow bucktail—a few strands of
    green and pearl Flashabou as well as chartreuse
    Krystal Flash are included in the wing

Thugmeister (Matt Supinski)
Hook: Up eye salmon, size 2-4
Thread: Black
Body: Silver tinsel over rear half, purple chenille
    then blue Flashabou
Wing: Purple marabou over purple Krystal Flash over
    brown Krystal Flash over two black saddles
    with a few strands of silver and blue Flashabou

Thugmeister Spey (Matt Supinski)
Hook: Up eye salmon, size 2-6
Body: Purple Flashabou through rear three-quarters
    and peacock herl for front quarter
Wing: Two black saddle hackles
Hackle: Purple schlappen
Collar: Natural guinea

Small Orange Spey (John Valk)

Hook: Kamasan B 220, size 8-12
Tag: Gold tinsel
Rib: Gold tinsel
Body: Orange floss
Wing: Orange Hoffman Chickabou
Head: Three turns orange ostrich herl

Joe's Leech (Joe Penich)

Hook: Daiichi 2051, size 7
Thread: Black
Rib: Red, silver or copper wire
Body: Black micro chenille
Wing: Black rabbit strip
Collar: Black rabbit strip guard hairs

Bear's Blue Guinea (Jeff Andrews)

Hook: Up eye salmon, size 6-8
Thread: Black
Tag: Silver flat tinsel
Rib: Fine oval silver tinsel
Body: Light blue floss
Underwing: White bucktail
Wing: Natural teal
Collar: Blue dyed guinea

Bush Weasel (Jeff Andrews)

Hook: Up eye salmon, size 4-8
Thread: Black
Tag: Flat silver tinsel
Rib: Flat silver tinsel
Body: Black dubbing
Hackle: Black schlappen through entire body
Wing: Teal
Throat: Teal
Collar: Black hen saddle

Olive OTL (Nick Pionessa)

Hook: Tiemco 200 OTL, size 2-4
Thread: Olive
Tail: Olive marabou
Rib: Copper wire
Body: Olive dubbing
Hackle: Mallard or wood duck
Head: Gold or orange tungsten bead

Purple OTL (Nick Pionessa)

Hook: Tiemco 200, size 2-4
Thread: Purple
Tail: Black marabou
Rib: Red copper wire
Body: Purple haze Salmon and Steelhead SLF
Hackle: Black schlappen
Head: Gold or orange tungsten bead

Purple Bunny Spey (Rick Kustich)

Hook: Up eye salmon, size 1/0-4
Thread: Purple 8/0
Rib: Small copper wire
Body: Purple haze Salmon and Steelhead SLF
Wing: Purple rabbit hair fastened matuka-style with rib
Hackle: Purple schlappen
Collar: Purple jumbo guinea

Black Bunny Spey (Rick Kustich)

Hook: Up eye salmon, size 1/0-4
Thread: Black 8/0
Rib: Small copper wire
Body: Rainbow Lite Brite
Wing: Black rabbit strip fastened matuka-style with rib
Hackle: Black schlappen
Collar: Natural jumbo guinea

White Bunny Spey (Rick Kustich)

Hook: Up eye salmon, 1/0-4
Thread: Red 8/0
Rib: Small copper wire
Body: Purple Haze Lite Brite
Wing: White rabbit strip fastened matuka-style with rib
Hackle: White schlappen
Collar: Natural jumbo guinea

Purple & Orange Marabou Spey (Rick Kustich)

Hook: Daiichi 2051, size 3-5
Thread: Purple 8/0
Tag: Silver tinsel
Rib: Silver tinsel
Body: Purple Steelhead and Salmon Dubbin
Hackle: Purple over orange Hareline marabou
    spey hackle
Collar: Purple jumbo guinea

Black & Chartreuse Marabou Spey (R. Kustich)

Hook: Daiichi 2051, size 3-5
Thread: Black 8/0
Tag: Chartreuse Uni-stretch
Body: Rainbow Lite Brite
Hackle: Black over chartreuse Hareline marabou
    spey hackle
Collar: Natural jumbo guinea

Devil's Advocate (Rick Kustich)

Hook: Daiichi 2051, size 3-5
Thread: Red 8/0
Tag: Orange Uni-stretch
Body: Polar Pearl Lite Brite, cut and dubbed
Hackle: White Hareline marabou spey hackle
Collar: Natural jumbo guinea

The Devil's Brother (Rick Kustich)
Hook: Daiichi 2051, size 3-5
Thread: Purple 8/0
Tag: Orange Uni-stretch
Body: Purple Haze Salmon and Steelhead SLF
Hackle: Purple Hareline marabou spey hackle
Collar: Purple jumbo guinea

P.P. (Rob McCormick)
Hook: Daiichi 2051, size 3-5
Thread: Olive 8/0
Rib: Gold oval tinsel
Body: Olive dubbing
Hackle: Olive Hareline marabou spey hackle
Collar: Green dyed guinea

Bad Hair Day (Rick Kustich)
Hook: Daiichi 2051, size 3-5
Thread: Orange 8/0
Body: Summer duck SLF
Hackle: Long brown marabou
Collar: Orange dyed pheasant rump

Milwaukee Spey (Bob Blumreich)
Hook: Daiichi 2051, size 1½
Thread: Black
Rib: Medium flat silver followed by fine oval
    silver tinsel
Body: Rear half hot pink, front half black seal
    or substitute
Hackle: Imitation heron belly dyed hot pink
Throat: Mallard flank dyed hot pink
Wing: Strips of black goose

Green Butt Skunk Spey (Bob Blumreich)
Hook: Daiichi 2051, size 1½
Thread: Red
Butt: Fluorescent lime floss, underwrap with
    silver tinsel
Tail: Golden pheasant crest dyed bright red
Rib: Medium flat silver followed by fine oval
Body: Black dyed seal or substitute
Hackle: Black schlappen or imitation heron
Throat: Mallard flank dyed chartreuse
Wing: Narrow strips of white goose or turkey

Winter's Hope Spey (Bob Blumreich)
Hook: Daiichi 2051, size 1½
Thread: Red
Body: Rear half flat silver tinsel, front half
    powder blue seal or substitute
Hackle: Imitation heron belly dyed powder blue
Throat: Purple schlappen
Wing: Strips of orange goose

Dark Water Spey (Ray Schmidt)
Hook: Tiemco 7999 sized for preference or water
    conditions
Thread: Bright red or cherry 3/0 monocord or single
    strand floss
Body: One red and one purple marabou plume, stripped
    down one side. Start with the red at halfway
    point on the shank and palmer forward. Tie in
    the purple at the red endpoint and palmer
    forward.
Wing: Four purple and two red Flashabou
Collar: One black marabou, stripped and wound at head

Orange and Red Spey (Ray Schmidt)
Hook: Tiemco 7999 sized for preference or water
    conditions
Thread: Bright red or Cherry 3/0 monocord or single
    strand floss
Body: Two orange marabou plumes, stripped down one
    side. Start first one at halfway point on the hook
    shank, palmered forward, followed by the second
    strand to finish wrap.
Wing: Six strands of red Flashabou
Collar: One red marabou strand stripped and wound in
    at head

Chartreuse Kingfisher Spey (Ray Schmidt)
Hook: Tiemco 7999 sized for preference or water
    conditions
Thread: Bright red or cherry 3/0 monocord or single
    strand floss
Body: Two chartreuse marabou plumes, stripped down
    one side. Start first one at halfway point on the
    hook shank, palmered forward, followed by the
    second strand to finish wrap.
Wing: Four strands pearl and two strands red Flashabou
Collar: One kingfisher blue marabou or schlappen
    strand stripped and wound at head

Purple Snow Spey (Ray Schmidt)
Hook: Tiemco 7999 sized for preference or water
    conditions
Thread: Bright red or cherry 3/0 monocord or single
    strand floss
Body: Two white marabou plumes, stripped down one
    side. Start first one at halfway point on the hook
    shank and palmer forward, followed by the
    second strand to finish wrap.
Wing: Four strands white and two strands purple
    Flashabou
Collar: One purple marabou strand stripped and wound
    at head

White Conehead Spey

Hook: Tiemco 9395
Thread: White
Tail: White marabou
Hackle: White marabou
Cone: Gold

Purple October (Rick Kustich)

Hook: Daiichi 2051, size 3-5
Thread: Purple 8/0
Tag: Silver tinsel
Rib: Silver tinsel
Body: Purple Steelhead and Salmon Dubbin
First Hackle: Purple heron substitute wound
    through front half of body
Second Hackle: Orange dyed pheasant rump
Collar: Purple jumbo guinea
Wing: Purple arctic fox

September Spey (Rick Kustich)

Hook: Daicchi 2051, size 3-5
Thread: Yellow 8/0
Rib: Silver tinsel
Body: Light golden olive Diamond Braid
First Hackle: Olive heron substitute wound
    through front of body
Second Hackle: Olive dyed pheasant rump
Collar: Olive guinea
Wing: Barred olive hackle

Orange Spey (Rick Kustich)

Hook: Daiichi 2051, size 3-5
Thread: Purple 8/0
Tag: Orange Uni-stretch
Rib: Gold tinsel
Body: Fluorescent orange SLF
Hackle: Orange heron substitute
Collar: Purple jumbo guinea

Olive Spey (Rick Kustich)

Hook: Daiichi 2051, size 3-5
Thread: Yellow 8/0
Rib: Gold tinsel
Body: Medium olive SLF
Hackle: Olive heron substitute
Collar: Purple jumbo guinea

Black Schmidt's Spey (Ray Schmidt)

Hook: Daiichi 2161, size 1 or 2
Thread: Black
Tag: Ultra green chenille
Rib: Gold or copper Krystal Flash
Body Hackle: Black pheasant rump
Body: Kaufman Blend dubbing (dark stone)
Collar: Black pheasant rump

Natural Schmidt's Spey (Ray Schmidt)

Hook: Daiichi 2161, size 1 or 2
Thread: Black
Tag: Ultra red chenille
Rib: Gold or copper Krystal Flash
Body Hackle: Natural pheasant rump
Body: Kaufman Blend dubbing (dark stone)
Collar: Natural pheasant rump

The Instigator (Charlie Dickson)

Hook: Daiichi 2055, size 1/0-3
Thread: Red 8/0
Tag: Gold tinsel and yellow floss
Rib: Oval gold tinsel
Body Hackle: Yellow
Body: Orange seal-type dubbing
Hackle: Orange teal

Nick's Purple Spey (Nick Pionessa)

Hook: Daiichi 2051, size 5-7
Thread: Red
Tag: Silver tinsel
Butt: Pink Uni-stretch
Body: Purple Steelhead and Salmon Dubbin
Hackle: Black schlappen wound through body, then
    a few turns of pink and a few turns of purple
    heron substitute at head
Collar: Orange dyed guinea

Nick's Olive Spey (Nick Pionessa)

Hook: Daiichi 2051, size 3-5
Thread: Olive
Butt: Green copper wire
Body: Chartreuse Steelhead and Salmon Dubbin
Hackle: Mallard gray heron substitute through body
Collar: Mallard or wood duck

Muddy Waters (Brian Slavinski)

Hook: Daiichi 2055, size 7
Thread: Orange
Body: Chartreuse Pseudo Seal
Hackle: Chartreuse heron substitute wound
    through front half of body
Collar: Orange soft hackle or schlappen
Wing: Orange Polar Aire

Sasa (Brian Slavinski)

Hook: Daiichi 2055, size 5
Thread: Orange
Rib: Gold round tinsel
Body: Rear two-thirds chartreuse Pseudo Seal,
    front one-third orange Pseudo Seal
Hackle: Orange dyed blue-eared pheasant
Wing: Grizzly saddle hackle
Collar: Orange dyed guinea

Adam's Fancy (Brian Slavinski)
Hook: Daiichi 2055, size 5
Thread: Orange
Tag: Silver tinsel
Tail: Red dyed golden pheasant
Butt: Black ostrich
Rib: Silver tinsel
Body: Rear half pink Uni-stretch, front half
    chartreuse Pseudo Seal
Hackle: Chartreuse dyed blue-eared pheasant
Wing: Pink rooster
Collar: Peacock breast
Shoulder: Kingfisher

Niagara Sunrise – Spey Style (Rick Whorwood)
Hook: Gaelic Supreme blind eye
Hook Eye: 20 lb. Dacron
Body: Rear half fine flat tinsel, front half red seal
    fur or substitute
Rib: Medium oval silver
Hackle: Schlappen purple or any color
Throat: Guinea or teal
Wing Style: Spey Style Strip Wing

Niagara Sunrise – Simple Married Wing (Rick Whorwood)
Same as above except wing
Wing: Simple married wing—purple, red, orange,
    and yellow goose

Niagara Sunrise – Dee Style Strip Wing (Rick Whorwood)
Same as above except wing
Wing: Dee style strip wing—red turkey

Green Highlander (Mark Conway)
Hook: Daiichi 2055, size 5
Thread: Black
Tag: Flat gold tinsel
Body: Fluorescent yellow, chartreuse and
    highlander green seal fur in dubbing loop
Throat: Chartreuse cock hackle
Wing: Married strips of yellow, orange and
    chartreuse goose tied in short
Topping: Yellow arctic fox

Gordon (Mark Conway)
Hook: Daiichi 2051, size 3
Thread: Black
Tag: Oval silver tinsel and yellow silk
Tail: Fluorescent yellow marabou
Butt: Black ostrich herl
Body: One-third red silk and two-thirds yellow silk
Rib: Oval silver tinsel
Throat: Fluorescent blue cock hackle

Underwing: Purple dyed golden pheasant tips
Wing: Married strips of fluorescent yellow,
    fluorescent blue and claret goose, florican
    bustard and fluorescent yellow goose on top
Cheeks: Jungle cock

Nighthawk (Mark Conway)
Hook: Daiichi 2051, size 3
Thread: Black
Tag: Oval silver tinsel and yellow floss
Tail: Blue marabou
Butt: Red ostrich herl
Rib: Oval silver tinsel
Body: Flat silver tinsel
Throat: Black cock hackle
Wing: Black goose topped with chartreuse
Cheek: Jungle cock

Sweep (Mark Conway)
Hook: Daiichi 2051, size 3
Thread: Black
Tag: Flat silver tinsel
Tail: Golden pheasant crest
Body: Black silk
Rib: Fine oval tinsel
Throat: Black cock hackle
Wing: Black goose with blue and gold macaw

Kate (Mark Conway)
Hook: Daiichi 2051, size 3
Thread: Black
Tag: Oval silver tinsel and yellow silk
Tail: Blue macaw and golden pheasant crest
Butt: Black ostrich
Rib: Oval silver tinsel
Body: Red floss
Throat: Yellow cock hackle
Wing: Married strips of fluorescent yellow and
    red goose and speckled bustard
Cheek: Barred wood duck

Yellow Floodtide (Troy Standish)
Hook: Daiichi 2051, size 3
Thread: Black
Tag: Silver oval tinsel
Tail: Red floss
Butt: Black ostrich
Rib: Flat silver mylar followed by oval tinsel
Body: Rear three-quarters yellow floss, front quarter
    fiery yellow Salmon and Steelhead SLF
Hackle: Yellow Hareline marabou spey hackle
Collar: Red schlappen
Wing: Married strips of peacock, yellow, red, then
    repeated
Eye: Jungle cock

Fuchsia Floodtide (Troy Standish)
Hook: Daiichi 2051, size 3
Thread: Black
Tag: Silver oval tinsel
Tail: Red floss
Butt: Black ostrich
Rib: Flat silver mylar followed by oval tinsel
Body: Rear three-quarters silver/gray floss, front
    quarter silver/gray Salmon and Steelhead SLF
Hackle: Fuchsia Hareline marabou spey hackle
Collar: Purple schlappen
Wing: Married strips of peacock, fuchsia, red, then
    repeated
Eye: Jungle cock

Purple Floodtide (Troy Standish)
Hook: Daiichi 2051, size 3
Thread: Black
Tag: Silver oval tinsel
Tail: Red floss
Butt: Black ostrich
Rib: Flat silver mylar followed by oval tinsel
Body: Rear three-quarters orange floss, front quarter
    jaffa orange Salmon and Steelhead SLF
Hackle: Purple Hareline marabou spey hackle
Collar: Orange schlappen
Wing: Married strips of peacock, pink, purple,
    orange, then repeated
Eye: Jungle cock

Gray Ghost Tube (Troy Standish)
Tube: Heavy copper
Thread: Black
Rib: Silver tinsel
Body: Yellow floss
Underwing: White bucktail
Throat: Golden pheasant crest
Wing: Four gray saddles over peacock herl over
    golden pheasant crest
Shoulder: Silver pheasant
Eye: Jungle cock

Tommy's Hot Bee (Tom Cornell)
Hook: Daiichi 2050, size 7
Thread: Orange 3/0
Tail: Yellow dyed squirrel
Body: Yellow then orange then yellow deer hair,
    spun and trimmed
Hackle: Orange
Post: Yellow dyed squirrel

Speed Skater (Nick Pionessa)
Hook: Daiichi 2051, size 3-5
Thread: Orange or red

Tail: Fine orange bucktail
Body: Yellow deer hair spun and trimmed
Collar: Orange deer hair
Head: Orange deer hair spun and trimmed

Bucky Bomber (Rob McCormick)
Hook: Daiichi 2051, size 3-5
Thread: Red
Tail: Yellow calf tail
Body: Orange deer hair, loosely packed,
    spun and trimmed
Hackle: Yellow palmered through body
Wing: White calf tail

Waller Waker
Hook: Daiichi 2051 or Partridge C542
Thread: Black
Tail: Stiff black bucktail or moose
Body: Black and natural deer hair spun and trimmed
Throat: Stiff black bucktail or moose
Wing: White calf tail

Black Surface Muddler (Brian Slavinski)
Hook: Up eye salmon, size 6-8
Thread: Black
Tag: Silver tinsel
Butt: Chartreuse yarn
Body: Black dubbing
Hackle: Gray saddle palmered through body
Wing: Natural squirrel tail
Head: Black deer hair neatly trimmed

Muddler Caddis (Rick Kustich)
Hook: Up eye salmon, size 8-10
Thread: Black 3/0
Body: Rusty orange dubbing
Hackle: Brown palmered through body
Wing: Bleached elk
Head: Natural deer hair spun and trimmed

Steelhead Red Quill (Bob Morrissey)
Hook: Daiichi 2151, size 10-12
Thread: Gray 8/0 Uni-stretch
Tail: Dark dun micro fibets
Abdomen: Dyed goose biot
Thorax: Red quill TCO dubbing
Hackle: Dark dun cock hackle
Wing: Dark dun deer hair

Rusty Steelhead Spinner (Bob Morrissey)
Hook: Extra strong dry fly hook, size 8-14
Thread: Gray 6/0 Uni-thread
Abdomen: Rust dyed goose biot
Thorax: Gray thread medallion and sheeting on top

Part III
A Guide to the Rivers

Great Lakes

N
W E
S

One inch 63 miles
One inch 39 kilometers

0   63 miles

Quebec

Ontario

Mary's River

Lake
Huron

Georgian
Bay

Owen
Sound

Meaford

Wasaga
Beach

Lake
Simcoe

CANADA

U.S.

Watertown

Sable River

Oscoda

Southampton

Owen
Sound

Bighead River

Nottawasaga River

Ganaraska River

Port Hope

Lake
Ontario

Black River

Pulaski

Maitland River

Saugeen River

Oak Orchard Creek

Point
Breeze

Salmon River

Goderich

Grand River

Rochester

Brantford

Niagara River

Genesee River

Big Creek

Irving

New York

Lake
Erie

Erie

Conneaut

Cattaraugus Creek

Elk Creek

Conneaut Creek

Pennsylvania

Ohio

Introduction to the Rivers

Although the Great Lakes tributaries offer a diversity of fly fishing opportunities for steelhead, many require perfect timing and a creative approach. And while nearly every drainage in the entire system gets a run of steelhead, not all provide ideal situations for the serious fly fisher. In some cases, those who would compare Great Lakes tributaries to those of the West Coast may be disappointed. Both man-caused and natural limitations characterize fragmented angling possibilities throughout this fresh-water system, and the proximity to urban centers often provides an abundance of anglers. However, it is the challenge that makes this fishery unique, and ultimately the fish that make the effort worthwhile.

Over the years, we both have fished many quality waters worth the attention of any serious fly angler. What follows is a brief profile of some primary fly fishing waters located throughout the entire Great Lakes system. This is not intended to be a detailed "where to" section, but rather an identification of some destination waters that embody the true spirit of the Great Lakes steelhead. This is the main reason that we did not include "tell all" detailed maps. However, we have found the state-by-state Atlas & Gazetteer maps produced by the DeLorme Mapping Company to be an excellent source for finding rivers and access to them. From these starting points, the curious angler can begin to explore endless other possibilities while building a personal knowledge base for future trips.

Although these recommendations do not come without other competing anglers, it is important to remember that many Great Lakes tributaries get strong pulses of fish for many months of the year, thus dispersing angling pressure throughout a long season. Remember also that there are many variable factors that contribute to a successful steelhead experience—run timing and water conditions top the list. The thrill of the chase cannot be ignored, for we have traveled many miles for just a few fish. But the experiences in doing so have been unforgettable.

We have found that it often takes three days to become familiar with any river's personality. In fact, most successful steelheaders spend years identifying high-probability water that suits their fishing styles and tastes. Some of the most memorable moments of steelhead fishing involve self-discovery.

Many rivers have experienced guides who have spent years unlocking the secrets of familiar waters. For the most part, Great Lakes fly fishing guides are not abundant, and the good ones are always in high demand. Because the fickle nature of many tributaries requires an astute understanding of local waters, the most successful regional guides are passionately connected to the resource. It is this dedication, however, that limits the potential number of guides who truly are masters of their profession.

Since inclement weather defines the Great Lakes region, steelhead fishing is not for fair-weather anglers. High water almost always brings fish into the tributaries, but the price paid is usually a weather system that brings rain or snow. When primary water gets washed out for a day or two, we have included a few secondary tributaries in each region that may hold some good opportunities under such conditions. Because too much information is often as useless as too little, we have purposely not mentioned hundreds of other streams with varying degrees of potential that may be worth exploration by the adventuresome.

Including seasonal streams, there are 3,000 or so tributaries in the Great Lakes, and we've seen most of them. But the number we have fished is slightly less than 100. You can spend time fishing different water every year or you can settle upon a few rivers you like and get to know them intimately. Although there is value in both approaches, steelheading success in terms of catching fish is often linked to familiarity, and that means knowing your water. Whatever your intentions, this section provides some quality starting points—the rest is up to you. For the purpose of us capturing the true character of a river and for the fact that both of us were not able to fish every river covered, each river section has been written by one of us individually. That person's initials appear directly after the title of each river.

11

Lake Superior

Baptism/Knife Rivers (JK)

Minnesota is the land of walleye and northern pike, not steelhead, right? Actually catching a steelhead in the Minnesota tributaries of Lake Superior falls into the category of monumental challenges, but the thrill of the chase is well worth the effort. As discussed earlier in Part I, the steelhead dwelling in this part of the lake have fallen on hard times. In the heyday of the 50's, 60's, and 70's, these streams produced runs of rainbow trout in great numbers. But for many reasons, the precipitous decline of the fishery in this region since that time has continued until present day. Although the prospect for the future may look bleak, fishery managers have not given up hope. In fact, their encouragement inspires the serious angler to search these waters for an occasional pleasant surprise.

After several years of experimental stocking, most of Minnesota's north shore streams are now being managed for natural reproduction. While research indicates that each stream supports fish genetically programmed to return to specific rivers, these are normally spring-oriented fish which start showing up in the tributaries some time in April. It seems that once the walleye season opens, most attention is diverted away from steelhead. So when another burst of fish arrives from late May to early June, these fish usually go unnoticed by all but the astute steelheader. It should be noted that fall rains can also result in an irregular push of fish into various waters from late September until freeze out.

Highway 61 leads northeast directly out of Duluth following a beautiful shoreline pathway up to the Canadian border. This scenic two laner passes over the lower section of every Minnesota tributary at a point below most of the upstream barriers, and there are many pulloffs available which provide ample access to many of them. The most charming of them all is the Baptism River. Its dark, rich water flows into the lake some 60 miles from Duluth. There is about 1.3 miles of fishable water available before encountering the falls that prevent the upstream passage of steelhead. This river of pockets and deep holes stretching through an enchanting canyon requires creative techniques to fly fish the river's variable characteristics. There is an easy access rest area off Highway 61 built in conjunction with the Tettegouche State Park. The park provides handy full-service camping facilities and a comfortable trail to the falls. Because the best fishing approach to these north shore tributaries demands skipping around rather than spending long periods on any one in particular (unless you find fish), the Baptism offers a logical location to set up a base camp for exploring the region. Additionally, there is a system of hiking trails available throughout the area accessing the upper reaches of many streams, providing fishing opportunities for native populations of brook trout.

The scenic Baptism River. Jerry Kustich photo.

Back toward Duluth, Split Rock Creek requires a bit of a walk to search out its steelhead potential. Backtracking even further gets the angler to Minnesota's other notable north shore tributary—the Knife River. Although the water here often runs with a bit of a tinge, rain can dirty it substantially. The river is moderate in size—40 to 50 feet wide. Below the fish way, there are a series of runs cutting through a hard rock channel accessed again from a convenient rest stop. The fish here can be mixed stockers (clipped fins) as well as a unique wild strain. The number of wild fish in this system has always been highly variable, but more and more efforts are being directed to enhance the Knife's wild fish capabilities. The fish way found below the Highway 61 bridge allows only hand-sorted wild stock to access the many miles of spawning water above the highway. The character of the system changes upstream as the river breaks into several tributaries with stretches of gravel and spawning riffles. Only portions of this water are available to the angler, however, and regulations should be checked before venturing forth to the upper Knife.

Going the other way from the Baptism, the next notable tributary northward is the Devil Track River near the town of Grand Marnias. This pretty stream offers a mile or so of fishable water along with an access trail off a local forest road. Minnesota's Brule River is big but provides only a short stretch of worthwhile water at the Judge Magney State Park. Other tributaries with some potential include Kimball and Kadunce Creeks. Remember, there are several other possible streams all along the shoreline with short stretches that could be explored, but the very nature of the region limits one's enthusiasm. The appeal here is to enjoy the challenge of finding a Minnesota wild steelhead.

Big Two Hearted River (JK)

It depends to whom you talk or what map you examine—this river can be referred to as the Two Hearted River or the Big Two-Hearted, with or without a hyphen. This is a river of Michigan's Upper Peninsula entering the southeast shoreline of Lake Superior not far from the resting place of the famous shipwrecked freighter, the Edmund Fitzgerald. In this region, it is said that "big" is usually added to the name of a tributary after all its forks come together. If that is the case, we are then concerned mainly with the Big Two Hearted portion of the river.

The Big Two-Hearted, with a hyphen, gets its notoriety from the pen of Ernest Hemingway, whose enchanting short story "The Big Two-Hearted River" has been acclaimed as one of the best fishing pieces ever written. However, according to Robert Traver, a.k.a John Voelker, author and judge who spent a lifetime angling the waters of the Peninsula, Hemingway used the Big Two-Hearted as an alias to disguise the real river of which he wrote.

Traver states that Hemingway intended "to fool and divert the multitude from the real place he had in mind" because such a man "is not going to snitch on any water he truly loves, least of all in writing." Oh, well. With that in mind we wandered off to locate the "famous" Big Two Hearted, with no hyphen, because of its reputation as excellent springtime steelhead water.

As it turned out, the river wasn't too easy to locate; maybe that was Hemingway's ruse all along. We made a few wrong turns, then a few correct ones that led us through sandy back roads and stunted conifers until we eventually reached the campground at the mouth of the river. Later we learned it would have been easier to take H37 north of Newberry to gravel road 410, turn right and follow that to the Reed and Green Bridge which crosses the river leading to 423, then left to the same location where we were standing. When we headed for the river's mouth, it was then we found that the Big Two Hearted is apparently a well-known destination point for many anglers who obviously had no problem finding the river. Lawn chairs were stretched for a hundred feet below the river's entry point into the chilled waters of the lake. The fishermen and women were chucking lures and bait to a run of fish that hadn't yet shown up. This river is supplemented with annual stockings of steelhead, but it is estimated that over half of the returning fish are naturally reared in the system.

A long, very cold winter that lingered into spring had probably delayed the run significantly. This is not uncommon in the Great Lakes under such conditions, and we learned subsequently that the fish arrived in full force one week later. Usually, we were told, the fish show up here in the middle of May and they hang around well into the early part of June. This particular year, the peak of the event was shifted back a week to ten days. Since there are always a few fish around at times when they should be, we explored the river with the undying optimism of committed steelheaders.

The character of the river's lower portion is a combination of broad gravel and deep runs very suitable for classic steelhead techniques. The blood-red tinge of the water, reflecting the abundance of iron in the region, is probably a coincidence given the river's name. Access here can be obtained from the parking area at the mouth by walking upstream to various sections of water. Access to the upper sections can be attained by following 410 back to the Reed and Green Bridge. The character of the river at this point above and below the bridge is much more typical of Michigan rivers. The water here is more contained within its forested banks; deep sand and gravel bars give way to even deeper holes and runs that undercut banks stacked in places with downfall or overhanging brush. Wading the edges was difficult, and crossing the river wasn't a good option. Traversing the bridge, we followed a side road downstream that accessed the river in spots between private property boundaries. It was here we talked to a few locals who confirmed the lack of fish in the river so far that year, but later in the day, we had the good fortune to spot two steelies as we fished downstream from the bridge.

The appeal of the Big Two Hearted lies in its remoteness. Michigan's Upper Peninsula or "U.P." offers a wide range of other natural activities as well. The bird observatory and the ship museum at Whitefish Point, Seney National Wildlife Area, and Pictured Rocks National Lakeshore are but a few other distractions for the avid steelheader.

The Big Two Hearted is also known for its fall runs of salmon, brown trout, and brookies. Like most Lake Superior tributaries, autumn runs of steelhead are weak and dependent upon rain, and normally severe weather and cold temperatures set in before the optimum time period for consistent fall steelheading.

There is certainly a vast area to explore within Michigan's Upper Peninsula, offering many options throughout late spring if an angler is willing to travel around. Since the nature of Lake Superior's spring steelhead runs are unpredictable, keeping all alternatives open may be an important consideration in determining a successful steelhead trip. In this spirit, through the wilderness of the Huron Mountains northwest of Marquette runs the pristine waters of the Huron River which can produce wonderful action for wild Superior steelhead. There are other waters available in this rugged portion of the UP, but an experienced guide is recommended.

From the town of Baraga at the base of the Keweenaw Peninsula, there are several other rivers that can also be explored during an expedition to this remote region of Michigan. Starting with the Sturgeon River, two other notables are the Ontonagon and the Firesteel Rivers. Of course, there are several other waters well worth looking into as well.

From the Big Two Hearted to the Montreal River on the western border between Michigan and Wisconsin, the Upper Peninsula offers many steelhead possibilities in a region of the United States which can still offer some exciting outdoor challenges to the adventuresome.

Brule River (JK)

In a land where only the hearty survives, the lovely Bois Brule River (commonly referred to as just "the Brule") cuts its way through a mixed forest of hardwoods and conifers until it empties into the south shore waters of Lake Superior in the far northeastern portion of Wisconsin. This unique corridor possessing just a touch of historical wilderness has been wisely designated the Brule River State Forest. Picturesque foot trails along a wooded shoreline and ample boat launch facilities provide ready access to its bounty. In close proximity to the city of Duluth, the river is frequented by many serious anglers from northern Minnesota as well as Wisconsin. Although the Brule is renowned for supporting natural populations of both brown and brook trout, the traditions of this water as a premier steelhead stream date back to the 1920's when fishermen came from great distances to challenge its big rainbow trout. In fact, the Brule produced two state record rainbow by the mid 1960's.

The Brule is a moderate-sized river offering ideal wading conditions for the serious fly angler. Although there are some easy-to-cross sections, care should be utilized depending upon the flow. The bottom consists of small rocks, sand, and gravel. Its series of riffles, runs, pools, and boulder pockets create classic holding water that is easy to reach with a variety of fly fishing techniques. Although catch rates here do not compare to the prolific production streams elsewhere in the Great Lakes, combined with a wonderful sense of connection to the "natural," visiting the Brule becomes more than just a fishing expedition. It provides a pleasurable outdoor experience on many levels.

Management techniques during the 1990's have been directed to restore the steelhead fishery that went through some lean times during the mid 80's. A relaxing of regulations leading to a year-round fishing season in 1982 seemed to precipitate the decline of the fisheries between 1984 and 1988. Overharvest by a growing number of anglers combined with increased offshore harvesting and improved techniques all spelled doom for the Brule River steelhead. This crisis prompted Wisconsin DNR to take drastic measures to preserve this unique strain of Lake Superior steelhead. The department's efforts are intended to restore this wild run naturally while using minimal hatchery influence. A seasonal closing of prime spawning water south of Highway 2 provides needed sanctuary once the fish wind their way unscathed through prime fishing water. A one fish over 26" bag limit has also been introduced, and an aggressive education program has been instituted preaching the values of catch and release for the future quality of this worthy Wisconsin fishery.

Timing is everything when visiting the Brule. Fish counts at the lamprey barrier/fish way indicate peak time on the river ranges from mid September to mid October and again from the end of March through mid April. Best fishing occurs when a flush of water from passing rainstorms allows fish movement upstream. Since the Brule runs through wooded areas influenced greatly by underground springs, water drops and clears quickly after moderate rainfall. The run usually stalls with the onset of cold weather conditions in November and begins again when winter's grip gradually fades in the spring.

The Cranberry and Flag Rivers are two other smaller waters worth checking out for wild fish in this vicinity of Wisconsin, particularly if the Brule is out of shape from rainfall. The avid angler may even consider taking a day to explore Lake Superior's shoreline northeast of Duluth to sample steelheading—Minnesota style.

The Brule River is easy to find. The fishable section flows northward through the town of Brule located on U.S. State Highway 2. There are about 12 fishable miles before the river enters Lake Superior. Ample access is available following County Forest Road H. Camping and lodging can be found in Brule, and state campgrounds can be found along the river.

Cypress River (JK)

Lake Superior's north shore journey picks up with many rivers of all shapes and sizes from the Ontario city of Thunder Bay 180 miles slightly northeast to the town of Marathon. The route along this section of shoreline provides one of the prettiest drives in North America. Breathtaking views and scenic panoramas offer a glimpse of unspoiled nature along the heavily traveled two-lane Highway 17—a portion of which is the main artery across Canada. Although all the tributaries entering the lake in this region share the same characteristic—a natural upstream barrier blocking the passage of migrating steelhead—each river differs in lengths of fishable water available. The size of the water varies greatly as well, and all are dependent on rain or snowmelt for a decent flow. Starting in late April near Thunder Bay, most steelhead in the region run up these Ontario tributaries to spawn in the late spring. The peak period occurs between May 15th and June 1st—the further north, the later the run.

Scott Smith masterfully covering some fast water on the Cypress River. Scott Smith photo.

Meeting Scott Smith for a day on the Cypress River, I realized that a guide is probably the best way to experience the tributaries of this region. But Scott is not only a guide, he is an avid fly fisherman, writer, and an active advocate promoting the conservation ethic along the entire north shore of Lake Superior. In his "other life," he is a S.W.A.T team commander in Thunder Bay. We chose the Cypress because of its extraordinary beauty as well as its convenient location to a series of other tributaries found in either direction, just in case things weren't happening on that particular piece of water. We could have accessed the Cypress at Highway 17, but Scott preferred using the rutted two track to get us to a trail we could use to hike into the river further upstream. This road, located on privately owned property, requires a modest fee to enter.

According to Scott, there are three miles of river below the impassable falls. When we arrived at the water's edge, it was like stepping into a wilderness. A mixed forest of conifer and leafless birch lined a broad area of gravel with the river winding through its defined channel. Although the water was low, it required a careful approach to cross safely. Impressive runs, pools, and rocky pockets awaited upstream. The water was tinged with red because of a high iron content, and the river rock was stained the same color. Because the downfall along the shoreline made some aspects of hiking difficult, this wasn't a trek for the weak of heart. Scott's ability to pack 40 pounds of equipment, everything needed for wilderness survival, was noteworthy.

We fished a series of holding runs all the way up to the waterfalls, and that day we were fortunate, for there were some fresh fish that had just moved into the river. The typical Lake Superior steelhead is small, hard, and scrappy— averaging three to five pounds. Scott assured me, though, there are fish that go ten pounds, and later I was whipped handily by a fish of substantial size. The falls were spectacular. It was only after lunch, just sitting and appreciating the day with Scott, that I realized the hike itself to this secluded location was the real treat. The fishing was just a bonus.

Fall rains can produce a fresh run of steelhead in the Cypress, but coho and pink salmon predominate the season along with a unique run of "coasters." This rather large lake-run brook trout, native to the waters of Lake Superior, struggles as a species to hang on to a precarious future.

To the west a short distance, the Jackpine River crosses Highway 17 with characteristics similar to the Cypress—reddish water, but swifter runs. The Jackpine is another well-noted north shore river offering springtime runs corresponding to those found on the Cypress. Access is attained only by trekking upstream and downstream along its banks. Back toward the town of Nipigon is found, of course, the famous Nipigon River. Fragmented by power dams, only the lower portion of this large piece of water gets steelhead. Requiring a creative approach, and likely a guide, this section of river can offer opportunities for rainbow well into summer. The upper portion of the river below Lake Nipigon can also provide unique opportunities for trophy brook trout in late May and June as well.

Backtracking another 20 miles or so toward Thunder Bay, another piece of water worth looking at is the Wolf River. This is a river of medium size with gravel runs that are pleasurable to fish. Although there are eight miles of fishable water, most of it is accessible only by floating. That option alone makes the Wolf intriguing. According to Scott, this river is an unusual north shore tributary for its flows are maintained by a spring-fed creek found further upstream. Because of its consistent flows, the Wolf also offers one of the best north shore possibilities for fall steelhead, along with some brook trout, beginning in late September.

Both private and provincial campgrounds can be found along Highway 17. The town of Nipigon offers accommodations, and its centralized location provides many fishing options in either direction. Scott's new book, *Ontario Blue-Ribbon Fly Fishing Guide*, provides valuable insight to this area.

Old Woman River (JK)

It is difficult to drive past the Old Woman River without stopping to fish its water. This small river enters Old Woman Bay in the northern reaches of Lake Superior Provincial Park, and the parking area overlooking the beach and the bay provides a peaceful rest along with a splendid view. If one squints hard enough, the face of the old woman for which the river and bay are named can be observed in the rocky cliffs across the water.

The river itself provides several easy-to-read fly fishing runs above and below Highway 17. Many times I have been drawn to fish its golden tea-colored water as if lured by some mystical powers. Unfortunately, the easily accessed water dissipates much too quickly, leaving the angler with few upstream options. Bushwhacking through thick growth can certainly limit an angler's eagerness to explore the water that beckons beyond the tangles. Although the Old Woman is not necessarily a destination river by itself, it is a must in a visit to this section of shoreline.

Another large tributary that calls out to passing anglers is the Agawa River found further south in the same Provincial Park. Its big water spills over gravel bottoms defining some classic steelhead runs, but gathering information about the Agawa has been a difficult process. Finding fish with any consistency in its broad waters is a problem that deters many anglers from spending much time there with any regularity. Although springtime flows make the river difficult if not impossible to cross, access is attained by walking up gravel bars and high banks from the highway bridge. Since the gravel bottom tends to erode away under one's feet, caution is advised in swifter currents. The Agawa is the kind of river that is found only in a steelheader's dreams. The appeal is to hit it right on some day! It should be noted that steelhead do tend to hang in the Agawa well into June, offering an extended time period to sample its wonderful potential. But it is the sheer beauty of the experience that makes fishing the Agawa so special.

The closest town in this area with any services is Wawa, located only about 15 miles from the Park's northern boundary. Highway 17 then leaves the lake's shoreline for 106 miles until coming back to the lake again at Marathon. The portion of shoreline far removed from the highway has only a few streams, and they are very difficult to access. Historically, Wawa was the location for the first Hudson Bay Company as well as the Northwest Trading Company. These days it is a service center for this isolated region while also providing fly outs to remote regions further north. Another of the north shore's significant steelhead rivers flows south of town.

The Michipicoten River is a large piece of water that provides challenging fly fishing opportunities in the broad riffles flowing below Scott Falls Dam. A tailwaters situation is unusual for the north shore, and the Michipicoten has been producing quality steelhead runs for years. Unfortunately, fishing pressure has diminished the quality of the area's steelheading within the last decade, but this river still offers worthwhile challenges for the dedicated steelheader. Depending upon the year, steelhead can hold in the river well into summer providing late season potential along with the possibility of dry fly action.

Fly fishing outfitters are a rare commodity along this stretch of the lake's shoreline. Although Eric Dicarlo is a local name associated with a highly reputable guide service, other commitments keep him off the river in this capacity these days. Word is he will share both his knowledge and his passion for the region's steelhead with anyone who may be interested.

Springtime on the north shore can be very uncomfortable. At that time, Lake Superior's water temperature can still be in the mid 30's, so any onshore breeze drops inland temperatures considerably. It is essential, therefore, to be properly attired. Temperature swings are not uncommon, and hypothermia is a real possibility under these conditions.

Pancake River (RK)

The vastness and beauty of Lake Superior's north shore rises as a symbol of the diversity of the Great Lakes system. Traveling west, sandy beaches give way to rock points and cliffs which project an image of a completely unspoiled shoreline, one that could be compared in splendor to some of the most remote coastal waters of the Pacific Ocean. Steelhead belong here. Cities and towns have been left behind, one-stop gas station/store/restaurants which service mostly travelers are monuments to this harsh climate which only few choose to inhabit. As we slowly drove up the gravel access road to the Pancake, the harsh nature was quite evident. It was the latter part of May, and buds on the trees were only just beginning to show.

The Pancake is an intimate river only forty to sixty feet in width for most of its winding path. There is heavy growth lining a good portion of the banks making the roll cast the popular choice from most casting positions. The Pancake's water travels briskly over mainly gravel and sand with depressions creating holding pockets. Numerous small runs are carved where the flow butts against a stable object such as a fallen tree or a logjam. Some longer runs could be found where the main current ran along steep banks. The Pancake is the type of river where constant analysis of the potential holding water is important as steelhead could be in any nook or cranny. Careful wading and approach will help keep fish unaware of your presence and from finding cover in the timber.

Due partly to its somewhat limited runs of steelhead, good timing can have a critical impact on success or lack thereof. In the spring, rains and warming temperatures should equate to fish movements. When we arrived, heavy rains had brought up the level and the water was stained with a sandy particulate. The level dropped and clarity improved over the next few days. It should have been the absolute perfect conditions. However, the fish were not there. The late blossoming of spring was most likely the culprit. In two days, I had only one brief connection with a steelhead to show for my efforts. This fish did leave its mark. Although only four to five pounds, its side shimmered of blinding silver in the afternoon sun, and before we parted ways, it flexed its muscles in a show of power. Wild Lake Superior fish are a special breed.

The gravel road which leads to the river can be found across from the Pancake Bay Provincial Park. Camping is allowed in the park, and during May, it is like having one's own peace of heaven as this is a few weeks ahead of the recreational campers. The frigid lake gives the effect of camping next to a very large block of ice. There are a few pullouts on the gravel road that lead to river access. As it turns out, choices can dramatically effect results. A rugged two track goes the final distance to the falls which mark the upstream limit to fish migration. We decided not to venture it and fished the middle part of the river for our two days. The steelhead we searched for in this section had apparently already passed us by. The rains had brought in a few fish and it seemed as though most had shot straight up as a couple days later we spoke with an angler who had hooked numerous steelhead in the deep slots below the falls. You just never know.

Mid May through early June seems to be the most consistent spring time frame. The Pancake also receives runs of fish in the fall; late September and October would be the most likely period. There are a number of other small or short rivers in the Pancake Bay area. One that is a pleasure to fish is the Chippewa River. There are only a handful of pools between the lake and a falls which prohibits upstream migration, but there is plenty of room for casting. The moderate flow of its pools drop into broad tailouts where a fly can swing seductively for fresh fish that have just moved in from the lake.

Steel River (JK)

The Steel River is far removed from any significant population center. It lies about 15 miles east of Terrace Bay and some 40 miles west of the town of Marathon. This is an impressively large river with classic-looking steelhead water that encourages traditional approaches. Unfortunately, there are only three miles or so of fishable water before a falls blocks the further upstream migration of steelhead. Because the river runs out of Santoy Lake, it rarely gets too dirty to fish, but it can get too high.

The Steel River is noteworthy because its steelhead are perhaps the latest running, naturally spawning fish in the Great Lakes. And though it is not uncommon to find fish spawning in early June, the steelhead of the Steel may linger in the river until July, depending upon conditions. This can open up another door for the fortunate angler. According to Scott Smith, bug hatches at this time of year can inspire some surface feeding by post-spawn steelhead dropping back to the lake. Since dry fly fishing for steelhead in the Great Lakes is a rare event, the Steel is on a short list of rivers that can provide such an opportunity. This is certainly not a dependable occurrence, but it is a consideration for the adventuresome.

The high bridge on Highway 17 crosses conspicuously over the Steel. Access can be attained from an undeveloped parking area on the west side. There are several nice stretches of water from the bridge downstream on both sides. There is also a west side trail that leads up to the falls on a very high bank, but getting to the river from the trail requires some caution.

In the vicinity, another tributary worthy of investigation is Mink Creek found west of the Steel. Although a pretty section of the river runs north of Highway 17, the creek must be accessed by the trail south of the highway to get below the falls.

12

Lake Huron

Au Sable River (RK)

Michigan's Au Sable River is a big, beautiful piece of water. Its dark flow winds through sandy, alder-lined banks. Many pools are filled with fallen timber. As I raced to the river in the remnants of the torrential rains that dramatically slowed my journey the night before, I just knew the river would be blown out. After all, well over an inch of rain had fallen, possibly pushing two inches. Between the rigors of the travel and fouling up my directions, I arrived at the boat ramp near Foote Dam almost an hour late. I quickly issued apologies to friend and author, Bob Linsenman and to Kelly Neuman, a young, knowledgeable, and enthusiastic Au Sable guide. Apologies turned to concern over river conditions, and I was shocked to find the Au Sable, while high and slightly stained, was still fishable. Bob and Kelly were quick to explain that the surrounding sand plain acts as a large filter and limits actual runoff. Good for us.

Our plan of attack included a drift boat, which is probably the best way to approach this section of the river. It was the last day of April, and the spring run was in full swing. There can be fishable numbers of fresh fish all through May. We fished some from the boat, but mostly at points where Kelly had skillfully slid the skiff to shore to explore various pockets and runs which could be covered quite easily by wading. It would be important for first timers to select the areas to wade very carefully as some would be too deep or dangerous. We repeatedly threw our flies into the dark, green areas behind shallow gravel bars. Some were obvious holds, while others were well hidden, being uncovered by Kelly through his personal experiences. The fish we found were right along the bottom, some being rather aggressive. We hooked fish on small wets, nymphs, and large buggers. All in all, a spectacular day as the rain held off enough to not be miserable, with each of us landing some fresh and spirited steelhead.

The Au Sable runs bank to bank and is probably one hundred fifty to two hundred feet wide through most of this lower section. Annoying, fly-stealing submerged timber can make some runs difficult or impossible to fish. The flows in many runs were quick, requiring proper weighting to place the fly at the desired level. The heavy flows combined with wading obstructions called for some skillful technique when fighting a fish. The scourge of the Great Lakes, the hydroelectric power dam, affects this river as well. The dam above the launch site restricts steelhead migrations to approximately six miles of river channel. But there is a tremendous amount of fishable water packed into this section before it reaches the lake at Oscoda, and it receives a considerable annual run of both wild and hatchery fish.

Kelly Neuman operates his Streamside Custom Rod & Guide Service from South Branch, Michigan. He represents an ever-growing contingent of

Kelly Nueman about to release a bright hen from the Au Sable.

professionals in the region who are concerned about the health of their fishery and the quality of the experience. The Au Sable is one of a handful of Great Lakes rivers where using a boat is a real advantage from a fly fishing standpoint and one would do well to hire Kelly's services for their first trip. Near the end of the float, Kelly pointed out some slow sweeping runs, comprised mainly of gravel bottoms, where he has been fishing large flies on sink-tips for fresh-run fall steelhead with some success. The water he showed us was beautiful, and it certainly whetted our appetites for a return visit some late September or October. Using a drift boat wasn't the only option as the following day I easily found two public access points along the south bank. The most popular was the Clay Banks where I fished some good water both up and downstream from where the masses huddled. As we had witnessed the day earlier, fishing pressure was pretty light during the week once away from the immediate access. However, following the river on foot, for the most part, is restricted either by the terrain or private land.

Bob Linsenman is passionate about his feelings for his beloved Au Sable. He is well-known throughout Michigan and the entire Great Lakes for his two co-authored books with Steve Nevala, *Michigan Trout Streams: A Fly-Angler's Guide* and *Great Lakes Steelhead: A Guided Tour for Fly-Anglers.* Both are good sources of information. Bob also guides on the river, mostly for its trophy wild trout in the upper reaches. His new book, *River Journal: Au Sable River,* published by Frank Amato Publications, gives new insight into uncovering some of the secrets of this spectacular place.

I left impressed with the river, the surroundings, the steelhead, and the company. The Au Sable is challenging water in terms of finding fish and bringing them to hand. It is certainly worth a visit. The Ocqueoc River well north of the Au Sable near Rogers City and the Rifle River located to the south which flows into Saginaw Bay are both medium-sized rivers receiving runs of steelhead. They provide some variety to the big flows of the Au Sable.

Bighead River (RK)

John Valk pointed to a barely visible submerged boulder and explained how the deep crevice behind it almost always held a steelhead when fresh fish were on the move. It was the first week of May, and spring-run fish had been trickling in each day. With the water in fine shape, our prospects were good. It took only a few casts to find the exact spot that John had so aptly described. The silver torpedo affixed to the end of my leader tore an opening in the surface of the water and bolted downriver. In the soft water of the pool below, the fish of six to seven pounds was brought to hand. The steelhead's body glistened in the early morning sun as it posed for a few quick photographs. Another handful of casts in the same spot found another bright fish, this one somewhat smaller but just as tough. It was obvious that John was very familiar with this water, a factor for which there is little substitute when it comes to success.

John owns and operates Grindstone Angling in Waterdown, Ontario, just outside of Hamilton. He has fished the Georgian Bay area for many years and has developed a deep appreciation for steelhead. He also operates a successful guiding operation on the waters in the two- to three-hour range from his shop for trout and steelhead. When water conditions are right, the Bighead is his personal choice. Those who know this river feel that almost every freshet brings in some fresh fish, provided water temperatures are agreeable. The Bighead will normally rise and color with a heavy rain, but clear quickly. Being there when the water is green is the key as extreme clarity sends the fish sulking into deep pools. It is an enchanting small river averaging 60 to 70

John Valk and a wild Bighead River steelhead.

feet in width through its lower reaches. Except for its lowest stretch where it meets with the Georgian Bay of Lake Huron at the town of Meaford, the Bighead runs through beautiful landscapes of forests and orchards.

This is great fly fishing water. Plenty of room for backcasting and the typical holding water is relatively shallow. There are numerous small pools and runs where utilizing a wet fly swing can work well. However, John's favorite approach is the most effective. He prefers to concentrate on the numerous pockets found throughout the river for fresh fish on the move. The softer water of the pockets often draws steelhead in for a moment of rest during their migration. These often-aggressive fish can be prime targets. John likes dead drifting nymphs with a long leader and an up and across cast. He fishes intensely and meticulously, plying his offering in any water that looks barely deep enough to hold a fish. Reading the water is extremely important. The Bighead can receive incredible numbers of steelhead, and John told stories of a few days where fish could be found in almost every good pocket in the run which we were fishing. The rule seemed to be to not pass any water that had at least a chance of holding a fish. Sadly, runs in the Bighead aren't what they once were; overharvesting seems to be a leading factor. A movement toward more restrictive regulations was recently cut short. However, for 1999 a reduction has been made to two per day. The runs in the Big Head are entirely wild, and it is disconcerting to see such shortsighted views by so-called sportsmen with no understanding or appreciation for such a special resource. It is sad that this is such a widespread problem throughout the Great Lakes region. We are our own worst enemy. And by the way, the Bighead occasionally sees some very large fish with a legitimate 20 pounder as a possibility.

Good access to the river can be found at a park on the west side of the river in Meaford. Where the river crosses a concession road outside of town also provides access to the river. When in this area, another river worth consideration is the Beaver. This river enters Georgian Bay at Thornbury. It is similar in size and character to the Bighead but is dammed less than a mile from the lake. This water below the dam sees a lot of fish and a lot of anglers. A hydraulic lift at the dam allows steelhead to pass above. There is probably five to six miles of fishable water above the dam which is characterized by pockets and small runs. Access to this stretch is limited but holds some significant potential since the fishing pressure on this water is extremely light. A fish count at the lift station provides a mechanism for determining the densities of fish in this area. This section above the dam is only an option in the spring and is closed to fishing from October 1 until the opening of trout season.

Maitland River (RK)

I first viewed the Maitland through the dim glow of the streetlights along the Highway 21 bridge. It was well after dark, and Jerry, Bob Morrissey and I had just arrived on the scene from a long, miserable late-autumn day on the Saugeen. Even in the faint light, I could detect something special about this river. It was very cold and blustery as lake-effect snow raced by us, and its horizontal path seemed to be sucked into the darkness rather than falling to earth. The relentless winds howled loudly, mocking our intentions of steelhead fishing. Later, at a Goderich restaurant, we heard the really bad weather wasn't to begin until after midnight. We were out of there; the Maitland would have to wait.

This brief sequence was not without significance. The image of the river flowing in the darkness was like a mirage, and its impression remained with me until I could visit it again the following spring. When I first viewed it in the daylight, my expectations were immediately exceeded. This was a steelhead river of little compare—big, open, and flowing unencumbered for miles and miles. Love at first sight. But another apparent reality is the weather. In this first return since that stormy night, Jerry, Scott Smith, and I met Larry Halyk on the river. It was nearly as miserable as the initial encounter. It seemed like a matter of coincidence until my next four visits saw various degrees of cold, heavy rain, snow, and gusting winds, the worst of which were strong enough to blow a person off his feet if they weren't firmly planted. Larry, who has fished this region for many years, assured me that the conditions were not always like this, but the statistics indicated otherwise. I can conclude that I ran into an incredible string of bad luck, but the certainty is that careful planning around the weather is a must as the Maitland is no place to be when the frigid winds sweep down from the north.

The Maitland is a big river, probably a couple hundred feet wide or more in some areas in its lower reaches. It has an inviting flow as subtle riffles give way to long pools and runs, some of which are too shallow to hold steelhead and others which fall into the black depths, too deep to be covered with fly fishing techniques. However, many are just right for fly fishing. The interesting aspect of water selection on this river is that the way a pool or run looks on the surface is not always the key indicator as to how well it will fish. The depth of the water and even current speed can be difficult to judge until it's experienced. The river's bottom is mainly comprised of gravel along with various-sized boulders and even exposed bedrock. Drops in the gravel, boulders in the main current, and cuts in the bedrock create high-percentage holding areas. It can take the investment of hours of plying with a fly to find the prime runs or, more likely, the one or two prime areas within the run where the ideal holding water intersects with that which can be effectively covered with a fly rod. In the eight years that Larry Halyk has fished this river and through hours of exploring, he has found a handful of runs which he can efficiently fly fish. The Maitland is a river where success doesn't come easy and, as I have experienced, requires one to pay his dues. With the fish spread out over 40 to 50 miles, big numbers are normally not part of the equation.

As with the Grand River, the current fishery is rather young and the runs are continuing to build. The Province of Ontario places a heavy emphasis on wild steelhead, and the run in the Maitland is comprised primarily of naturally reproduced fish. This is in large part due to the concern and involvement of local groups such as the Maitland Valley Anglers, Nine Mile Steelheaders, and Ontario Steelheaders who have successfully rehabilitated spawning habitat

Finally a fish from the Maitland! Rick Kustich poses with his first.

on a handful of tributaries. There is a direct correlation with this effort and the building numbers of returning adults. Due in part to the effort involved for success and the fact that the current fishery is relatively new, the Maitland is lightly pressured. There is pool after pool, some of which see very few anglers. It provides the perfect opportunity to spread out, cast a long line and utilize traditional techniques. The fact of being alone in such a beautiful place speaks for itself. I have only seen one other fly fisher as fly fishing for steelhead has yet to become popular in Ontario. However, there are a few who have made their mark with a fly rod on this river. Ken Collins, owner and operator of the Grand River Troutfitters in Fergus, Ontario, has been successfully fly fishing the Maitland for years. When speaking of the Maitland, he approaches the subject with a guarded reverence for a place that obviously means very much to him.

The Maitland commonly runs low and clear through September and October. The first good fall rain which brings up the level will normally produce a run of steelhead. November and December seem to host the most consistent fishing. Water temperatures can vary dramatically in the fall depending on weather patterns, and fly fishing opportunity increases when the water temperatures are in the 40's or at least high 30's. We have experienced that the window of optimum temperatures and good fish numbers can be quite short in some years. The Maitland clears quickly and can withstand fairly heavy rain. This is one river that, when the conditions are right, it is time to move. Only the water below the Highway 21 bridge, which encompasses a few nice pools, remains open to fishing year-round. The extended fall season, from October 1 to December 31, allows for steelhead fishing from the Highway 21 bridge upriver for over 30 miles to Highway 4 in the town of Wingham. By late November, steelhead are usually distributed throughout this stretch. The entire river opens again with the trout season, the last Saturday in April. There is normally a good three to four weeks of spring fishing for a combination of fresh fish and drop-backs. Access can be found at any one of the five bridges that cross the river up to Auburn. There is some good water near each bridge and plenty to explore in between.

After a significant rain, the Maitland is often unfishable for a couple days as bank-full conditions make fly fishing an impossible task. Two other smaller rivers of significance found in the Maitland region can be quite good when the Maitland is out. The Bayfield River is about fifteen miles south of Goderich and the Nine Mile River is about the same distance north. Even though the Bayfield and Nine Mile will normally run dirtier than the Maitland when in spate, they each offer a much higher percentage opportunity as they commonly maintain a fishable size and character. Although smaller, if fished selectively after a rain, they are nice-sized rivers for fly fishing. The Bayfield generally receives less fishing pressure than the lower Nine Mile. Highway 21 crosses each river providing access both up and downriver. Look upriver of Highway 21 for lighter fishing pressure.

Nottawasaga River (RK)

I have only had the occasion of fishing the Notty, as it is affectionately referred to, a couple of times. Through the hospitality of avid steelheader Chris Atkinson, fisheries researcher Chris Weland, and Aquatic Biologist for the Nottawasaga River Conservation Authority Fred Dobbs, I found myself in the middle of a beautiful run on a crisp November day. Some fresh fish rolled to be certain that we knew they were there. Chris Atkinson, Chris Weland and Fred all hooked and landed some fish on gear. After about two hours, the swing of my fly concluded with the thump of a take and a heavy fished shook violently at the end of my leader. After a brief toe-to-toe tussle, it raced upriver as I struggled in a useless attempt to keep the line tight. As is the common outcome of such a situation, the fish was gone. It had sliced my leader on a sharp edge along the bottom, possibly a clam shell. This was all the river was willing to give me on this day despite there being reasonable numbers of fish present. The disappointment of the missed opportunity grew large as the day drew to a close.

The Nottawasaga flows into Georgian Bay at the community of Wasaga Beach. Under normal fall flows, the lower end is quite manageable with a fly rod. Spring runoff drains a considerable area which can create heavy flows. In the spring and early fall, the lower river naturally carries a green tinge caused by an algae that is present in the water. It is rare for the lower Notty to run very clear.

There are almost two distinct rivers within one. The lower river consists of the two to three miles of water up from the Highway 26 bridge in Wasaga Beach. A road along the river's east bank provides a couple access points to this water. Here the Notty consists of various pools and runs, some with slow to moderate current flow. There are also various small pools, pockets, and tailouts which can hold resting fish on the move. After working the water with Chris Atkinson, it was clear the Notty involves a fair learning curve to determine the subtle holding spots which consistently attract steelhead and which can be efficiently fished with a fly rod.

Above this lower stretch, the river runs through a long, stale swamp where there is no water for steelhead angling. This is where the lower river picks up the green coloration. However, above this point, from the town of Alliston downstream some ten to twelve miles, the river flows freely once again. It is somewhat smaller than the lower stretch but maintains similar characteristics in terms of potential holding water. Access is limited, which consequently leads to light fishing pressure. This is in contrast to the lower stretch which does receive a moderate amount of angling effort. Since it is located above the swamp, the water is generally clearer in this upper area.

Chris Weland, Chris Atkinson, and Fred Dobbs are quite proud of the wild population of returning adult steelhead and contend that the fish of the Notty are the hottest fighting fish in Ontario. From my brief encounter, I could not argue. There can be good fall runs through October and November depending on water conditions. December fishing can be best in the upper stretches when concentrations of fish can possibly be found. The Notty also receives good runs in the spring. I witnessed some fish that had only spent one year in the lake in the size range of 15 to 18 inches all the way up to three- and four-year fish exceeding ten pounds. One of the days I spent on the Notty I heard of an eighteen-pound steelhead taken earlier that morning, and Chris Atkinson confirmed that a few legitimate twenty-pound fish are caught here. That is something to always keep in the back of your mind when you fish the Notty.

Saugeen River (JK)

The Saugeen River enters the main body of Lake Huron at the town of Southhampton, less than 25 miles west of Owens Sound. This is beautiful, gentle water that winds its way through approximately 120 miles of pastoral hills and picturesque farmlands. Its upper sections and tributaries support quality habitat for native trout. The Saugeen is a quiet river that meanders for miles without great definition, particularly in the middle section. It is a large river with a substantial base flow. Traditional techniques are very much at home on its placid flows. Most steelhead fishing occurs, however, in the popular section below the cement lamprey control barrier called Denny's Dam just outside of Southhampton. From this point downstream, the river possesses several runs and pools that rival the best steelhead rivers anywhere. Unfortunately this section is short lived, and as the river approaches the lake, it flattens out a few miles below the dam. There is a considerable estuary area before the lake.

In terms of angler success, the Saugeen is one of the top steelhead-producing rivers in Ontario, and though steelhead are known to migrate many miles upstream, most fish are harvested in those sections below Denny's Dam. The Saugeen supports a substantial natural run of fish, but it is also stocked annually to supplement these wild populations. This action is necessitated by the demand of the casual angler to be able to keep his catch.

When the weather conditions are right, steelhead can be caught in the lower section of the river throughout most of the year. This piece of water is easy to access, and it can accommodate many anglers. And because the movement of fish has been slowed historically by the lamprey barrier, anglers are able to catch good numbers of fish in this lower stretch under certain

The big water of the lower Saugeen.

conditions. Access to the dam area is obtained on the north side of the river at the Fisherman's Park maintained by the Ontario Steelheaders, or on the south side at the Ministry of Natural Resources (MNR) parking lot. There is another large pulloff on Highway 21 across from the golf course which allows entry to the lowest runs from the north side. The river is deceptively large at this point and impossible to cross. Though quite wadable on each side, care is advised.

In the summer of 1995, the MNR modified the south side of the dam with the help of the Ontario Steelheaders. Improvements were made on the barrier which increased water flow; therefore, more fish are drawn in that direction to utilize the ladder. Other modifications on the ladder allow better passage of the fish during the cold months. Because the fish are now able to get upstream more efficiently, they are less vulnerable to the large numbers of anglers fishing below the dam. Also, the increased number of fish able to reach prime spawning gravel upriver should lead to greater productivity of wild fish.

Although the runs below Denny's Dam offer some excellent opportunities for the fly fisherman using a variety of techniques, crowds can certainly be discouraging at times. However, the improvements at the dam have also improved fishing opportunities for many miles above the barrier as well. The Saugeen is a good example of a cooperative effort between sportsmen and the ministry in the area creating more angling options. Fishable numbers of steelhead now reach the town of Walkerton, and improvements at a barrier there should allow fish access to many more miles of water in the future. Also, an extended season now allows anglers to fish this stretch until the end of December.

The 50-mile section of river from Walkerton downstream to Southhampton is not without some drawbacks. It is not only difficult to access many miles of the river, the subtle steelhead runs are often separated by lengthy stretches of flat water. Walking from bridges at Walkerton, Paisley, and Port Elgin offer some alternatives. Floating the river may also open up many other opportunities for the exploring angler.

We have fished the Saugeen River on several occasions over the years. It has become very evident to us during those visits that the weather in the region can be rather severe during the prime months of steelhead season. Lake-effect storms can regularly roll in accompanied by prevailing north winds and unpleasant gusts. This is a part of the steelhead experience in the area. In general, fish movement depends on the rain and snow. The Saugeen is no exception. Heavy rains raise and dirty the water in the river significantly, but the Saugeen can turn around rather quickly. There are even times when the water remains fishable through a deluge. Since the drainage is huge, the factors affecting the river's flow are many. Often, the best fishing on the Saugeen occurs during these periods.

One of the most uncomfortable days we have ever experienced steelhead fishing was spent on the beautiful section of water that runs through Walkerton. There are several well-defined runs from the cement structure all the way down below the town bridge. The river here is still quite large, carrying a good volume of water. It can't be crossed. The day was in the 20's, the snow was falling, and the wind was howling. Our efforts were punctuated with hourly breaks at the donut shop located conveniently on the bank of the river. By day's end, we had not even seen a fish, but the memories of the experience will last a lifetime. We consumed a quantity of donuts and copious amounts of coffee that day, and conceded that the future looked bright for this particular shop, especially during steelhead season.

There are still many unknowns associated with the Saugeen, especially if this upper section continues to improve. And though spring fishing above Denny's Dam starts on the opening of the general trout season at the end of April, there are still fish moving into the system at that time. Also, fishing for post-spawn fish lasts well into May. Although angling for drop-backs may not appeal to some anglers, often Great Lakes fish returning to the lake are in great shape, and they provide spirited action on the fly rod. It is possible to locate pods of surface-feeding drop-backs as well, particularly during the famous Hendrickson hatch. The Saugeen River holds much potential for the fly fishing steelheader and, quite possibly, many surprises.

St. Mary's River (JK)

Some of the earliest records of fly fishing in the Great Lakes waters occurred on the famous strait that connects Lake Superior to Lake Huron near the city of Sault Ste. Marie known as the St. Mary's River. This unique piece of water is less than a mile in length, and it is defined by a vast series of riffles, holes, and white water across its substantial width. Because of these characteristics, this portion of the river is often referred to as the St. Mary's Rapids or the Sault Rapids. Easily accessible from a well-developed waterfront park near downtown, the St. Mary's provides long fishable periods for steelhead that can start in late April, last into July, and then pick up again in early October.

Most fishing in the St. Mary's takes place off a cement berm that separates the main channel from a smaller channel created specifically for spawning purposes. This smaller piece of water possesses many stream-like characteristics while offering some classic holding water well-suited for the fly fisher. Since there is a retaining barrier across the entire width of the river as it leaves Lake Superior, water levels in both channels can be controlled. The flow in the spawning channel is steadily maintained, but the water in the

This photo demonstrates the vastness of the St. Mary's rapids.

main body of the river can vary greatly from spring until fall depending on the amount of water generated within the entire Superior drainage.

In late April and throughout May, most angling is to fish setting up spawning redds on both sides of the berm. Caution is advised, however, on wading through the spawning channel to the cement wall. It is not only difficult to cross at points, care should be taken as well not to step on redds. The flow will determine the fishability of the main section on the outside of the berm, and though steelhead can be found throughout the great expanse of this short river, many will be out of the angler's reach. Only a limited amount of wading can occur on the river side of the wall at this time of year, and, again, it is not advised to wade through redds for the purpose of reaching other fish. For those not interested in fishing to the redds, moving fish can be hooked swinging flies through the deeper pockets as fresh steelhead continue to pulse into the system through June.

Once the spawning process has been completed, fish will remain to feed in the St. Mary's through June. And since the water flowing out of Lake Superior is always quite cool, the tailwater nature of the river can produce some exciting steelhead potential throughout a portion of July as well. With the onset of summer conditions, abundant hatches of caddis can occur, and during this period, many migrating rainbow can be found in the river feeding on the various stages of emergers. Regular plants of Atlantic salmon over the years could also result in a surprising hookup now and then. This time of year offers an exciting opportunity for anglers willing to explore the possibilities.

In early fall, steelhead arrive again in good numbers. Since the water flow is generally lower at this time of year, the river itself is open to more wading potential. Steelhead can then be found in deep depressions behind the redds of spawning salmon. An accidental release of pink salmon earlier this century has resulted in a prolific naturalized run during August that by itself has drawn the interest of many fishermen during recent years. Because climatic conditions can get quite severe in this part of the Great Lakes, fall fishing is subject to many variables that can end abruptly with a winter blast which can occur any time after October arrives.

We have had difficulty finding the St. Mary's in its prime. Late runs, high water, and tough weather conditions have plagued our efforts. Often, guide Karl Vogel can be found on the cement berm with a client, or in the parking lot offering advice to anyone willing to ask a question or two. His love for the St. Mary's is quite apparent, and his enthusiasm is contagious. He believes the two-handed rod has a great future on the big river, especially during high-water years. Karl also believes that the St. Mary's demands the use of many specialized flies designed for the region, particularly if one is to expect consistent results hooking steelhead in this intriguing piece of water. Despite our setbacks, the river's potential has been enticing. Maybe it is the river's history, or maybe it's the ghost of Hemingway, but the St. Mary's allure, without question, beckons yet another trip. Maybe next time we'll get it right.

13

Lake Michigan

Kewaunee River (JK)

The last time I saw my favorite 9½ foot, 8 weight Winston was on the top of the pickup in a parking lot on the lower Kewaunee River. A very hard, cold rain had just begun to change to snow that day in late April, and in the rush to find a hot cup of coffee, the mistake was made. The rod had fallen off somewhere on route to the restaurant, never to be found again. After years of dodging similar deluges, such a mental slip seemed inexcusable. In fact, the Great Lakes steelheader usually prays for rain until the waters rise, then he usually prays for it to stop. It is this pendulum of weather patterns that keeps the steelhead on the move, and the steelheader on alert. For many reasons then, the steelheader can't afford to lose concentration—or hard lessons are learned.

The Kewaunee River is ranked as a Class I stream by the Wisconsin Department of Natural Resources (DNR). Found near the town of Kewaunee at the base of the Door Peninsula some 25 miles southeast of Green Bay, it is one of the prettiest river corridors in the Great Lakes. Unique within the state's ranking system, the Kewaunee has no dam preventing migrating fish from reaching the upper portions of the river and its notable tributaries, thereby providing approximately 22 miles of free access for steelhead and salmon runs. For this reason, the Kewaunee system has also been known to support some natural reproduction over the years.

The Kewaunee is one of two Wisconsin rivers used to gather feral brood stock to maintain the stocking program for the state's portion of Lake

Michigan. The migrating fish are diverted to the C.D. "Buzz" Besadny Anadromous Fish Facility by a cement weir. The fish then pass through the gathering stations. Some fish are taken away to the state hatchery while others are allowed to naturally continue upstream. Although this artificial barrier slows the migration, it merely delays the upstream movement, according to the DNR.

The state of Wisconsin spends much effort securing access to its Class I rivers. A large section of the lower Kewaunee falls within the C.D. "Buzz" Besadny Fish and Wildlife Area. From the fish facility to the river's mouth, there are several runs and pockets ideal for the fly rod. A beautiful six-mile section of river located above the facility all the way up to the third County Highway "C" bridge is also included within this area. Winding through a forest of hardwoods, a series of gravel flats and defined runs entice the fly fisher in this upper section. In fact, this piece of water invites some traditional dry line techniques. The park area is opened the entire year.

The Kewaunee gets a run of coho and brown trout in the fall along with a full compliment of three strains of steelhead filling in throughout a long season. And though appropriate conditions can provide steelheading opportunities from late fall until spring, April offers some of the best timing for this river's steelhead. We witnessed plenty of activity in the third week of April, and the action in the river was supported by the actual fish count at the passage facility. It should be noted, however, that the annual sucker migration in late April can stifle an angler's enthusiasm. As many suckers move upstream

The lower Kewaunee River.

from the lake to spawn in the river, it becomes more difficult to swing a fly without attracting the big mouth of this native bottom feeder.

As we fished the river, we mostly enjoyed hiking through the upper section, occasionally spotting a fish here and there, hooking a few in the deeper runs. These fish were colored up, some had already spawned. In the water below the weir, the fish were fresher, and the few we caught were bright. The major rain that began to fall on our last day drove us from the river as the waters began to visibly rise. This surge would surely bring in more fish, but it would be a few days before the river was fishable again. It was time to leave anyway. Unfortunately, we left too quickly. Hopefully someone got a nice rod in the process.

North of the Kewaunee on the Door Peninsula, there are a few other options. Both Silver Creek and Stoney Creek are small streams that offer excellent potential for the exploring fly angler. Several other small tributaries there are also well worth a look.

Big Manistee River (JK)

The Big Manistee is another of the prominent Great Lakes rivers with a substantial natural run of steelhead that dates back to the turn of the century. It is big water with many West Coast characteristics. And since the fish can ascend the river no further than Tippy Dam near Wellston on State Highway 55, this is a favorite area that attracts many anglers. State access sites at the dam on both sides of the river make this upper portion of the Big Manistee easily attainable, and for those willing to walk, there are several other good runs available downriver. Also, the use of a drift boat opens up many miles of prime water downriver from the dam. This is becoming an increasingly popular method for anglers to spread out throughout the system.

Since the river's size inspires the fly fisherman to extend his casting range to allow for maximum coverage, the Big Manistee provides the fly angler many opportunities to utilize various traditional steelheading techniques. This river is perfect for spey rod advocates. Along with some well-defined riffles and runs, there are numerous gravel flats and bars that drop off into slots and deep pockets. When the fish are moving upstream to spawn during March and April, many will hold in the dark water below the gravel areas. Often these are fresh fish or drop-backs, both willing to grab a well-presented fly with aggression. In some sections, logjams lining the shoreline, along with blind pockets in the river, make chasing a fish downstream very difficult, so it is best to make a stand wherever the fish is hooked.

On our visit to the Big Manistee, we were fortunate to encounter prominent Great Lakes fishing guide Ray Schmidt taking a break along the shoreline with a client. Ray is a leading conservationist as well as an outspoken advocate for the wild steelhead of Lake Michigan. His passion for the sport, the fish, and this river were very evident in our conversation. Ray owns and operates Schmidt Outfitters in Wellston, near the banks of the Big Manistee, which includes a fly shop, lodging, and guide service. He willingly shared a few tips that were converted into a number of hookups later in the day. In the fall, the Big Manistee gets some of the earliest Michigan runs. Ray begins fishing the river in September and continues throughout the fall until the weather gets too severe. Winter can also provide some angling opportunities when conditions are mild enough.

Throughout the day, we could see numerous steelhead on gravel bars in the middle of this sizable water, but in several cases we couldn't reach them. The rain that started later in the afternoon definitely got the fish moving. Utilizing the information garnered from Ray, we were in position to intercept a pulse of fresh fish from a slot that gradually dropped out of sight behind a long gravel bar. Using a dry line, long leader, and small Egg Sucking Leeches, a forty-foot cast would swing the fly nicely down into the drop-off. The fish we hooked were big, hot, and they readily manhandled us. We only landed two. The rain fell steadily throughout the night.

We were scheduled to leave the area the next morning, but decided to look at the Big Manistee before we took off to see how it was taking the rain that still continued to fall. From a high cliff, the water appeared to be in perfect shape. It was with much reluctance that we pointed the truck toward New York and took off. But as we headed down the road, we came to our senses. Since this was too good of an opportunity to drive away from, we put everything on hold, turned the truck around, and rushed back to the run we had left behind the night before. Again, we continued to hook fish until the water started to rise and turn off-color by early afternoon. When it comes to steelhead, we have learned from past experiences never to "walk away" from a sure bet—if there is such a thing in the world of steelheading.

For those who enjoy covering the water with a boat or watercraft, the daylong float from Tippy Dam to High Bridge provides a wonderful opportunity. The upper part of this section is characterized by gravel upwellings and elevated bars followed by pockets and dips which can be quite productive when covered with a swinging fly. Further down, the river takes on a more clay-bottomed type of character punctuated by deep pools and logjams where many steelhead can be found. Foot access to this section of water is difficult, but local knowledge obtained from area fly shops could be helpful in this regard. For the serious Great Lakes steelhead enthusiast, fishing this section of the Big Manistee is a must for both the fish and the splendid opportunity to sample a fine outdoor experience—Michigan style. Utilizing the services of a guide may be the best way to see this water. The ten miles or so

A Big Manistee buck.

of water below High Bridge has similar character to that just above it and also represents a good section for traditional fishing.

The Little Manistee River can be found south of the Manistee, and it is the most important drainage in Michigan. Both rivers flow into Manistee Lake, one of several lakes located on Michigan's western shoreline that subsequently empties into Lake Michigan a short distance away. The Little Manistee has become the sacred trust of Michigan's steelhead program. It is a stream-sized tributary with endless gravel runs, riffles, and pools that provide perfect fish-rearing capabilities. Smolts are then able to retreat to the security of the inland lake before enduring the rigors of the big water that lies beyond. Fish entering the Little Manistee are a naturalized strain, referred to as the Michigan or Manistee strain, that has maintained a genetic purity dating back to the origins of Michigan's stocking program. Feral fish are taken from the Little Manistee and the eggs are hatchery reared to maintain steelhead stocks throughout the state. Both Manistees produce some of the finest wild steelhead in the world, and the importance of these two rivers to the integrity of the Great Lakes steelhead program cannot be overstated.

The Little Manistee provides many excellent small-river fly fishing opportunities, but because of its significance, some rules apply. Checking the regulations is advised. There are several other tributaries further northward toward Traverse City that can also provide notable activity depending on run timing for each drainage. The Betsie River is a winding, low-gradient tributary with characteristics similar to the Pere Marquette. The Platte and Boardman Rivers are two other pieces of water worthy of the serious fly angler's attention.

Manitowoc River (JK)

About 80 miles north of Milwaukee via Interstate 43, the Manitowoc River flows eastward out of the farmlands of northeastern Wisconsin through the city of Manitowoc into Lake Michigan. Although the river provides some 20 miles of water accessible to moving steelhead before the Clarks Mill Dam inhibits upstream progress, for a number of reasons this river is more or less designed for the serious steelheader interested in prospecting for fish utilizing a variety of traditional methods. Of the four times I attempted to fish the Manitowoc, the river was too high one spring, too low upon another occasion, and blizzards interrupted the other two efforts. It must be the enigmatic allure, however, of an inviting rural river with long stretches of excellent-looking fly water that keeps me headed in that direction whenever the opportunity arises.

Unlike several other Wisconsin rivers flowing into Lake Michigan which can at times produce dependable, somewhat prolific runs, steelhead migrations on the Manitowoc are neither as predictable nor as abundant, a fact that can be quite appealing to the dedicated angler looking for a variety of challenges. When flows are adequate in the fall, sporadic spurts of bright Skamania summer runs can scatter up and down its entire length, particularly in conjunction with the Chinook salmon migration throughout October. And though freezing temperatures and low flows can limit opportunities in the dead of winter, a January rain or thaw can bring in some Chambers Creek strain steelies throughout the cold months followed by a run of the Ganaraska strain fish which starts in early spring. Naturally, balancing timing with the right conditions can be exasperating, as I have found out over the years.

In times of moderate flows, the Manitowoc is a gentle gradient river of medium size from 40 to 50 ft in width. In the upper reaches, boulder-strewn runs along with flat riffles provide the perfect situation for swinging unweighted or slightly weighted flies on a dry line. Local experts prefer the use of spey flies which provide a rather lively action to entice fish from somewhat shallow lies. Even under the most ideal conditions, the waters of the Manitowoc display a murky twinge. Since it is not uncommon for steelhead in this situation to feel more secure in the shallows, particularly on bright days, a fly with some action or color can often encourage an exhilarating take.

With plenty of water for steelhead to spread out in the Manitowoc, it is unlikely to find large concentrations of fish as on other rivers. Since fish will be found one here, one there in the process of thoroughly hunting the water, this river offers the fly fisher a taste of what West Coast steelheading is all about. Therein lies the challenge. Methodically searching with the appropriate technique for the conditions can be a rewarding experience, especially for the avid angler who enjoys this kind of opportunity. Look for the subtle breaks along the shoreline and behind rocks, or in the depressions left behind salmon spawning redds. Steelhead here could be located just about anywhere.

Unofficial access to the river can be obtained at several bridges, and I am told that in Wisconsin, as long as one wades the edges, an angler avoids breaking any trespass laws. One should be advised, though, that slick rocks can provide testy wading, especially with higher flows. Since the Manitowoc has been targeted by the Wisconsin Department of Natural Resources for priority management considerations because of its great potential, the river's future looks promising as well. But if the Manitowoc isn't fishable, one should not despair, for there are several alternatives available. While some choices have been featured elsewhere in this section, the Pigeon River north of Sheboygan and the Sauk River at Port Washington are other selections that are highly recommended.

The Sheboygan River is another appealing tributary of moderate size that attracts many steelhead throughout the spring. Although there are many miles of suitable fly water all the way to Sheboygan Falls, the river west of Highway 43 flows through the property of Kohler Industries, the world-famous plumbing fixture manufacturer, and it restricts fishing privileges on company land. But since it is possible to purchase a permit to fish this section, it may be a worthwhile investment if there are fish around. After the Sheboygan flows under the interstate and through the city of the same name, the public water available offers a continuation of decent fly water well worth the time and effort.

Muskegon River (RK)

The old adage of what a guide does on his day off is true—he goes fishing. After spending some thirty straight days on the river guiding clients to steelhead, Matt Supinski readied his jet boat so the two of us "could just go fishing." Matt and I have come from similar beginnings, with Matt spending his youth in Western New York, living for a time less than a mile from my home. Ironically, even though we traveled in similar circles it wasn't until the night before this April morning that we had actually met, on the banks of what is now Matt's home river. There is one common denominator; our love for steelhead has been greatly influenced by what is now my home river and what was during Matt's youth—the mighty Niagara.

Matt and his wife Laurie own and operate a beautiful, quaint lodge on the banks of the Muskegon called the Gray Drake. The lodge is run in the style of a bed and breakfast with a gourmet meal prepared for you to start the day. As part of their operation they offer a complete guide service for steelhead, trout and salmon. One need not be a guest at the lodge to utilize the guide service. Next year they hope to add a small fly shop.

The Muskegon is an intriguing river. It is big, powerful and running bank to bank. It is the type of river that takes years to know and a lifetime to uncover its secrets. In the spring, finding steelhead is not all that difficult. The water below Croton Dam and continuing downriver for the next five miles consists of many gravel bars. Spawning fish can be readily spotted on the gravel and holding steelhead can be found in the dark water above and below the gravel. In the fall and winter, finding fish is not so easy. A working knowledge of steelhead water combined with trial and error of suspected lies is the only way to determine consistent holding water. Matt has spent considerable time over the past few years learning consistent holding water and shared with me photos of chrome-bright fall and winter fish caught while using some of his innovative approaches.

This April day we found some willing participants that took nymph patterns, small wet flies and even smaller egg patterns. The fishing had been as it had on my previous two spring visits, plenty of fish and with persistence a few would take a fly. I lost the fish of the day at the net. I had carefully worked the bright hen upriver after it had peeled off most of my fly line only to break the tippet during a momentary loss of sanity. An embarrassing rookie mistake, and Matt didn't hide his disappointment. I promised myself and Matt to return to chase some fresh fall fish.

Since the water is big and difficult to wade during full flows, a boat is a real asset on the Muskegon. Many of its runs, pools, and gravel pockets need to be fished from the boat. While a drift boat or even a personal floating craft will allow an angler to drift to good water, a jet boat is probably the best tool

Matt Supinski fishes a dark pocket on the Muskegon river.

for the swift currents of the river. It is difficult to row upstream against its flow and once you have passed prime water it may be impossible to return. I am not a big proponent of jet boats, the whine of their motor tends to break the mood of a steelhead river, but this is one river that does beg for their use. I did see a number of guides skillfully using their drift boats to allow their clients to properly cover the water. This is certainly one river where a guide will be a significant advantage, even to a seasoned steelheader.

The Muskegon does not eliminate the wading angler. Actually, some good access to quality water does exist. Access points can be found just below Croton Dam on Croton Road, at Pine Street about two miles below the dam, and at the M-37 bridge in Newaygo. According to Matt, Newaygo is about twelve river miles from Pine Street. Walking upriver from the Pine Street access there is some prime water consisting of runs, gravel and pockets that can be easily reached and fished by wading anglers. I have had some fair success fishing this water during past visits.

In the spring, the busiest part of the river is the section between the access below the dam and Pine Street. Below Pine Street the pressure can be lighter, but on the weekends there will still be considerable pressure and competition for prime areas. Boat ramps and adequate parking can be found at all three of the access points noted above.

The Muskegon is clearly a fly fishing river, and I always leave with the sense that by paying your dues it will yield wonderful rewards. Some of its deep, long pools lend themselves perfectly to traditional techniques, especially in the fall and winter, but also for fresh spring steelhead. Matt, as well as some other guides working the river, have encountered consistent success fishing big spey flies on heavy sink-tips. There is a lifetime of learning here. Matt has begun this process by spending a considerable amount of time in the fifty or more miles of river from Newaygo down to the lake. The Muskegon also sees some very large steelhead. Legitimate twenty-pound fish are a possibility.

The Muskegon is certainly to be considered one of the Great Lakes prime steelhead rivers. With its runs apparently building each year, its future looks bright. The run consists of a mix of wild and hatchery fish. The Muskegon is only about forty-five minutes from the Pere Marquette, creating a good combination when visiting the area for an extended time.

Oconto River (JK)

The city of Green Bay conjures up images of football teams entrenched in mortal battle being played on a frozen tundra in temperatures that rival the Arctic. These are hardly conditions that would inspire any steelhead angler. Yet 20 miles further northward flows another river famous for hard-fighting steelhead that migrate out of the northwestern reaches of Lake Michigan. The Door Peninsula which juts into the lake northeast of the city forms a body of water known as Green Bay. The Oconto River is a tributary that empties into the bay near the town of Oconto. And on those occasions when weather patterns moderate, the Oconto provides fly fishing opportunities for steelhead that last from fall well into springtime.

The section of the Oconto River that flows into the impoundment above the dam at the town of Stiles is a beautiful, meandering, medium-sized trout stream. But below the dam, the river changes character. There it is big and broad, but simple; tannic in appearance, but very clear. The long flat riffles below the dam still bear the scars of past spawning activity, though there were no fish visible anywhere at the time of my visit. Easily waded stretches, both runs and depressions throughout the width of water, define the entire area that can be observed from the old bridge site. Because wading across the entire section could be difficult at times, access can be obtained on both sides of the river. And though there has been some difficulty attaining a consistent flow in recent years, local sportsmen groups have reached some favorable agreements with the Oconto Electric Cooperative which operates the hydroelectric facility at the dam. A regularity of releases from the small reservoir should provide more predictable conditions that will benefit the fishery as well as the fishermen. These releases also provide ice-free fishing conditions that can last throughout the winter.

The Oconto gets strong runs of Chinook in early fall, followed by a substantial run of brown trout. During this late fall period, winter steelhead start showing up also, and these fish are likely Chambers Creek strain stocked by Wisconsin for cold-weather fishing opportunities. The spring runs are probably of Ganaraska origins. It is still unclear whether the river's potential for natural reproduction that we had heard about for years actually occurs. Some officials do believe this is a possibility for the future if a stable flow can be maintained.

The way to find this upper portion of the Oconto is to follow Highway 141 to Stiles. The river there provides a long length of fly fishable water that gradually becomes less defined a few miles down from the dam. From that point downstream, floating the river opens up other possibilities including more fishable breaks at various locations. A set of riffles accessed by following County Road J can also be a good ambush point to intercept migrating steelhead.

While the Oconto presents the fly angler with a broad range of possibilities for a long period of time, the best of other local options occurs in the series of rivers southeast of Green Bay. The Peshtigo River north of Oconto gets a solid steelhead run, but its big water is more suited for the angler who enjoys a challenge. Most activity there occurs below the dam.

Pere Marquette (RK)

Even though I have fished its waters a few days of nearly each of the last ten years, I hardly feel worthy to speak of its hallowed flows. This is the quintessential Great Lakes river. There are miles of free-flowing currents uninterrupted by dams or other indiscretions. The PM, as it is affectionately known, turns and winds and doubles back on itself as it meanders over sand and gravel aimlessly through thickly forested banks. Initially its currents look soothing and lazy, but when you step in, its flows are forceful and gain instant respect. The PM is protected under the Natural Wild and Scenic River Act. It would be unfitting for it to be any other way. Its beauty is spectacular and its steelhead are wild. With the exception of some summer runs, the returning fish are all Michigan strain steelhead produced in the high quality of the Pere Marquette watershed. Cool summer flows are fueled by numerous spring seeps and small overgrown tributaries which create perfect habitat for smolt production. The PM truly has it all.

In many ways, the Pere Marquette is typical of Great Lakes water flowing through a bank-to-bank channel with holding water being characterized by a series of runs, pockets, drops in the gravel floor, and sweeping bend pools. It is different from classic West Coast water but a few of these elements can be found in some deep placid pools, particularly on the lower end, and in broad tails found at the conclusion of a number of runs. The PM is also home to a significant population of resident trout. This, combined with a limited run of summer steelhead, creates a near year-round fishery. The PM has a rich history, one that includes interesting personalities and some of the first steelhead guides in the Great Lakes. Zimmy Nolph, who had surpassed 90 years old before recently passing away, is known to be one of the first. Guide Bob Nicholson, who owns and operates the Baldwin Creek Motel, is now the river's elder statesman with many years under his belt. The river's quality has attracted and developed a new core of guides, some of the best in the Great Lakes region. Names such as John Kluesing, Walt Grau, Tom Johnson, Jim Johnson, Jac Ford, and Kelly Galloup are closely associated with a quality experience, high ethics, and the development of the techniques and flies which are popular on the river today. Jim Johnson now has only a limited guiding schedule and, along with Shaun McDonald, concentrates on the management of Johnson's Pere Marquette Lodge located in Baldwin along the banks of the PM. This is a full-service operation geared toward ensuring that a trip to the river will be an enjoyable one. The rooms at the lodge are very comfortable and include breakfast and dinner. A complete guide service covers all the nearby rivers and the fly shop is stocked with everything one needs to chase steelhead. The best part is that the lodge is in walking distance of the upper PM.

The Pere Marquette can be loosely split into two areas. For the most part, the upper boundary to the quality steelhead water is the M-37 bridge.

From this point downstream to the Gleason's Landing access comprises the famous flies-only section. While only a scant few miles by way of the crow, this stretch is estimated at about seven river miles considering all its twists and turns. The upper water is quite intimate and brushy, about as small as I prefer to go in terms of steelhead water. After the Baldwin River meets up with the PM less than a quarter of the way through the flies-only section, there is a noticeable gain in volume, and I find the water from this point down to Gleason's to be comfortable fishing. At the peak times of the season, you will encounter a fair amount of pressure throughout the flies-only section. The access to the river is quite good, and once to the river, state law allows you to fish private property by staying in the stream and getting out to wade around obstructions. There will also be a fair amount of drift boat traffic at certain times. Many are operated by guides who are quite respectful of the wading angler. Fishing with a guide is a great way to experience this river. In his book *River Journal: Pere Marquette*, Matt Supinski places into detail some specific things to know about the flies-only water including access points and water selection. This book gives a great concise coverage of the entire watershed.

The water below Gleason's Landing becomes quite large, possibly reaching 90 feet or so in width. In this big water, crossing and even wading can be a little difficult. There is less gravel, more sand, and some deep, dark pools. The access points are more spread out than above. The river runs through an increased amount of federal land, meaning the number of cottages decreases and the scenery gets even better. In the spring, more steelhead will be condensed into the gravel-laden flies-only water, but one will find more elbow room on this lower section. It may take a little more time to uncover its secrets, but it is worth the effort. I have had some successful fishing all the way downriver below the town of Walhalla.

Most of my experience on the PM has been in the spring. While my preference is for fall steelhead, throughout the spring, fresh fish continue to arrive, and I have found these to react similarly to fall fish. The spring runs commonly intensify in late March and peak through the first few weeks of April. Weather conditions can shift the best fishing ahead of or behind this time frame. The PM is quite dependable in the spring. Because of its sandy banks, it can withstand significant moisture, taking heavy rains to wash it out. The river's groundwater influence assists in maintaining decent flows even in years of little moisture, but when low water persists, a freshening rain can draw large numbers of steelhead. Fresh fish can be found into May at a time when angler numbers can be quite low. Fall runs can be encountered in October and November and vary in intensity from year to year. In the fall, it becomes important to learn a few pools that are productive and to fish them intently. It is equally important to gain familiarity with the many contours of the bottom of a particular run as some that are full of deadfalls can be a nightmare for the

Jerry Kustich attached to a Pere Marquette steelhead.

fly box. However, fall fish swimming in optimum water temperatures are known to move to a fly. In his work *Michigan Steelhead Fly Fishing Manual,* Bob Colson gives accounts of his dry line experiences on Midwestern rivers, most of which related to the Pere Marquette. There are some opportunities from December through February, and they will be directly dependent on weather patterns and water conditions.

Clear water usually calls for fine tippets of 3 to 4x. It is only wise to go this light when the rod being utilized is capable of handling such low breaking strengths. Small flies with a natural look and color along with small egg patterns will be productive in low, clear water. A stealthy approach is also important when these conditions exist. Because of the river's numerous tight pockets or runs and quick currents, many of the fly anglers are currently utilizing the running line approach. However, a long single-handed rod, or a two-hander combined with a floating line and a long leader, or a variety of mini-tips with short leaders are all effective ways to cover the PM's water while appealing to a more traditional style. Aggressive fish will not shy away from heavier tippets. River guides John Kluesing and Walt Grau advanced two-handed rod fishing on the PM in recent years. They have even utilized the greater length of the two-hander for maximum line control for nymph fishing.

To know the PM is to love it. It is one of those special places where a certain warmth is generated by the mention of its name. A warmth that can be read on a person's face before any words are spoken. My fondest memory of the Pere Marquette occurred only a few years ago. I met Jim Johnson in the morning to fish Michigan's Muskegon River. Bright sun, clear water, and the lack of fresh fish made for a tough day. With only a few hours of daylight left we sped to the PM. With the confidence that can only be gained through years of experience and an intimate knowledge and love of a river, Jim paraded us to a sweet run. Our hooking was better than our landing, but we did intense battle with some fresh fish. A few pointers from that night led directly to a beautiful, bright fish brought to hand the next morning which was and still is my finest Wolverine State steelhead.

The PM is a shining gem. It is a must river for the serious Great Lakes steelhead fly fisher.

Root River (RK)

Although not fitting the model of a complete fly fishing steelhead river, this book would not seem complete without a discussion of the Root River. It enters Lake Michigan at Racine, Wisconsin. Located between Milwaukee and Chicago, the river is surrounded by a solid population mass up and down the lake shore. Combat fishing was how it was first described to me, and upon a visit, I found this to be rather descriptive but exaggerated. What I actually saw was a lot of anglers fishing together, hooking steelhead and having a good time. This was a few years back and today it probably wouldn't interest me that much, but the Root provides opportunity for anglers and could be the starting point for some future steelhead fly fishing enthusiasts.

A dam just upstream from Route 38 restricts steelhead migrations to the lower few miles of the river. The water just below the dam and downstream is the most popular. The Root is heavily stocked and normally receives heavy returns, a reason it is a favorite among anglers. After a rain, fall or spring, there is almost always some fish present, sometimes of incredible numbers. The Root muddies easily from rain, but those that fish it prefer the off-color water. This water below the dam is fairly nondescript and runs bank to bank making it a chore to land a fish in higher water. Most techniques will involve adding weight to the leader to offset the swift flow. Because of this and the people factor, it may not be a good river to try any traditional techniques. However, I did find some water further downriver accessed through Brose Park where very few anglers could be found. Access to some good water can be gained at Lincoln Park as well.

In 1994, the Root River Steelhead Facility was constructed through a cooperative effort. Its main purpose is to provide brood stock for Wisconsin's Lake Michigan steelhead fishery. In order to fully utilize the facility, the following research objectives were established: to develop a long-term index of Chinook/coho/steelhead populations returning to the Root River by tracking the (1) abundance of returning adults, (2) age-specific growth and condition factors, (3) size and age distribution of returning adults, and (4) return to creel of these stocked species. An annual report is published each year detailing the yearly observations.

The Root falls into the category of making the most of what you have. Because of the dam and agricultural development, there is no hope for natural reproduction. But annual stockings are able to provide a productive fishery for many to enjoy.

St. Joseph River (RK)

The St. Joe has its headwaters in the state of Michigan, dips down south into Indiana, and then flows north back into the Wolverine State before dumping into Lake Michigan at the town of St. Joseph. The word here is opportunity—one that has been improved and even created in recent years through a cooperative effort by the Michigan and Indiana departments of natural resources as well as the U.S. Fish and Wildlife Service. A handful of dams built on the river from 1868 through the early 1900's for hydroelectric purposes had restricted fish migration to the lower 23 miles, blocking off most of its better water and a number of tributaries. Through the St. Joseph River Interstate Anadromous Fish Project, two new fish ladders were constructed in each state and another existing passage was improved. In addition, a hatchery was constructed to supply fingerlings to establish a fishable run of steelhead. The finished product, which now has opened up the river to a total of 63 miles to be accessed by lake-run fish, is the result of a 12-year effort at a cost of 11 million dollars. By all accounts, especially in terms of recreation and economics, it is a very successful project. A number of other rivers come to mind where such a project could see similar results.

The St. Joe is a big river with broad, sweeping flows. Some of the river runs deep and slow with little opportunity for fly fishing. As one moves up the system, the fly fishing water increases. The river runs through a combination of agricultural fields and various-sized population centers. The water running through the various towns does not detract from the opportunity or experience. The section of river near South Bend and Mishawaka and above represents significant possibilities for the fly rod as a more manageable-sized river combines with runs, riffles, and gravel. The access in this section is very good with no less than 16 official access points from the Indiana/Michigan border to the Twin Branch Dam which marks the end of the upstream migration. Access can also be found near and around the dam sites at Berrien Springs, Buchanan, and Niles in Michigan. A map which describes the project as well as detailing access points is available through the department of natural resources of either state.

This is certainly a case where the use of hatchery fish can clearly be supported. A steelhead fishery now flourishes in a river which never had significant runs. This created situation allows more people to enjoy the pursuit of steelhead fishing. The St. Joseph is heavily stocked with a combination of winter-run fish from Michigan and summer-run Skamania-strain steelhead produced at the Richard Clay Bodine Fish Hatchery near the Twin Branch Dam. The result is a near year-round steelhead fishery when favorable conditions exist. The winter-run fish provide good opportunity in the fall and spring and the Skamania-strain fish, which typically migrate beginning in June, provide opportunity throughout the summer right into late fall. Skamania are known for their aggressive behavior toward a fly. Combine this with often favorable water temperatures and it is the perfect recipe for traditional steelhead techniques.

Water temperature is the key when in pursuit of summer-run steelhead. I found that out firsthand on an August stop at the St. Joe. A few days of sweltering heat had left the river in the mid to upper 70's. I fished some nice water below the Berrien Springs Dam but the heat had the fish laying low. Two key items when fishing for summer runs on the St. Joe. When there is a string of cool weather combined with offshore winds bringing cooler water near shore anytime from June through the end of September, get to the river. When water temperatures are high in the main river, search out cooler water which could be in the form of a spring seep or a cooler tributary. It is a good bet that fish will be concentrated there. One of the main tributaries, Dowagiac Creek, adds cool water to the system which commonly holds summer-runs. The Skamania on the St. Joe are known to feed on its blanket caddis hatches. On the evening of the aforementioned day, cooler air prevailed and clouds of caddis appeared toward dark. I witnessed a few huge boils in the tail of a long pool, which I would like to think was the result of a feeding steelhead. I cast to the area in vain but thought it would be fun to try again someday. Fresh St. Joe steelhead will take big flies in an aggressive manner. When the water is low and clear, the best strategy is to concentrate on natural patterns—nymphs, caddis larvae and eggs. There is much to be learned about this fishery, and in time it may establish itself as a premier river in the Great Lakes region. Matt Supinski has been learning some of the big, lower water via his jet boat and is uncovering some significant opportunities. Getting together with Matt could be a good way to see the river.

14

Lake Erie

Big Creek (JK)

That particular day in late November was as dreary as it gets. The clouds and fog draped the entire region in a twilight type of aura that lasted from morning until dark. When we left the Buffalo area, every stream in the region was swollen and muddy from a few days of constant rain. In fact, most creeks were running outside their banks. Our intention was to explore a little-known tributary entering Lake Erie from Ontario's north shore, and though we figured it, too, would be unfishable, the opportunity would afford an evaluation of this creek under the worst possible conditions.

Big Creek enters into the deep eastern basin of Lake Erie at Long Point Bay, a piece of water created by a long finger of land stretching into the main body of the lake. The spring creek-type nature of this tributary is unique in the Lake Erie basin. Flowing out of the Norfolk Sand Plain, the constant charge of groundwater added to the base flow gives the creek similar characteristics to those of the famous Michigan rivers entering Lake Michigan's east shore. Senior Management Biologist for the Ontario Ministry of Natural Resources, Larry Halyk grew up fishing Big Creek with his father. He recalls the steelhead that they would catch years ago before there were any active stocking programs in the lake. Those fish were sleek, silver, wild, and hard to forget. And though the environmental problems of the 60's and early 70's severely impacted this wild run, a significant naturalized run now occurs there once again, spawned in the gravel and reared in the consistency of Big Creek's flow.

To our surprise, the creek was running high but still fishably clear when we located the portion that runs under Route 16 near Lynedoch. The water there was deep, bending around cutbanks and weaving through years of collected downfall. The current carved out distinct runs, and there were a number of obvious places to find moving steelhead. Landing them may have been a problem among the tangles. The creek at that point was a very comfortable size for angling, but it required some unique tactics to fish it adequately. According to Larry, such periods of high water were perfect for Big Creek. Since the lower sections of the creek are very deep and much slower, fall fish will stay there until a push of high water invites them upstream. Intrigued by the investigation, we fished this area only briefly. With the little amount of dismal light still available, we headed up to look at another section of water Larry recommended.

The stretch of river below the town of Delhi presents a series of gravel-type runs and pools. This section of water is known to gather fish for spawning purposes, but historically the Quance Dam in Delhi has impeded the progress of the run beyond this point. However, the dam is no longer a barrier to steelhead as a fishway was constructed in 1996. According to Larry, there are good numbers of steelhead successfully spawning in Big Creek and its tributaries upstream of Delhi. Electro fishing surveys during the summer of 1998 showed impressive results of wild juvenile steelhead and brown trout at all stations on Big Creek and its high-quality tributaries. In addition, juvenile densities below Delhi are higher than the previous year and many times higher than five years ago. The run here is building. Much of the credit goes to the Delhi District Anglers Association who have been quietly conducting habitat improvement and operating the Quance Dam fishway. Because the steelhead usually get up to the Delhi area in late November, Ontario has extended its steelhead fishing season on Big Creek until December 31st. Unlike the Great Lakes tributaries in the States that stay open all year long, the Province of Ontario closes many sections of prime steelhead water to protect natural populations of spawning brown trout occurring during late fall. Some of Big Creek's best steelheading opportunities take place in December. By the time we explored the creek and found the access points, it became too dark to fish. No doubt, Big Creek is a sleeper well worth future investigations.

Venison Creek is a well-known tributary of Big Creek with a vibrant history. Its reputation as a premier trout stream brought folks to fish its waters from all around Lake Erie earlier in the 1900's. After years of habitat degradation, these days the creek is coming back, and though it provides little value as a steelhead stream because of closures, it does contribute many wild steelhead to the system. With an increased interest in wild fish throughout the continent, studies of the entire Big Creek drainage may inspire a wild fish management plan that could restore the fish still living vividly in Larry's memory.

Young's Creek flows into Lake Erie in close proximity to Big Creek. This small stream gets the same groundwater influences from the sand plain, and it supports a good population of wild fish as well. Although its size limits fly fishing potential, it does offer options to the creative angler.

Cattaraugus Creek (RK)

It was the early 70's when I first fished the "Cat." Our brother-in-law Danny Flutur led us on a winding trip along Zoar Valley Road to a point where an official access point now exists. Back then, I remember access being a little tenuous. I can recall the day as though it were yesterday. Soft October light illuminated the golden-orange foliage creating a nearly surreal setting. The creek's soft, greenish flows split the valley in half as it turned and wound with the contours of the earth. Even at that young age, the Cattaraugus struck me. Looking back, it wasn't just its beauty but its mystery and intrigue. It was a wondrous new world, one that included lake-run fish that we knew little about. It was wild and untamed, such a dichotomy for Western New York. I seemed to find an immediate connection. We fished with hardware in those days, and I hooked a large Chinook that I so badly wanted to land, but which spit the hook after a violent struggle. Jerry lost an acrobatic 18 inch, what we called a rainbow, but which certainly was a steelhead. This occurred a year ahead of any steelhead stocking programs, quite possibly a fish with direct genetic connection to those stocked in the 1920's. I have often reflected on that day and contemplated its significance. Without us fully realizing it, that day was our first step to a lifelong love affair with steelhead.

The Cattaraugus Creek seems misnamed as it flows with the size and character of a small river. It averages 60 to 80 feet in width with some areas sprawling out even wider. Riffles blend into long runs and pools, many which conclude with wide, slow tailouts. Various pockets and tight runs can be found between the runs and pools, and can hold fish when they are on the move. The floor of the Cattaraugus is a combination of gravel, slate, and various-sized boulders. The steelhead water flows from a dam near the village of Springville approximately 40 miles to Lake Erie near the town of Irving. The Cat possesses some of, if not the most, conducive water in the entire Great Lakes region for traditional steelhead fishing. When water temperatures and conditions are right, there should be no other way to approach this river. Various spey flies fished on dry lines, sink-tips, or with sinking leaders work quite well and are the most satisfying manner in which to catch a steelhead. Leave the running lines at home.

The Cattaraugus may be more famous for its water conditions than it is for its water. The main flow and its various tributaries drain vast miles, much of which runs through clay banks that quickly stain the water and keep it that

A very fresh, wild Cattaraugus Creek steelhead that came to a swung fly.

way for days. You must pick your times carefully when fishing here, and the successful Cattaraugus angler constantly keeps abreast of water conditions and is very flexible. This unpredictability is the one factor that has kept the Cat from being popular among traveling anglers. There have even been years when rains and runoff have timed themselves to a degree that literally resulted in no fishable days for an entire season. In an average year, possibly 50 to 60 percent of the days in October will find fishable conditions and maybe 25 percent in November. It normally goes down from there. The fact that hitting this river right takes such calculation is one reason that success here is so sweet.

The Cattaraugus can roughly be broken into three sections. The first section runs from the town of Gowanda down to the lake. Most of this water runs through the Cattaraugus Indian Reservation which requires a special Seneca Nation Fishing License. While a few pools near the town of Versailles are located off the reservation as well as some of the water near the lake, it is wise to have this special license when fishing any of the water below Gowanda. The lower eight miles has good access from Route 438 via a number of dirt roads that lead to the river. The second is a ten-mile stretch that ends at Gowanda and runs through a spectacular gorge with very limited access. Many of the pools in this section are slate bottomed, and the fish do not seem to hold as well as in many of the upper pools. The upper section runs from the dam in Springville down some fifteen miles to a New York State access point. There is an informal public access near the dam. In general, this upper section has fairly limited access as well.

The Cattaraugus is certainly a better fall river than spring, with winter fishing only possible in the mildest of seasons. In years with sufficient water flows and cool-enough temperatures, fishable numbers of steelhead can often be found in the lower reaches by early to mid September. Normally good numbers exist through October, and the peak of the fall fishing probably occurs in the last week or two of October and the first few of November. The first good rain of the fall is required to distribute the fish throughout the entire river system. For traditional techniques, September through early November is the best timing. Fresh fish combined with water temperatures in the 40's and 50's create the perfect combination. When the conditions prevail, spring fishing is normally at its best in late March and early April. I have caught some very spirited drop-back fish through mid May.

Typical Cattaraugus steelhead average 22 to 28 inches in length, some of which are as exciting a fish as I have encountered. There are some wild fish in the mix which makes this place all the more special. The Cattaraugus provides the full steelhead experience. Miles of water for fish and angler to spread out, an unspoiled setting, and beautiful runs and pools for fly fishing. The strategy that this river requires adds to its appeal and challenge. Any day you catch a steelhead on the Cat is a good day. This is a river where one can find peace, escaping the competition of life and of other more heavily fished waters. The Cat seems to cleanse the soul as its inviting current seems to flow right through me instead of around.

There are a handful of other steelhead streams in the general area that do clear much quicker than the Cattaraugus. Moving southwest along the Lake Erie shoreline, both Canadaway Creek and Chatauqua Creek receive decent runs of steelhead. Chautauqua is probably the better of the two with more consistent runs and some natural reproduction. Heading north from the Cat, Eighteen Mile Creek provides good fly fishing opportunity in both the fall and spring.

Conneaut Creek (RK)

Our previous two visits had turned into little more than nature walks. Although we saw a few steelhead, some alive and some dead, none had come by way of connection to the end of our leader. It was time to call on some expertise. Jerry, Brian Slavinski, and I met Jerry Darkes on a brisk first of December morning near interstate 90. Jerry Darkes is a good friend and knowledgeable steelhead guide/instructor and fly tackle rep from the Cleveland area, and through his trips and classes has built a solid reputation throughout

Ohio. He had been fishing the Conneaut extensively and promised us the grand tour some time in the fall. With the season winding down, today was the day. Jerry guided us through a variety of pools and runs. While the water was a little lower and clearer than what would be considered perfect, our prospects were good. By the end of the day, we had each tasted success, including a couple good fish pushing the ten-pound mark. With the cold water, the fish had not come easy; in fact, persistence was clearly the word of the day. In the end, it finished with one of those overwhelming feelings of satisfaction—we had beat the elements, encountered the object of our visit, and had shared it all with good company.

The Conneaut runs through the eastern end of Ohio entering Lake Erie less than ten miles from the Pennsylvania border. On its way to the lake, it runs through a combination of farmland and lightly forested hardwood stands. It averages 40 to 60 feet in width, and because of its low gradient, the Conneaut flows sluggishly from pool to pool. Actually, the holding water is mainly comprised of pockets and short runs that give the fish adequate security. The Conneaut runs over a mix of shale and gravel. The cuts, drops, and ledges of the shale often produce some of the prime holding lies, especially when low water predominates. As we found out, locating such ledges can be extremely important. The cuts and ledges will not necessarily be visible when the water is up a little, but it is important to make mental notes of this type of structure

The upper reaches of the Conneaut Creek.

during low-water periods. In the areas with gravel bottoms, some deeper pools have been formed. There are also numerous gentle tailouts which will hold resting steelhead, most often when the water is off-color.

This is a true spate river. When rains freshen the water and turn it green or even brown, there will normally be a movement of steelhead. Timing can be extremely important as it will drop and clear quickly. Aggressive, fresh-run Conneaut fish will grab a fly feverishly in green water but may need extra coaxing in clear water. This is one river where careful planning can mean everything.

Good runs of fish are often encountered when the proper conditions prevail throughout October and November. December can also be good with a combination of fresh and older fish. The upper reaches begin to fish better during this time period. There can be some winter fishing in years when the weather is mild. In recent years, the spring fishing, which normally begins in early March and runs through April, has been very good. Jerry Darkes has filled me in on the details of some big fish at this time as well, including a few in the 14- to 17-pound range.

The Conneaut travels some 40 or 50 miles with its headwaters actually flowing from Pennsylvania. The lower ten miles is consistently the best water. Along Route 7 between I-90 and the lake, there is a popular access point as the creek runs under the road. In this area, there are numerous small pools and runs offering a good starting point. There are a few other access points to the creek on the lower end as well. The upper water is smaller but quite fishable. The creek makes a big bend to the west and then horseshoes back to the east. Route 7 crosses the river again upstream, and while it is only a few miles by road, it may be twenty or more by way of the water because of this big bend. We found access at a couple of bridge crossings on this upper water.

Overall, the Conneaut is an enjoyable steelhead stream but does not represent Ohio's only contribution to the Great Lakes fishery. For those in the Cleveland area with a few hours to spare, try the Rocky River. It has some characteristics very similar to the Conneaut. Access can be gained through the Metro Parks. The Grand River, between Cleveland and the Conneaut, is big water which is often unfishable but has large, gentle pools perfect for more traditional techniques.

Elk Creek (JK)

Elk Creek enters Lake Erie near the city of Erie, Pennsylvania. Over the years, this tributary has gained the reputation for being one of the top steelhead producers in the country. In fact, this blue-ribbon stream has been the subject of many articles. And while it may yield many fish annually, Elk Creek is certainly not typical of most steelhead streams found anywhere else throughout the Great Lakes. This pretty creek of small to moderate size carves its way through a beautiful ravine, and its water flows over a bedrock and slate floor that change little from year to year. Runs, holes, nooks, crannies, pockets, crevices, and ledges all provide security for the many steelhead that wander into this tributary throughout the season. When the water is in perfect shape, the deep holes take on an emerald hue, presenting an inviting enticement for any angler gazing upon its waters.

The secret behind Elk Creek's amazing success is simple. Pennsylvania's Fish and Game Commission inundates its portion of Lake Erie with close to one million steelhead per year. Since Elk Creek is the largest of Pennsylvania's tributaries found along its 41 miles of shoreline, it is the prime benefactor of this aggressive program. A good percentage of steelhead surviving until adulthood eventually find their way back to Elk Creek or some of the state's smaller neighboring tributaries. At times, Elk Creek can be alive with fish. And though this can provide one of the most unique fishing opportunities anywhere, the experience needs to be tempered with a balanced perspective. Rumors of thirty hookups per day at one time were not uncommon, but such reports can wreak havoc with the psyche of any angler, particularly those avid steelheaders more accustomed to the conventional expectations from other regions of the Great Lakes basin.

Elk Creek depends greatly on fall rains to draw steelhead into its waters. The base flow of any slate-bottomed creek is typically very low because the system is able to gain little recharge from groundwater seepage. Under the proper conditions, fish can enter the creek as early as late September, and unbelievably, the run can last all the way until spring. Winter fishing opportunities are totally dependent upon air temperature. Creeks of slate tend to freeze readily.

Knowing the rhythms of Elk Creek is important. Heavy rains can raise the water in any slate creek rather quickly. We experienced such a situation a few years back when a steady downpour elevated the water about one foot in a few hours, but as the water was on the rise, the fish turned on rather significantly. They shut off immediately, however, as the water continued to get dirtier. Water drops and clears quickly in a slate-bottomed creek as well. Less than two days later, the water was in perfect shape and fish were everywhere. As the water continues to drop, it is believed that many fish retreat back into the lake to wait for the process to repeat itself once again. Although this may be true, many fish still remain in the variety of holding lies found the entire length of the creek.

Fishing techniques can vary greatly from day to day as well as season to season. Under rapidly changing conditions when water is on the rise, swinging large, bright flies works well. As the water drops, the same techniques with smaller flies will continue to be an effective approach. Then, when the water

Water conditions are the key to success on Pennsylvania's Elk Creek.

settles into various states of moderation and clarity, a wide range of nymphing methods can be employed. As the water conditions get very low and clear, avid Elk Creek steelheaders utilize small flies and very light leaders. Landing fish up to ten pounds on 4x or 5x tippet can present an entirely different kind of challenge. In the cold months, this same small-fly technique is the preferred method used to entice steelhead in the grips of midwinter lethargy.

Most angling activity centers near the town of Girard, west of Erie, where many anglers target the lower several miles of the creek. As word of the Elk's prolific nature has increased over the past several years, so has the fishing pressure. These days it is much more difficult to duplicate the per angler success rates of former years because the resource, in terms of fish and space, is shared by so many. A long season helps disperse the pressure somewhat.

Although the Elk can provide wonderful steelhead fishing at times, it should be emphasized that this experience does not represent "normal" steelheading situations where much of the day can be spent searching for just a few fish. The avid angler familiar with the Elk Creek fishery would be advised to adjust expectations when visiting other steelhead rivers elsewhere in the Great Lakes or on the West Coast.

Other creeks in the area get plenty of Pennsylvania fish as well. Walnut Creek and Sixteen Mile Creek both provide options for anglers looking for some variety. Twenty Mile Creek on the New York border is another pretty slate stream worth looking at, particularly after a freshet of rain.

Grand River (RK)

We all love a good news story, especially when the news is about a steelhead river. Ontario's Grand River is a good news story. Its upper reach is an already famous tailwater trout fishery producing big browns that feed on dry flies. But little is known of the lower steelhead water which is just beginning to emerge. The Grand flows into Lake Erie at Port Maitland, less than an hour from Buffalo, NY. In the late 1980's, the deteriorated Lorne Dam finally gave way to the point where fish passage was possible and opened access to a handful of tributaries which provide ideal spawning habitat. Runs of wild fish are building each year and have reached the point of fishable levels. The origin of the steelhead that have established the run is still a mystery, but genetic studies which will shed some light on the subject are currently under way.

There is still one dam at Caledonia, some 30 miles from Lake Erie, which the steelhead must swim over to reach the spawning water. The fish will stage in this area, and there is approximately 10 miles of fly fishing water below the dam. This section contains gentle riffles that drop into runs and pools which average four to five feet in depth. While this entire section will hold steelhead, higher concentrations will be found nearer to the dam. This is especially true once the water temperature dips below 40 degrees F. as the fish will have more difficulty in clearing the dam. The pool at the dam receives much pressure, but the next half-mile represents good fly water. The water below Caledonia generally runs off-color until late fall. Wade with care as fractured bedrock creates an uneven bottom and the off-color water can disguise dangerous drop-offs. Aggressive fish are known to chase large white flies when properly presented in the water below the dam. Above the dam, one must travel to arrive at suitable fly water. The water from just below Brantford up to the dam at Paris, some 20 miles, represents the heart of this river's steelhead holding water. Brantford is located nearly 60 miles upriver from the lake. This area simply looks like steelhead water. Moderate to gentle flows moving over a bottom of gravel, bedrock, and sand. Boulders of various sizes are strewn throughout the pools and represent perfect holding lies in the smooth glide of a tailout. The Grand is big water, the way I like it. Near Brantford it is approximately 200 feet wide—plenty of room to air out long casts. In normal flows it is difficult to cross, and I found myself wading to the extent of my abilities in attempting to cover all the water from one side of the river.

There is one slight problem. The fishery has grown faster than its regulations. Prior to 1998, the fishing season for trout, which includes steelhead, closed on September 30 and reopened with the trout season the following spring. Beginning October 1, 1998, the open season for rainbow and brown trout will be extended to December 31 for the water 25 meters below Wilkes Dam in Brantford downstream to Lake Erie. The kill limit for this extended season is restricted to one for a regular license and catch and release for a conservation license. The Wilkes Dam is a low-head structure that does not really affect steelhead migration except for the middle of winter. This still leaves much of the prime water outside of this new extended season. However, an effort is being made to apply an extended season which would cover the remaining water up to Paris. Since the management of the spawning brood stock is recognized as a top priority, more restrictive regulations are intended for this section. Such special regulations require the politics of public consultation. Jack Imhof, Aquatic Ecologist for the Ontario Ministry of Natural Resources, is coordinating this effort through his "exceptional waters" program. It seems simple, but it appears that Ontario fisheries management is ruled by the same bureaucratic lunacy all too often found in the Great Lakes states. Senior Management Biologist, Larry Halyk, along with others, has recognized the need for an extended fall season for quite some time. Warren Yerex, Supervisor of Aquatic Resources for the Grand River Conservation Authority, has always been supportive of this concept. Such special regulations for steelhead will go a long way toward elevating its status.

Larry Halyk fishing a dry fly on the Grand River.

There is also some discussion of a catch and release winter season for the water below Caledonia.

The lower Grand is a fly fishing river. Broad runs and pools of moderate depths are perfect for slowly swinging flies that entice steelhead. And as this fishery emerges, so does an incredible opportunity—steelhead on a dry fly. Larry Halyk called me one evening with reports of returning adult steelhead rising to the heavy caddis hatches found on the Grand. Anytime I hear such a report it is worth checking out. It was late September, and the air was brisk, summoning an early fall. We fished a pool that had "dry fly" written all over it—gentle flows, fairly shallow, and intermittent boulders. It reminded me of a pool where I had successfully fished dries on the Bulkley River in British Columbia. Larry graciously allowed me the first pass. About midway through the pool, the tranquil of the early autumn morning was shattered as Larry shouted out loudly. I looked back in time to see the heaving boil left by a large, bright steelhead that had followed Larry's bomber into the placid inside seam. The fish wasn't hooked, but the enthusiasm that it generated was instant. I walked up to his position to receive a full account of the events. Larry is a very avid and accomplished steelheader who has caught more than his share of fish, but this occurrence left him shaken, fumbling to tie on another pattern. It was wonderful to witness such excitement. That was the only fish that showed to our fly that day, but Larry returned two more times, hooking a fish on the surface on his next trip and landing a six-pound male on his last which gently took a skated moth pattern. Three fish to the surface in three trips for Larry is fantastic dry fly fishing. I am very interested in the future potential of this river.

The spawning tributaries that feed the Grand are smaller creeks that are scarcely large enough for enjoyable fly fishing. However, the largest is the Nith River, a good-sized piece of water which receives a run of wild fish. With its run building, a serious fishery could develop here as well.

15

Lake Ontario

Black River (RK)

As I pulled into the parking lot of J. Patrick's Outfitters in Watertown, New York, in the predawn hours, I could see Pat Doldo tying a last-minute fly to take to the river. He was beaming with anticipation, if not for the day of fishing before us, then for the future of the Black River steelhead fishery. Pat, a licensed guide, has owned and operated his fly shop for ten years, but it has only been the last few, after a fish ladder was added to a dam in Dexter, that steelhead can migrate up through Watertown. The spring runs are currently the most consistent with the peak normally occurring in mid April and lasting into May. And there are some big fish. Steelhead weighing in the mid to upper teens and even pushing 20 pounds are caught each year. The real news is that the river appears to be producing a significant number of wild steelhead smolts. There is no indication at this point of how the wild fish are contributing to the return of adults, but it does add to the overall positive feeling of the direction of this river.

The Black is big, powerful water some two hundred feet in width. The current in the middle moves at considerable speeds with a slight roar to give a constant reminder of its force. Not a place for light tippets. Pat directed me to a run downriver from an official access point right in the city. The run was actually a couple-hundred-foot current break caused by a small rise in the bottom which was showing through as a small island on this day. The result was softer, quieter water which created the perfect respite for migrating fish. The bottom is a combination of gravel and uneven small boulders which stole

Pat Doldo fishes a current edge on New York's wild and forceful Black River.

a few of my flies. Looking at the river as a whole, these current breaks would seem to comprise the majority of the holding water although there were a few obvious pools which could be fly fished.

Pat is a proponent of traditional fishing, preferring large spey flies fished on weighted leaders, but admits that when the fishing gets tough, smaller black stonefly nymph patterns can work quite well. Certainly larger hooks combined with heavy tippets will favor the angler when a fish decides to move to the middle of the river since in some runs there is little opportunity to follow. In the run we fished in the morning, fighting a steelhead from the spot it was hooked would be the only way for a successful landing. Pat did hook one fish in the morning on an orange spey which promptly wrapped him around one of the aforementioned small boulders. I blamed the low pressure and miserable weather for our lack of hookups through the rest of the day, but it wasn't for a lack of fish as we witnessed a handful of steelhead roll on the surface.

I liked the look and feel of the Black. Wild and untamed, it's the right match for steelhead. The Black requires the utmost of respect when wading as its forceful flows have claimed a number of lives over the years. Unfortunately, early settlers found the need to try to tame it as another dam a mile or so above where we fished ends the upstream migration of steelhead. This leaves about six miles of water from this dam to Lake Ontario where it enters at Henderson Harbor. Currently, the access point where we started is the only official site and entry to most of the river is either restricted or dangerous. However, funds have been set aside and New York State, working in cooperation with the city of Watertown, is in the process of establishing more access. At this point, there are many stretches of the river that go unfished. Even where we parked, fishing pressure was light, and the encouraging part was the only three other anglers I saw or spoke with were all fly fishing, which points to the possibility of building a fly fishing tradition on this river.

The Black River clearly falls into the category of an emerging fishery with tremendous potential. With increased access, the opportunity for a lifetime of exploration is possible. I for one am encouraged, and I know I will be back.

Ganaraska River (JK)

Perhaps the Ganaraska River is one of the most significant steelhead tributaries in the entire Great Lakes basin. Entering Lake Ontario 60 miles east of Toronto at Port Hope, this short, modest, creek-sized "river" supports a substantial run of wild fish. Over the years, the steelhead of the Ganaraska have independently evolved into a genetic strain of fish unique to this specific drainage. Feral fish from the river are used to provide eggs for the Province of Ontario's supplemental stocking program, and these fish have been planted in small numbers in the Canadian portions of both Lake Erie and Lake Huron. Ganaraska progeny have also been introduced successfully into similar short drainages on Wisconsin's side of Lake Michigan. The Ganaraska strain has evolved into a heavy-bodied rainbow, and some of the fish returning annually are quite substantial, especially when compared to the size of their home water. Additionally, the run numbers an amazing 10,000 to 20,000 fish annually.

Known primarily as a spring-running fish, steelhead start entering the Ganaraska in late winter. Because the river above the cement lamprey control barrier called Corbett Dam is considered sanctuary water, it is closed to all anglers from late fall until late spring. At the dam, the fish readily proceed upstream utilizing a fish ladder and lift system. Although the short section of fishable runs found below the Highway 74 bridge downstream to Lake Ontario is open all year round, the piece of river immediately below the dam is permanently closed to further protect returning fish from angler harvest. These restrictions provide many benefits. By the time the regular trout season opens on the last weekend of April, many steelhead will have already spawned in the river's upper sections. This upstream closure also provides protection for a substantial native brown trout fishery, allowing late fall spawning activities to proceed without angler harassment.

When the season finally does open, there is a long stretch of slow water accessible to the public immediately above the dam. Although this holds some fly fishing value for the creative angler, most fly rodders head upstream to the Sylvan Glen Conservation Area. At this point, there is an excellent stretch of fly water available upstream above the bridge, allowing for a variety of fly rod techniques. The section below the same bridge readily encounters private water a short distance downstream. Although membership is required to fish this particular piece, it may well be worth the investment if there are any openings available. There is a series of classic fly fishing runs and pools available in this private section. Also, this portion of the river gathers many steelhead dropping back to the lake once the spawning cycle has been completed. So when conditions are right, it is not uncommon to find these large drop-backs taking mayflies off the surface in early May as they get recharged for another season in Lake Ontario.

We knew the river would be high as we were driving out of the heavy traffic east of Toronto. It had stopped raining, but the puddles in the area indicated that a major downpour had recently passed through. The run on the Ganaraska had been late; maybe this rain would finally bring some of them home for the spawning season. Since trout season had just opened the

The Ganaraska River above Sylvan Glen.

preceding weekend, we also knew there should be quite a few people on the stream this week as well. When we arrived at Port Hope, the river was high, dirty, and there surely were many anglers.

As we checked the section of river below the dam, we noted that several folks were hooking fish in the murky flow. We also noticed many fish flicking the surface the entire stretch. There was no doubt about it, a fresh run of steelhead had just arrived. When we checked the dam the next morning, hundreds of steelies were swimming in the pool below the barrier. They were also jumping high and slapping against the flow that trickled over the cement wall in a desperate attempt to get upstream. Other fish conveniently found the ladder. This impressive display provided a small glimpse that supported the Ganaraska's reputation. Because the river is relatively short, the water dropped and cleared throughout most of the day. We were able to hook our share of fish, too.

Although the Ganaraska is a pretty stream, it is not breathtaking as it winds through farm lands and new growth forests. For obvious reasons, the "Ganny," as it is affectionately called by locals, attracts many anglers from this very heavily populated section of Canada. Hopefully, this oasis will stay healthy as the area continues to grow. And though most fishing takes place in the lower 4 or 5 miles, there also are other locations worth exploring upstream.

Many serious north shore anglers fish several other tributaries in the area, though many of them are rather small. Wilmot Creek receives a good run of wild fish genetically geared for that specific drainage. Back toward Toronto, Duffin's Creek is also a good bet. And in Toronto, many anglers catch steelhead out of the Humber River in an urban setting. Many steelhead found along this shoreline are wild and well worth the hunt. Southwest of Toronto are two other smaller tributaries worthy of consideration—the Credit River and Bronte Creek. The Ganaraska is one of a kind, however, and despite the crowds, it is a must for the seasoned steelheader looking for the complete Great Lakes experience.

Genesee River (JK)

When Paul Jacob invited me to fish the Genesee River with him one day in a recent November, I jumped on the opportunity. Though it has long been on my "to do" list, favorable water conditions never seemed to coincide with time available in the past. The Genesee has the reputation for being a difficult piece of water to fish due in part to the fact that it isn't always in decent fishing shape. But despite episodes of high, dirty water, perhaps it is the rumor of trophy steelhead that has kept the desire to fish the "Genny" alive over the years. Paul is a young, accomplished angler, and since he grew up in close vicinity of the river, it didn't take long to realize that he had done his homework quite well. This particular year the water was low and clear, and the one Sunday we fished together provided exceptional fishing for steelhead up to 15 lbs. The rather large size of the river allows fish maximum room for fighting, but keeping these dynamos from heading full force back to Lake Ontario without hanging up on a boulder seemed futile at times.

Of the steelhead we landed that day, several showed no signs of fin clips or distorted dorsals indicative of hatchery fish. It is possible that some of these heavy-bodied nomads were wild fish from the Canadian tributaries located across the lake, a definite bonus to those of us who care about such matters. Some believe fall steelhead enter the Genny merely to gather food,

Paul Jacob caught this beautiful Genesee River steelhead on a swinging spey fly and a two-handed rod.

eating the salmon eggs released by the plethora of Chinook which clog the river throughout the fall. This same behavior is exhibited on the Niagara River. By spring, though, the river is stacked with many steelhead attempting to spawn. It doesn't always happen, but at least on that day, thanks to Paul, everything fell into place.

The Genesee River is a unique but temperamental piece of water which flows northward out of Pennsylvania through New York, bisecting Rochester a few miles above its entry into Lake Ontario. Although there is only about a mile of water below the impressive falls and the adjacent power plant which could be considered fly fishable, this section can hold many steelhead anytime between November and early May. Depending upon the volume of flow, the stretch includes a few well-defined runs, boulder-strewn pockets, and flat tailouts which can provide the fly angler some exciting possibilities for both traditional and nymphing techniques. In fact, Paul recently treated Rick to a day where a dozen or more fresh fish were hooked swinging spey flies on sink-tip lines. The water is wide and uncrossable, but it does fish well from both sides.

Although the Genesee River gorge provides a rather unlikely but beautiful respite from the urban setting which surrounds it, the cast of characters fishing the river could be unsettling to some. Because snagging and other illegal fishing activities seem to be a way of life on the Genny, many ethical anglers find this aspect of the experience quite disturbing. Unfortunately, authorities seem to have no intentions to patrol this area for abuses at this time.

Nonetheless, access into the gorge on the west side can be obtained from a city park, down a trail requiring a rather tricky hike, especially in the snow or rain. Descending to the river on the east side is done on a moderately sloped service road accessed from Seth Green Street. Once there, walking along the angular rocks can be difficult and wading the edges to fish pocket water can be downright treacherous. Much care is advised! Since the Genesee is a long, vast watershed, moderate rains or melting snow can adversely affect fishing conditions for extended periods.

Like so many Great Lakes tributaries, being there when all the conditions are favorable requires much research, and even more luck. But when things are right, this short reach of the Genesee River can provide classic steelheading opportunities in a surprisingly pretty setting.

Although most alternative options found along this shoreline of Lake Ontario have been covered in other sections, Irondequoit Creek, east of Rochester, can provide an opportunity for big fish—particularly during the winter months. Both its location as well as overcrowding when fish are around, however, are considered major drawbacks. But still, it is worth a look if you are in the area.

Niagara River (JK)

There is not a more challenging piece of water in the entire Great Lakes than the mighty Niagara. Its huge, tumultuous water is not only extremely dangerous for the intrepid angler, to catch fish consistently from this roaring dynamo requires an uncommon knowledge of the many forces that affect fish behavior in a massive vortex of eddies, boils, and raging rapids. Except for the summer months, good numbers of steelhead can be found throughout the entire river below Niagara Falls from September until May. The peak of the run starts irregularly in November, and while fish counts build throughout the winter, weather can severely limit the angler's ability to chase after these exciting fish that spend a portion of their lives growing heartily in the deep waters of Lake Ontario.

Steelhead enter the Niagara for many reasons. For one, its sheer size may merely be interpreted by many fish as an extension of the Lake. Also, because

Jerry Kustich and a silver Niagara River hen.

of extensive power generation at sites on both shorelines, the water in the lower river tends to be warmer at certain times of the year than in Lake Ontario, an attractive respite for roving steelies. Additionally, in the fall large runs of spawning Chinook and lake trout attract a following of these nomadic rainbow interested in munching on various stages of eggs deposited from both species. Then, after all spawning activity ceases, the steelhead turn their attention to the colossal numbers of baitfish found in the lower Niagara during the winter months which include shiners, shad, and smelt. This phenomenon alone could account for the increase of winter fish. The cycle subsequently ends with an impressive spawning effort in May where steelhead can readily be observed working redds in the select areas that provide gravel for such activity. And though wild fish productivity may not be substantial in the river, there has to be some contribution to the total stocked population from this source. However, at present, fishery managers will officially acknowledge that very little, if any, significant naturalized spawning actually does occur in the river.

Steelhead are caught both from the shore and out of boats. Needless to say, boat anglers need a sturdy, safe craft. Most offshore fish are taken by drifting with the current while casting a variety of deep sink lines or shooting heads and manipulating the fly to ride as naturally as possible in the turbid current. Shoreline anglers find breaks along the massive river that will catch a natural swing taking the fly along with the erratic flow. Stripping bait patterns through back eddies can also produce numerous takes from lake trout as well as steelhead.

Understanding the dynamics of the flow regime in the river is critical to a successful outing. Daily water releases from the American and Canadian power generation plants, located on each side of the deep gorge below the Devil's Hole area, pulse a huge amount of water previously siphoned from the upper river through a sophisticated system of intakes and diversion pipes. These releases intercept the tremendous flow coming from Niagara Falls. Fishing success depends upon timing the resulting swells so as to catch the right drift with a well-presented fly. When the water is too clear, however, the steelhead then position themselves too far from shore to reach effectively. Usually the astute angler will wait until strong storms blow the contents of shallow Lake Erie into a brown broth. This water then winds its way from Erie over the Falls and into the lower river. During the two- or three-day period it takes for the water to clear, the fish follow tight to the shore, and it is then that they are more takable by the bank fly rodder.

Access is available on the American side at Whirlpool Park, Devil's Hole, and Artpark in Lewistown. The scenery is exquisite, and the history associated with these sites is vibrant. Excellent water is also available at the corresponding parks on the Canadian side as well as at the town of Queenston. Long, demanding walks are required to descend the gorge via sets of old stone stairways at Whirlpool and Devil's Hole. Although user-friendly stairs can be found in a limited area at Artpark, walking around the rocks near any portion of the river demands extreme care, and this fact cannot be overemphasized.

Landing a steelhead in the lower river is as demanding as hooking one. Usually the fish are heavy shouldered, extremely lively, and they utilize the full force of the river to great advantage. Losing steelhead in this vast water is a common occurrence. The heat of battle is most certainly the time when the angler must use extra caution not to make a wrong step. We have both slipped partially into the water while fighting fish, or tumbled hard on slick boulders. Although a hookup or two now and then is all anyone can expect in the Niagara, landing one can provide a memory of a lifetime.

Oak Orchard Creek (RK)

We reluctantly peeked over the ridge a hundred feet down to the water. We had held out some type of false optimism, but that quickly vanished. Oak Orchard Creek resembled a scene from Willie Wonka's chocolate factory, with the flow pushed to the extents of its banks. There was no mistaking it, even in the dim glow of first light. My good friend Keith Myott had driven all night long from Albany to fish the spring steelhead runs for a couple of days. But overnight, April showers grew into torrential rains which drained off the miles of agricultural development. A quick drive confirmed what we already knew—all the surrounding creeks and streams were in even worse condition. By comparison and with a little imagination, the "Oak" almost looked fishable. Our options were very thin—fish high muddy water or don't fish at all. Since fishing is almost always better than not fishing, we selected the former.

This stands out in my mind as one of the greatest steelhead decisions ever made. Prospecting some of the soft seams of the normal holds actually resulted in two hookups and one landed fish on big, bright flies. What happened in the afternoon is a blur. Luckily the rain was warm, raising water temperatures to the mid 40's, bringing with it an incredible number of fresh-run fish. We had spectacular fishing, landing a couple steelhead of up to 14 pounds. We each lost bigger fish due to the raging currents. The water conditions which easily could have sent me to the nearest cup of hot coffee had kept everyone else home. We had the river to ourselves. It was a special day.

Being fairly close to my home, I have spent many days on the Oak's accommodating flows. It is mainly these special times or instances that I am most fond. Significant runs of large spring steelhead have occupied many a day. The Oak Orchard is now more of a sentimental favorite than it is an esthetic one. Actually, many of the features that I cherish of an exceptional steelhead river do not exist here. Solitude is now restricted to winter fishing. The true handicap of the Oak Orchard is its length or lack thereof. One of the many small, inefficient dams found on New York's Lake Ontario tributaries blocks upstream migration and limits the available fly fishing water in high flows to about two miles at best. It is a shame because above the dam and resultant reservoir is a beautiful twelve-mile stretch of pockets, runs, and gravel. A fish ladder would give this river a rebirth. It has been discussed and is a possibility. As for now, my closest connection lies in the past. It is in its dark waters that I first fished for lake-run fish with a fly rod. It is where I caught my first steelhead, my largest Great Lakes steelhead, and have had some of the most intense battles that I have experienced. I will always be grateful for its part in developing my interest in steelhead and to Terry Wurster for introducing me to its bountiful currents many years ago.

Oak Orchard Creek enters Lake Ontario at Point Breeze which is a few miles north of Albion, NY. The steelhead water begins at the dam which is approximately six miles up from the lake. Access to the river is allowed by the utility company which operates the dam. Parking is available at a lot on Park Avenue. There is another access and parking area at the lower end of the fly fishable water which is provided by cooperative efforts of Orleans County and New York State. The upper part of the steelhead water is actually split into two branches. One that runs out of the turbines and one that is an overflow for the reservoir in high water. The channel that runs from the turbines

The Oak Orchard has gained a reputation for its large steelhead.

provides the bulk of the fishing opportunity. The upper water runs through tight woodlands and much of it lacks clear definition. There are some seams and pockets which provide obvious holding lies, but most will be determined through experience. In moderate to low flows, steelhead will lie in the depressions and subtle troughs of the creek's floor.

Midway through the fly fishable water the two channels meet, the river widens, and gradually opens to a point where there is plenty of room for backcasting. There is a series of seven or eight pools or runs of various sizes which can hold many fish. By far the most popular piece of water is the Archery Pool named for the archery club that occupies the west bank. Kind of an odd name considering that in twenty years I have yet to see an arrow actually take flight. The Archery Pool just feels like steelhead water. When pressure is light, a wet fly swing approach can bring exciting results for fresh spring fish. I can recall a number of brisk spring evenings where I have had the pool to myself or shared it with a companion. While wading waist deep and concentrating on the cast and mending, my thoughts have often drifted. With everything feeling perfect on this picturesque water, I could have been on any steelhead river in the world.

Even though its popularity has created less opportunities for solitude, some possibilities still exist. Despite pressured situations, a quality experience can be found at most times of the year. The Oak does not receive the fall runs of steelhead that I can remember of the mid 1980's. There is no known reproduction in its waters as summer temperatures are simply too warm. The lower fall runs can only be speculated upon, but stocking practices certainly have contributed to the situation. The first weeks of November seem to be the most consistent time frame for fall runs with the two weeks prior and into December providing opportunity. The fall does see a now-famous migration of big, beautiful lake-run brown trout. Oak Orchard has become mostly a spring steelhead fishery with the last two weeks of March and first two of April consistently providing the best opportunity. Actually, the activity in the spring is normally at its height when the water temperature maintains the 40 degree F. mark. This occurs a little later than on some other of New York's Lake Ontario tributaries because it takes a longer period to warm up the reservoir. Mid to late March fishing can be some of the best, combining increasing numbers with the opportunity for chrome-bright steelhead. If favorable weather, water conditions and reasonable fish numbers intersect during January and February, this will be my preferred time to fish Oak Orchard. Solitude can be found in nearly every pool and run at this time of year.

Water flows can fluctuate dramatically because of the dam. The utility company attempts to control flows for sportfishing, but some improvements are still needed. Hopefully a water management plan will be created and employed some day in the future which will encompass a more strategic use of power generation along with utilizing water from the Erie Canal to subsidize periods of low flows.

If Oak Orchard's water conditions are not favorable or the fishing pressure is high, there are other alternatives in reasonable proximity as one heads east. Sandy Creek in Monroe County is a small stream that meanders through farm fields and is characterized by small pools and runs which can hold some nice steelhead under the right conditions.

Salmon River (RK)

When I think of the Salmon River, I think of two rivers. The first is beautiful, with clear, dark water running swiftly over combinations of gravel, boulders, and bedrock. It glides its way through hardwood-lined banks which place an exclamation mark on its beauty come autumn. It bends slowly, then abruptly changes directions before righting itself again on its path to Lake Ontario. Its current is hard and fast—one must be respectful and play by the river's rules. Fast pockets and shallow runs give way to the haunting flows of deep placid pools. It is broad, big and untamed—a steelhead river by any sense of measurement.

The second river is not such a pristine and pure vision. This is a river shrouded in controversy. One tarnished by the barbarity of snagging Pacific salmon. Today regulations prohibit such activities, but the effects of this abuse linger like a toxin which may take generations to flush clean. Its negative impact has formulated the attitude and approach of some so-called fishermen. This second river is also known for its crowds—throngs that have been lured by heavy runs of large Chinook salmon, possibly looking for some type of fulfillment, but mainly just filling their coolers. To this callous lot the river is nothing more than a meat pit. It is also a river driven by economic policies where some commercial operators have such an influence on management to a point of controlling fisheries' decisions. Shortsighted views of a dollar in hand today restrict the development of a high-quality fishery and experience for tomorrow.

I have had the occasion to frequent the Salmon over the last twelve years, becoming somewhat familiar with its politics. Many of the same issues exist on other rivers in the Great Lakes region within proximity of a large population base, but these are rivers where I am not so close to its management process. With the Salmon I feel an attachment, making it easy for me to pass judgment.

Let there be no mistake, the Salmon is a great river, one of opportunity and challenge. And despite the fishing pressure, a quality experience can always be found. Its headwaters begin in the near-wilderness surroundings of the foothills of the Adirondack Mountains. Its natural flow is interrupted twice by power generation dams, the larger of which creates the Redfield Reservoir.

Brian Slavinski fishes a section of the Salmon River near Pulaski.

Below the second dam, the river runs free for some 16 miles to its confluence with the lake at Port Ontario. The water is diverse and at times intimidating. Salmon River steelhead will utilize a wide range of water for holding and movement. Careful reading of the flows is essential.

There are two fly fishing only, catch-and-release areas on the river located at the upper end of the steelhead water in Altmar. Both sections are short, each containing a handful of pools perfect for fly fishing along with some riffle and pocket water. Since the upper fly fishing area is above the hatchery, it sees less fish. There are state access points and parking lots for each section. In recent years, I have tended to stay clear of the fly fishing areas because of the intense pressure they receive. The entire river has suitable fly fishing water, and there is no reason to feel crammed. Actually, the two or three miles below the lower fly fishing area is some of my favorite water. Accessed from either the Altmar lot or the Ellis Cove access on the north side of the river, a variety of runs, pools, bends, and pocket water can be found. This stretch can occasionally see significant numbers of fish. Fresh-runs will combine with those that have been in the river for a few weeks creating a concentration of fish.

There is very good public access to all but the last few miles of water. With a combination of state, county, town, and even private landowner cooperation, there is no less than 13 public access points from the upper fly fishing area to the village of Pulaski. And once on the river, public easements along most of it down to Pulaski ensure the ability to travel the banks without trespassing, allowing the adventurous wading angler to cover most of the river. A few years back, the utility company which operates the dams on the river provided for the sale and easements to the state which has resulted in permanent public fishing rights for future generations. Good water can be found at each access. Some of the access points lead to the river's most defined and consequently heaviest fished pools. I use these points to access much of the least-fished water between the main pools. When water temperatures are above 40 degrees, steelhead will often be found in the offbeat runs and pockets above and below the well-defined water.

Including one pool above the infamous Black Hole, the lower two and a half miles of water suitable for fly fishing is privately controlled and known as the Douglaston Salmon Run. Access to this area is gained through a parking lot on the north side of the river and requires a small daily fee. Unethical behavior is not tolerated in this section of river and the daily limits are below those dictated by state regulations. The fee limits the amount of fishing pressure on a daily basis. Since this water is close to the lake, it is possible to encounter fish that have only entered the river within hours or even minutes. There are numerous runs, small pools, and pockets which can be easily covered with a fly rod. Some of the lower pools readily accommodate more traditional techniques.

Water levels fluctuate widely because of the dams. There is a water release policy in place which attempts to stabilize the flow and benefit the fishery. However, deviations from the plan are commonly caused by heavy rainfall or runoff. Before embarking on a trip to the Salmon, try to check the water levels. Water flow of 375 to 750 cfs provides for good fly fishing conditions. Water in the 1000 to 1500 cfs range can still be fly fished, but the level, combined with the flow, begins to make it quite difficult and restricts the water that can be fished.

The length of the annual steelhead opportunity of the Salmon River rivals that of any fishery in the country. Steelhead can be found as early as September, but good numbers normally begin to show by the second or third week of October. November is my favorite month as it commonly combines good numbers of fish with water temperatures in the 40 degree F. range. The river stays mainly free of ice all year, and there can be outstanding winter steelhead fishing from December right into the spring. The spring runs begin in March, and there will normally be fishable numbers of steelhead existing into May.

There are some wild fish returning to the Salmon. This is one river where we would like to see a greater emphasis on wild steelhead management. One factor that may encourage this is a change in the water release plan which was placed in effect in 1996. The impact will be cooler temperatures in the summer which not only will improve smolt production and survival, but possibly provide a summer steelhead fishery for Skamania-strain steelhead.

There are numerous services available along the river and in Pulaski including lodging, fly shops, and restaurants. Whitaker's Sport Store just off route 81 specializes in fly fishing equipment and guided trips. There are a few guides who specialize in fly fishing, including Dave Barber who owns and operates a lodge in Altmar called the Fish Inn Post, Greg Liu who owns and operates Oswego Outfitters, and Mark Kinniston who operates Upland Fishing and Hunting Guide Service.

The heavy flow of the Salmon does require some innovations. For this reason, the running line approach has become quite popular. However, with such a wide variety of water available, I have found weight forward lines with weight added to the leader or heavy mini-tips to provide effective coverage. Casting, mending, and concentration are the key when applying more traditional approaches.

If the Salmon is too high to fish or for a change of pace, there are two medium-size streams to the north which receive fishable runs of steelhead. These are South Sandy and Sandy (known locally as North Sandy) Creeks. There is public access to each, and some of the fish are wild. Also to the west of the Salmon is the Oswego River. This is a big river, but the steelhead water is restricted to about a mile stretch below the dam. It receives good runs of fish; the lower area is probably best fished from a boat. Guide John Dembeck can provide some interesting fishing. There are talks of a fish ladder which would open up miles of productive water.

Epilogue:
The Complete Angler

In today's modern world, there seem to be people fishing everywhere. An increase in population coupled with rekindled enthusiasm for the restored fisheries in many parts of our country thanks to the Clean Water Act in 1972 has made recreational fishing one of the top lifetime sports in America. As the "boomer generation" starts to approach retirement age, this trend will persist as long as there continue to be quality fishing opportunities for everyone into future years. Although the picture-perfect fishing scenario has long been synonymous with peaceful solitude, modern era fishing will certainly change perceptions and expectations of what a fishing outing should be. While private times on the water can still be sought and found, learning to get along with others on our favorite rivers will be key to many future adventures. As a friend once stated: three inconsiderate anglers can be a crowd, whereas hundreds of polite anglers can blend harmoniously into the backdrop of a beautiful day.

Traditionally, there has been a mystique built into fly fishing—some may even call it snobbery. It has been assumed that many who fly fish are looking for a deeper connection to the sport of fishing in general, and for some, this goal is attained with fly rod in hand. Whatever the perception of fly fishing may be, it cannot be denied that the anticipation of presenting a finely tied fly on a long, sensitively light fly rod to a lurking steelhead conjures up quite a thrill—a hookup is positively unequaled. Add this to the many other related art forms associated with fly fishing and the whole experience can become somewhat poetic. Indeed, the ardent enthusiast can get quite passionate about the pursuit, even to the point of believing that fly fishing is the only way to catch a steelhead—hence the snob factor.

There will be no debate here on the purity of fly fishing. Everyone fishes for a variety of reasons at different levels of meaningful, and not so meaningful, expression. While the technology that fly fishing demands requires a financial commitment on the part of the angler, the knowledge to catch fish on a fly consistently in a variety of situations requires a commitment of time and dedication. While it may be the many levels of commitment that really do set the fly fishing public apart from many other approaches to fishing, pursuing steelhead with a fly rod can also provide the framework to understanding fishing in a much broader sense as well. It could be said that fly fishing provides a wonderful opportunity to become a complete angler.

The complete angler should try to understand every technical aspect of the sport while strictly adhering to the rules of fair play. The complete angler should also understand all the factors that affect the dynamics of one's fishery while leading the way in conservation issues regarding that resource. The complete angler should offer other anglers assistance when needed on the water and report abuses when encountered. Most importantly, the complete angler should demonstrate unwavering respect for the environment, private property, the fish and fellow anglers.

Learning the proper methods of utilizing high-tech gear is not only rewarding, it can relieve much frustration while creating more opportunities on your favorite waters to catch fish. For example, an understanding of where steelhead may lie within a system coupled with the appropriate skills to properly present a fly to that piece of water can result in more steelhead encounters while at the same time fishing in less congested water. On the other hand, an inept approach may result in consistently foul-hooked fish and even worse. We have witnessed many incapable anglers consciously foul-hooking fish in areas "stacked" with a high density of fish under the guise of "fly fishing." Using methods that define good sportsmanship, these fish were quite takable with refined skills.

As stated in earlier chapters, we all must take an active stance in managing our waters based upon an understanding of fishery biology and good management practices. Throughout the Great Lakes, there is a contingent of dedicated biologists and managers who work hard to keep this resource in balance with its ecosystem. The importance of wild fish cannot be understated if we want steelhead for the future. Learn about your resource and take care of it. If nothing else, history has taught us that demands cannot be placed upon a fishery beyond its capabilities.

All of us have either witnessed or even done some dumb things on the water that may have angered someone at one time or another. Many things are done inadvertently and could have been avoided with a little conscious effort. A good rule of thumb: if you have made someone angry, you were probably out of line. Know the rules of each particular river you fish. These rules of etiquette traditionally vary from one place to the next. Most rivers, however, are governed by common sense. If there is a question as to the proper behavior in a given situation, the best course of action is to simply ask. It is rare to receive anything but a courteous response to an inquiry of another angler's intentions. Most of the time, it is greatly appreciated. In the same context, it doesn't hurt to politely assist someone on the river who seems out of step with the program. They usually appreciate the help, and a potentially unsettling conflict is diffused. Rotating through a pool or run is good sportsmanship on any steelhead river. By rotating, and encouraging others to do the same, all anglers get an opportunity at prime lies.

Unfortunately, every river has its share of anglers who just don't get the total picture, and these folks actually violate legal regulations in open public. Exceeding limits, chumming, killing fish just for the eggs, snagging, etc. are but a few common transgressions. Report violators; and if you feel secure enough, announce your intentions to the transgressors. Knowing folks are watching may make them more wary in the future—or it may even educate them. It's your fishery—take charge of it!

Respect the environment. Keep your fishing areas free of litter. There really is nothing more disturbing than to see the mess of various kinds left behind by many so-called sportsmen. This certainly encroaches upon the sense of nature that we all presumably seek in the quality outdoor experience. Also, be aware of the environmental impacts that are taking place in your favorite areas of the Great Lakes and be an active voice. The past has taught what can happen when vigilance is lax. Right now, throughout the country, there are organized attacks on the clean water legislation that has been responsible for our renewed fisheries. As long as man exists, there will be someone trying to take a good thing and screw it up, especially when it comes to the environment—history has taught us that as well.

Respect private property. Nothing can be more depressing than to read a "No Trespassing" sign at an access to a river that was previously open to the public. Many of these signs where inspired by the inconsiderate activities of fellow "sportsmen." Even where there is a legal corridor, it often borders private property. Treat that property as if it were your own.

Respect the fish. If you keep a fish, dispatch of it quickly. Keep it cool and utilize it wisely. Witnessing folks tossing steelhead into the back of a pickup truck like a piece of cordwood really demonstrates an ignorance and disrespect for the gauntlet of adversities it takes for a steelhead, wild or hatchery, to return to their tackle in the first place. Many believe in the misperception that all of our steelhead in the Great Lakes are stocked, and since *they* can just stock more, "keep 'em all." As detailed in the text, this couldn't be further from the truth. Stocking cannot keep up with an insatiable demand; and in many cases, these fish are poor but expensive substitutes. You can bet these same individuals complain loudly about the cost of government services in the form of taxes—probably even while they are bonking fish. Because of the biological importance of wild fish, we should release *every* one of them. Since steelhead do not die like salmon, even many stocked fish return back to the lakes only to run again another season. So remember: today's 24 inch hatchery fish is the future's 30 inch or larger trophy.

Respect your fellow angler. The world is getting more crowded by the day, and as unpalatable as that may be for those who care about our dwindling resources, it is a fact that will become more and more evident on our rivers as well. Since camaraderie has always been associated with anadromous fishing anyway, it is important to develop a sense of cooperation along the rivers we choose to fish. In today's world of socialized fishing, a kind word can go a long way. A quality fishing experience is not always defined by the amount of fish caught.

The Great Lakes provide unequaled world-class fishing opportunities, but the respect this fishery has garnered over the years is by far substandard. Overlooked and taken for granted, it is time to raise the consciousness of angler appreciation throughout the region (as well as the country) to a level commensurate to the magnificence of this resource. One only needs to observe the staggering condition of West Coast steelhead populations to recognize the true treasure the Great Lakes has to offer. The future, however, still depends upon understanding the value of steelhead, economically and spiritually, while implementing the concept of wise use based upon the most judicious of management practices.

Bibliography

Bates, Joseph D., Jr. *Atlantic Salmon Flies & Fishing*. Stackpole Books, Harrisburg, PA, 1970.

Behnke, Robert. "Wild Salmonid Genetics: An Impending Crisis?" *Trout*, Summer, 1995.

Burzynski, Thomas. *Wisconsin's Lake Michigan Salmonid Stocking Program*. Wisconsin Department of Natural Resources, 1997.

Colson, Bob. *Michigan Steelhead Fly Fishing Manual*. Bob Colson, 1992.

Combs, Trey. *Steelhead Fly Fishing*. Lyons & Burford, New York, 1991.

Denley, Peter. "Fly Fishing the Sault Rapids." *Ontario Out of Doors*, 1992.

Donarski, Dan. "Great Lakes Steelhead." *The Flyfisher*, Autumn, 1994.

Dueck, Lucy A. *Lake Ontario Rainbow Trout Genetics*. (Thesis), 1994.

Dueck, Lucy A. and Danzmann, R.G. "Matriarchal population structure of introduced rainbow trout (Oncorhynchus mykiss) in the Lake Ontario Watershed." *Can. J. Fish. Aquat. Sci.,* Vol. 53, 1996.

Filkins, Kenn. "St. Mary's Rapids Pink." *American Angler*, September/ October, 1992.

Fish Passage Protocol. Wisconsin Department of Natural Resources, 1995.

George, Jon. *The Status of Rainbow Trout in the Canadian Waters of Lake Superior Based on Frequency of Repeat Spawners 1991-1993.* Ontario Ministry of Natural Resources, 1994.

Halyk, L.C., Weland, C., and Danzman, R.G. *Genetic Stock Identification of Rainbow Trout from Ontario Tributaries to Lake Erie.* (Funding Proposal), 1997.

Jones, Michael L. and Kocik, John F. "Pacific Salmonines in the Great Lakes Basin." *Great Lakes Fisheries Policy and Management: A Binational Perspective.* Michigan State University Press, 1999.

Krueger, Charles C., Perkins, David L., Everitt, Rebecca J., Shreiner, Donald R. and May, Bernie. "Genetic Variation in Naturalized Rainbow Trout (Oncorhynchus mykiss) from Minnesota Tributaries to Lake Superior." *Internat. Assoc. Great Lakes Res.*, 1994.

——May, Bernie. *Genetic Comparison of Naturalized Rainbow Trout Populations among Lake Superior Tributaries: Differentiation Based on Allozyme Data.* (Draft), 1995.

Kustich, Rick. *Fly Fishing the Great Lakes Tributaries.* West River Publishing Company, Grand Island, NY, 1992.

——*River Journal: Salmon River.* Frank Amato Publications, Portland, OR, 1995.

Lake Michigan Integrated Fisheries Management Plan. Wisconsin Department of Natural Resources, 1995.

Linsenman, Bob. *River Journal: Au Sable River.* Frank Amato Publications, Portland, OR, 1998.

——Nevala, Steve. *Great Lakes Steelhead: A Guided Tour for Fly-Anglers.* Backcountry Publications, Woodstock, VT, 1995.

MacCrimmon, Hugh R. and Gots, B. L. *Rainbow Trout in the Great Lakes.* Ontario Ministry of Natural Resources, 1972.

Marcogliese, Lucian A. and Casselman, John M. *Scale Methods for Discriminating Between Great Lakes Stocks of Indigenous and Hatchery Rainbow Trout with a Measure of Indigeny in Lake Ontario* (Draft), Ontario Ministry of Natural Resources, 1996.

Maxwell, Mike. *The Art & Science of Speyfishing.* Flyfishers' Art & Publishing, Delta, BC, 1995.

Meyer Deke. *Advanced Fly Fishing for Steelhead.* Frank Amato Publications, Portland, OR, 1992.

Michigan Fisheries Centennial Report 1873-1973. Michigan Department of Natural Resources, 1974.

Minnesota Steelhead Plan Progress Reports: 1992-1996. Minnesota Department of Natural Resources, 1991.

Murray, Charles K. and Hoopes, Rickalon L. *Lake Erie Steelhead Fishing—Lake Erie Survey April 17, 1993 through April 15, 1994.* Pennsylvania Fish and Boat Commission, 1995.

Nagy, John. *Steelhead Guide: Fly Fishing Techniques and Strategies for Lake Erie Steelhead.* Great Lakes Publishing, Pittsburgh, PA 1998.

Niagara River Remedial Action Plan. New York State Department of Environmental Conservation, 1993.

North Shore Steelhead Plan. Minnesota Department of Natural Resources, 1991.

Rand, Peter S., Stewart, Donald J., Seelbach Paul W., Jones, Michael L. and Wedge, Leslie R. "Modeling Steelhead Population Energetics in Lakes Michigan and Ontario." *North American Journal of Fisheries Management*, 1993.

Reisenbichler, Reg. "The Risks of Hatchery Supplementation." *The Osprey*, The Steelhead Committee of the Federation of Fly Fishers, June, 1996.

Rudstom, Lars, Editor. *A Review of the Current Status of Lake Ontario's Pelagic Fish Community.* A Report from the 1996 Lake Ontario Technical Panel. Cornell University Biological Field Station, 1996.

Schreiner, Donald R., Editor. *Fisheries Management Plan for the Minnesota Waters of Lake Superior.* Minnesota Department of Natural Resources, 1995.

Seelbach, Paul W. "Effect of Winter Severity on Steelhead Smolt Yield in Michigan: An Example of the Importance of Environmental Factors in Determining Smolt Yield." *North American Journal of Fisheries Management*, 1987.

——"Smolting Success of Hatchery-Raised Steelhead Planted in a Michigan Tributary of Lake Michigan." *North American Journal of Fisheries Management,* 1987.

——"Population Biology of Steelhead in a Stable-Flow, Low-Gradient Tributary of Lake Michigan." *North American Journal of Fisheries Management*, 1993.

——Whelan, Gary E. "Identification and Contribution of Wild and Hatchery Steelhead Stocks in Lake Michigan Tributaries." *North American Journal of Fisheries Management*, 1988.

——Miller, Barry R. *Dynamics in Lake Superior of Hatchery and Wild Steelhead Emigrating from the Huron River, Michigan*. Michigan Department of Natural Resources, 1993.

——Dexter Jr., James L., and Ledet, Neil D. *Performance of Steelhead Smolts Stocked in Southern Michigan Warmwater Rivers*. Michigan Department of Natural Resources, 1994.

Smith, Scott E. *Ontario Blue-Ribbon Fly Fishing Guide*. Frank Amato Publications, Portland, OR, 1999.

Soverel, Pete. "Requiem for the Steelhead." *The Flyfisher*, Autumn, 1994.

Steelhead population dynamics and management alternatives: Lake Michigan. Fishery Division, Michigan Department of Natural Resources, 1995.

Supinski, Matthew A. *River Journal: Pere Marquette*. Frank Amato Publications, Portland, OR, 1994.

The Life Story of a Brule River Steelhead. Wisconsin Department of Natural Resources, 1991.

Vincent, Jim. *Basic Spey & Two Handed Fly Rod Casting*. Rio Products, Blackfoot, ID, 1994.

Index

Agawa River (Ontario), 207–208
alewife, 38, 39, 40, 42, 70, 86–87
Andrews, Jeff, 171
Ashtabula River (Ohio), 78
Atkinson, Chris, 218–19
Au Sable River (Mich.), 66, 211–13

bacterial kidney disease (BKD), 40, 76, 83, 87
Baldwin River (Mich.), 236
Baptism River (Minn.), 61, 199–201
Barber, Dave, 268
Bayfield River (Ontario), 218
Beaver River (Ontario), 68
Behnke, Robert, 47, 48
Betsie River (Mich.), 229
Big Creek (Ontario), 83, 241–43
Bighead River (Ontario), 66, 68, 213–15
Big Manistee River (Mich.), 227–29
Big Two-Hearted River. *See* Two-Hearted River
biodiversity, 48, 54
Blackhoof River (Minn.), 60
Black River (N.Y.), 89, 253–55
Blumreich, Bob, 171
Blust, Bill, 59
Boardman River (Mich.), 229
Borgeson, Dave, 70–71
Boyne River (Ontario), 68
Brule River (Wis.), 51, 58–60, 201, 203–205

Canadaway Creek (N.Y.), 245
Casselman, John M., 90

Cattaraugus Creek (N.Y.), 79, 80, 243–45
Chagrin River (Ohio), 78
Chautauqua Creek (N.Y.), 245
Clean Water Act of 1972, 39, 81, 269, 271
Clearwater River, 50–51
Collins, Ken, 217
Colson, Bob, 237
Columbia River, 49–50
Combs, Trey, 18
commercial fishing, 30–31
Conneaut Creek (Ohio/Pa), 78, 245–47
Conway, Mark, 171
Cornelius, Floyd, 80
Cornell, Tom, 172
Cranberry River (Wis.), 204
crowding, 19
Culligan, Bill, 79
Cypress River (Ontario), 205–206

dams, 45, 49
Danzman, Roy G., 87, 88
Darkes, Jerry, 245–46
Dembeck, John, 268
Devil Track River (Minn.), 61, 201
Dicarlo, Eric, 208
Dickson, Charlie, 172
Dobbs, Fred, 218–19
Doldo, Pat, 253–54
Dowagiac Creek (Mich.), 240
Dueck, Lucy A., 87, 88

Eighteen Mile Creek (N.Y.), 245
Elk Creek (Pa.), 247–50
equipment, 124–34
Erie Canal (N.Y.), 54
Erie, Lake, 70, 76–84, 241–52
extinctions, 25

fishery, steelhead
    history, 27–34
    management, 35–52, 53–92
Fitzhugh, Daniel, 28
Flag River (Wis.), 204
flies, 159–84
Flutur, Danny, 243
Ford, Jac, 235
French River (Minn.), 60–61

Galloup, Kelly, 172, 235
Ganaraska River (Ontario), 88, 90, 255–57
Genesee River (N.Y.), 257–59
genotypes, 46
Georgian Bay (Ontario), 65, 68, 214–15
gill netting, 64
Grand River (Ontario), 78, 82, 83, 247, 250–52
Grau, Walt, 172, 235, 237
Great Lakes basin, formation, 27–28
Great Lakes Fishery Commission, 56
Great Lakes Fishery Policy and Management, 37
Great Lakes Steelhead, 213
Great Lakes Water Quality Agreement, 81
Green, Seth, 28, 32

Haig-Brown, Roderick, 18
Halyk, Larry, 82, 84, 216, 241–42, 251–52
hatcheries, 25–26, 28–30, 32, 38, 45–52, 53, 66,
    69, 72, 82–83, 87, 90, 204, 258
Hemingway, Ernest, 201–202
Huron, Lake, 65–70, 211–24

Illinois, 74
Imhof, Jack, 251
Indiana, 73

Jackpine River (Ontario), 206
Jacob, Paul, 257–59
Johnson, Jim, 235, 238

Johnson, Tom, 235
Jones, Michael, 37

Kadunce Creek (Minn.), 201
Kewaunee River (Wis.), 75, 225–27
Kimball Creek (Minn.), 201
Kinniston, Mark, 268
Kluesing, John, 235, 237
Knife River (Minn.), 60, 61, 62, 199–201
Kocik, John, 37
Krueger, Charles, 58, 61

lamprey (sea lamprey), 33, 38, 54–55, 67, 69–70, 77,
    84, 90, 220
Linsenman, Bob, 211, 213
Little Manistee River (Mich.), 51, 66, 70, 229
Liu, Greg, 172, 268

Maitland River (Ontario), 70, 215–18
management. *See* fishery, management
Manistee Lake (Mich.), 229
Manitowoc River (Wis.), 230–31
Marcoliese, Lucien A., 90
May, Bernie, 58, 61
McCormick, Rob, 172
McDonald, Shaun, 235
McFadden, James, 71
McMillan, Bill, 18
Michigan, Lake, 70–76
Michigan State, 54, 63–66, 71–73, 201–203
Michigan Steelhead Fly Fishing Manual, 237
Michigan Trout Streams, 213
Michipicoten River (Ontario), 208
Miller, Barry, 63
Mink Creek (Ontario), 210
Minnesota, 60–62
Morrissey, Bob, 172, 215
Muskegon River (Wis.), 231–33
Myott, Keith, 262

Nemadji River (Minn.), 60
Neuman, Kelly, 211–13
Nevala, Steve, 213
New York, 79, 105, 253–55, 245, 257–68
Niagara River (N.Y./Ontario), 77, 85–86, 90, 259–62

Nicholson, Bob, 235
Nine Mile River (Ontario), 218
Nith River (Ontario), 252
Nolph, Zimmy, 235
Nottawasaga River (Ontario), 66–67, 68, 218–19

Oak Orchard Creek (N.Y.), 90, 105, 262–65
Oconto River (Wis.), 233–34
Ocqueoc River, 213
Ohio, 77–78, 103, 245–47
Old Woman River (Ontario), 207–208
Ontario, 62–63, 79, 205–10, 213–24, 255–57
Ontario Blue-Ribbon Fly Fishing Guide, 207
Ontario, Lake, 84–92, 253–68
Oswego River (N.Y.), 90, 268
overfishing, 31, 45, 68, 72, 204

Pancake River (Ontario), 208–10
Penich, Joe, 172
Pennsylvania, 77–79, 103, 105, 247–50
Pere Marquette River (Mich.), 235–38
Peshtigo River (Wis.), 234
Pigeon River (Wis.), 231
Pike Creek (Wis.), 59
Pionessa, Nick, 172
Platte River (Mich.), 229
pollutants and pollution, 18, 31, 43, 77, 81, 84, 91
Pratt, Dennis, 59
presentation, 134–53
Rifle River (Mich.), 66, 213
River Journal: Au Sable River, 213
Rocky River (Ohio), 78, 247
Root River (Wis.), 75, 238–39
ruffe, 55–56

St. Joseph River (Mich.), 73, 74, 239–40
St. Mary's River (Ontario), 65–66, 222–24
Salmon River (Idaho), 23, 49, 50–51, 81, 89, 90
Salmon River (N.Y.), 265–68
Sandy Creek (N.Y.), 265, 268
Saugeen River (Ontario), 219–22
Sauk River, 231
Sault Ste. Marie, Ontario, 62–63, 66, 222
Schmidt, Ray, 173, 227–28
Seelbach, Paul, 35, 48, 63, 71
Sheboygan River (Wis.), 231
Silver Creek (Wis.), 227

Sixteen Mile Creek (Pa.), 249
Slavinski, Brian, 173, 245
Smith, Scott, 173, 206–207, 216
snagging, 18, 19
Split Rock Creek (Minn.), 201
Standish, Troy, 173
steelhead, 21–26 and passim
    behavior, 99–110
    condition of, 108–110
    feeding, 110
    positioning, 105–107
    runs, 100–105
    sunlight, effect of, 106–107
    See also fishery
Steelhead Management Plan for Lake Erie, 78–79
Steel River (Ontario), 210
stocking programs, 23, 28–34, 37, 39, 43, 73, 75, 79, 82–83, 87–91, 258, 271–72
Stoney Creek (Wis.), 227
strategies. *See* techniques and strategies
Sucker River (Mich.), 63
Superior, Lake, 57–65, 199–210
Supinski, Matt, 173, 231–33, 236, 240
Swanson, Rob, 59
Sydenham River (Ontario), 68

Tanner, Howard, 36, 71
techniques and strategies, 18, 20, 108–10, 111–58
Tody, Wayne, 71
Twenty Mile Creek (N.Y./Pa.), 250
Two-Hearted River (Mich.), 63, 201–203

Valk, John, 173, 213–14
Venison Creek (Ontario), 242
Vincent, Dick, 47
Vogel, Karl, 224

Waller, Lani, 18
Walnut Creek (Pa.), 249
Washington State, 51
water
    quality, 18, 106
    reading, 111–22
    temperature, 101–102, 107
Wausugal River (Wash.), 51
Weland, Chris, 218–19
Welland Canal (Ontario), 54

whirling disease, 82, 90
Whiteman's Creek, 83
Whorwood, Rick, 173
wild fish, 53, 67, 70, 74, 77–78, 110, 258, 270
        See also hatcheries
Wilmot Creek (Ontario), 88, 257
Wisconsin, 58–60, 64, 74–76, 204, 225–27, 230–31
Wolf River (Ontario), 207
Wulff, Lee, 18
Wurster, Terry, 263

Yerex, Warren, 251
Young's Creek (Ontario), 243

zebra mussel, 42, 55, 77